# SELF-DECEPTION AND WHOLENESS IN PAUL AND MATTHEW

DAN O. VIA, JR.

D1203028

Fortress Press

SELF-DECEPTION AND WHOLENESS IN PAUL AND MATTHEW

Scripture quotations unless otherwise noted are from the Revised Standard Version of the Bible, copyright © 1946, 1952, and 1971 by the Division of Christian Education of the National Council of Churches.

"Ethical Responsibility and Human Wholeness in Matthew 25:31-46," by Dan O. Via, Jr., in *Harvard Theological Review* 80 no. 1 (1987). Copyright © 1987 the President and Fellows of Harvard College. Used by permission. "The Gospel of Matthew: Hypocrisy as Self-Deception," in *SBL 1988 Seminar Papers* 27 (1988). Copyright © 1988 the Society of Biblical Literature. Used by permission. "Narrative World and Ethical Response," *Semeia* 12 (1978). Copyright © 1978 Scholars Press. Used by permission. "Structure, Christology, and Ethics in Matthew," in *Orientation by Disorientation,* ed. R. Spencer. Copyright © 1980 Pickwick Press, Allison Park, Pa. Used by permission.

Interior design: Publishers' WorkGroup
Cover design: Patricia Boman

---

Library of Congress Cataloging-in-Publication Data

Via, Dan Otto, 1928–
    Self-deception and wholeness in Paul and Matthew / Dan O.
Via, Jr.
        p. cm.
    Includes bibliographical references.
    ISBN 0-8006-2435-1 (alk. paper)
    1. Self-deception—Biblical teaching. 2. Bible. N.T. Epistles
of Paul—Criticism, interpretation, etc. 3. Bible. N.T. Matthew—
Criticism, interpretation, etc. I. Title.
BS2545.S33V52 1990
226.2'06—dc20                                        90-33416
                                                       CIP

---

The paper used in this publication meets the minimum requirements of American National Standard for Information Sciences—Permanence of Paper for Printed Library Materials, ANSI Z329.48-1984.   ∞™

---

Manufactured in the U.S.A.                            AF 1-2435

94   93   92   91   90   1   2   3   4   5   6   7   8   9   10

*In memory of*

# JOHN A. HOLLAR

# Contents

# Preface

While self-deception may have come to be of uncommon interest in the modern world, the phenomenon has been profoundly observed since ancient times and often by religious thinkers. Recent approaches to it have been quite varied, and we shall see that it has been questioned whether there is such a thing as bona fide cases of self-deception.[1] Needless to say, I go with those who believe that there is. I can deceive myself about many different areas of reality: myself (character, beliefs, actions, property), others, my relationships with others, the world that surrounds me. And the specifics about which one can deceive oneself are endless. The alcoholic believes that his drinking is under control; the alienated couple do not notice that their marriage is a sham; the compulsive spender does not know that she spends more than she makes; the threatened professor convinces herself that her colleague's success is due to ruthless ambition; the AIDS patient believes that he has a fifty-fifty chance of getting well.[2] The bibliography on self-deception is enormous, and my analysis of the phenomenon in chapter 1 will look at only a few sources.[3]

I use the concept of self-deception as a vantage point for understanding something about Paul and Matthew. I have chosen Paul and Matthew for two basic reasons: (1) they both make use of the concept of self-deception and thus attract the concept in a natural way as a hermeneutical lens; (2) the similarities and dissimilarities of these New Testament writers make for a fruitful and interesting comparison. This tension expands our understanding of the problems and possibilities of faith. Looking at the New Testament writers from the angle of the experience of self-deception should expand our understanding of both the texts and the experience.

My method is existential in a broad sense. I am asking about the nature of a pervasive phenomenon of human existence with some attention being given to psychological aspects. And my approach to the text will be focally literary-critical. I have done close readings and paid attention to formal patterns, but I have also exploited the role of the reader in turning a text into a work and have observed the deconstructive tendencies of the language. I have attended to the impingement of historical contexts and occasionally have dealt with issues that belong to sociological exegesis. But with all of that, this study is primarily exegetical and interpretive— aimed at theological understanding—and is not intensively methodological. Since self-deception is a deformation that affects individuals, I have paid attention primarily to the subversion of the self and the recovery of wholeness. At the same time, self-deception is a social phenomenon, and I have given some consideration to its social causes and implications.

I want to thank Duke University for a sabbatical leave during the spring of 1989 which enabled me to finish writing this book. I should like as well to express my profound appreciation for the encouragement and constructive criticism that Dr. John A. Hollar gave me over a number of years and to attest to the deep sorrow that so many of us feel at his untimely death. I should like also to thank Timothy G. Staveteig, Fortress Press, for his painstaking editorial work and to thank Scott Andrews and Gregory Linton, my graduate assistants, for their careful proofreading and indexing. And without the conscientious work of Gail Chappell the typescript would not have seen the light of day.

I am also very grateful to the Religion Department of Wake Forest University for inviting me to deliver the Robinson Lectures there in the spring of 1986 and for the gracious hospitality extended to my wife and me on the occasion of the lectures. It is those lectures that have been revised and enlarged to become this book. In addition I should like to thank the Seventh and James Baptist Church in Waco, Texas, for inviting me to deliver a version of the lectures and for receiving them, and us, warmly.

# 1

## THE NATURE OF SELF-DECEPTION

When my love swears that she is made of truth
I do believe her though I know she lies
—William Shakespeare, Sonnet 138

$S$elf-deception is the act and state of actually holding a belief about or an image of oneself, or a vision of one's situation in reality, while at the same time knowing that the belief, image, or vision is not true. In self-deception the person is simultaneously the victimizer who lies and the victim who is lied to. The self-deceiver knows he is lying to himself and therefore knows the truth. At the same time, he believes his own lies and therefore does not know the truth.

For the sake of discussion I identify lying with ordinary deception, that is, interpersonal deception or deception of the other. Lying, then, is misleading someone intentionally with a message the deceiver does not believe. The message may be expressed in many ways—speech, writing, action, gesture, inaction, silence.[1] Self-deception is like ordinary lying—lying to another—in that it is an intentional misleading. But it is ambiguous with regard to the deceiver's disbelief in the misleading message. Since deceiver and deceived are the same person, the self-deceiver both believes and disbelieves the message.

The concept of secrecy also helps us to understand our phenomenon, since lying and secrecy overlap. The secret is that which is hidden or concealed and set apart or separated from the nonsecret. It is easy to confuse lying and secrecy because lying always involves keeping something secret: A person says that she was on R Street to keep secret that she was on M Street. But not all secrecy is meant to deceive.[2] Self-deception, then, is intentionally keeping secrets from ourselves.

Note that self-deception entails having a false belief but also having a veiled awareness that the belief is false, that is, a veiled awareness of the truth. The term *veiled* signifies that knowing the belief is a lie—knowing the truth—is less accessible than believing the lie. Self-deception may be distinguishable from what some call self-caused deception or single-minded delusion, in which one believes what is false without question.[3] The negative and unwelcome truth that is veiled or concealed may be called the "real" story, while the positive and untrue belief that conceals it may be called the "cover" story.

I have asserted—and will continue to assert—that self-deception is analogous to other-deception or interpersonal deception. The interpersonal model for self-deception creates the paradox of lying to oneself, simultaneously knowing and not knowing the same thing, keeping secrets from oneself.

Some find the paradoxical element in this interpersonal model of self-deception troubling, and the analogy has been denied.[4] For Sissela Bok the concept of self-deception is a compelling, useful, perhaps necessary, metaphor for describing certain internal conflicts and for enabling us to see the paradox of the human failure to perceive and react. But the metaphor short-circuits understanding by leading us away from the complexity that underlies our experience of paradox; it is a "premature ultimate."[5]

My inclination is to accept the paradox without apology. By *paradox* I mean a combination of ideas that is logically contradictory but is nevertheless believed to be necessary to portray the nature of human existence at its mysterious depth. To evade, resolve, or explain the paradox is to lose it.[6] My inclination to accept this paradox finds some corroboration in the Bible, for which the hidden core of humankind, the heart, is certainly mysterious. Consider two books as different as Jeremiah and James. According to the prophet, the heart—the seat of understanding and will—is deceitful and corrupt, impossible to understand in its foolish subversion of its own highest good, its relationship with the divine source of life (2:10-13; 17:1, 9-10). In James the person who hears the "word" and experiences it internally but does not act on it is self-deceived, divided against herself, living in forgetfulness of who she really is (1:18-24). This self-division comes to expression again in 3:5-12 where the tongue becomes a synecdoche for the divided self. Here we see a self out of touch with itself, so colossal in its self-contradiction that it can only be described in cosmic terms: The tongue is itself a fire igniting the cycle of nature and ignited by hell. The tongue both blesses and curses. It is like a spring producing water both brackish and fresh.

Within a paradoxical understanding of self-deception it is possible to explain why people deceive themselves, to explain without explaining away the paradox. Paul and Matthew provide an explanation when they suggest the reasons we deceive ourselves. Furthermore, while they do not explain how the phenomenon can be rendered nonparadoxical in its conceptual expression, they do explain—give a basis for—the overcoming of the phenomenon as an existential reality, that is, they confront it with the gospel. But they differ regarding the content of self-deception and how the gospel addresses it.

### THREE EXAMPLES FROM LITERATURE

Hulga Hopewell—the protagonist of Flannery O'Connor's story "Good Country People"[7]—had a wooden leg, a weak heart, and a Ph.D. in philosophy (not a promising combination). She clearly believed she was superior both in intellectual knowledge and self-knowledge to her mother and to all the others who peopled her rural Southern setting. One day Manley Pointer, a young man selling Bibles, visited their farm. He called himself a simple country boy, talked about his commitment to Christian service, and claimed that every home needed the word of God. Hulga contrived to seduce him and to lead him into hitherto unknown philosophical depths. But as it turned out, she was more seduced than seducer.

The seduction began on their way to a picnic the next day. She informed him that love was a word she did not use, that she did not believe in God but had seen through to nothing, and that this bitter knowledge, free from illusion, was the only kind of salvation anyone could have. The seduction proceeded despite all this philosophical talk as he pressed her to say she loved him and asked her if she did. She resisted using the word love, but in a moment in which passion conquered intellect she finally complied: "Yes, yes." "Okay then," he said, "prove it." Then she asked him, "How?" Instead of the expected "Let me make love to you," he shocked her with "Show me where your wooden leg joins on."

This began the final crisis in which she learned that one of the salesman's Bibles was a hollow box containing a flask of whiskey, a pack of obscene playing cards, and a box of condoms. Pleadingly she asked, "Aren't you just good country people?" "Yeah," he replied, "but it ain't held me back none." When she appealed to his being a Christian, he rejoined, "I hope you don't think that I believe in that crap!" His last words to her were, "You ain't so smart. I been believing in nothing ever since I was born." Hulga's mind stopped working, and she was reduced to helplessness.

Hulga's smug philosophy and her self-image as a nihilistic intellectual were shaken by the ambiguity she encountered in the designing Bible salesman. She was made to discover that there were dimensions in herself and in the world that had been concealed from her and of which she had not taken account. What she would do with this crisis of disillusionment, this puncturing of self-deception, the story does not clearly tell us.

In another O'Connor story, "Everything That Rises Must Converge,"[8] we meet Julian, a young man just out of college who had been given his education and was now sacrificially supported by his widowed mother. She was a kind-hearted woman, guilty of paternalistic racism, who found her identity in an aristocratic ancestry and in fantasies about happy childhood days at her grandfather's mansion. Julian did not like to think about all that she did for him and dealt with the knowledge of it by convincing himself that her sacrifices were necessitated by her own lack of foresight. Maintaining that culture was a matter of the mind rather than the heart, he felt that he was really the only one who could appreciate the elegance of the old family mansion. Julian believed that from his own intellectual resources he had wrested a first-rate education from a third-rate college. He especially believed that, in spite of his mother, he was free of racial prejudice and was prepared to face the new interracial world of the South. Furthermore, he believed he had cut himself free emotionally from his mother. But beyond this he had an evil urge to break his mother's spirit. He wanted to teach her a lesson about the true nature of the new world and her moral duty in it. He gets his chance in the story.

Julian was accompanying his mother on the city bus to an exercise class intended to help her high blood pressure. As they got off the bus, she handed a little black boy a penny, and the child's mother, enraged by her condescension, struck her a blow that knocked her to the ground. Julian's reaction to his mother's plight was one of gleeful anger: "I told you not to do that," "You got exactly what you deserved," "I hope this teaches you a lesson." But then when she said, "Tell *Grandpa* to come get me," and he saw the fierce distortion on her face, he realized how serious the trauma had been. He cried out, "Mother," "Darling, sweetheart, wait." Then he cried, "Mamma, Mamma."

By means of his picture of himself as a socially liberal intellectual, free from dependence on his mother, Julian kept himself unaware of other layers of his own reality of which he had given no account.

Dostoevsky's "Notes from the Underground"[9] is a classic portrayal of various aspects of self-dividedness and self-deception, but I limit myself to the place of power in self-deception. The underground man desired freedom as the power to rebel against a logically and mathematically ordered society that would reduce him to a piano key played by someone else. He wanted to smash things even if that went against his logical self-interest. He wanted to realize all of his possibilities, not just to exercise his reason. He believed, in fact, that this was a moral obligation and that people should not reconcile themselves to the stone wall of arithmetic and the laws of nature. They should not accept the stone wall even if it was not possible to knock it down. But he knew that he would not follow out this way of living and that his talk was only a joke—although he might be joking with a heavy heart.

Having been denied this dimension of power, he sank to a much lower level of power seeking. He humiliated a gentle prostitute named Lisa because he wanted power, telling her that he could not live without feeling that he had someone completely in his power, some human being to tyrannize. But he knew that this exercise of power was motivated by his need to compensate for an abasement he had suffered at the hands of some acquaintances. He actually knew himself to be desperately afraid of a world he despised, a world whose conventions he slavishly followed in order not to appear ridiculous—despite all the talk about smashing the system and despite the fact that he thought himself cleverer than everyone else. And while telling Lisa about his desire for power, he was also telling her that he was much worse than she, that he was in fact "the most horrible, the most ridiculous, the most petty, the most stupid, the most envious of all the worms on earth who are not a bit better than me, but who—I'm damned if I know why—are never ashamed or embarrassed, while I shall be insulted all my life by every louse because that's the sort of fellow I am."

Looking back at the three stories, we observe that Hulga is made to discover that she does not really have knowledge that will give her a nihilistic solution. Julian finds out that his moral superiority does not make him free or secure. Both believe something about themselves that they also know at some level is not true, although the two characters hardly glimpse the hidden dark side at all until the final crisis. Then they are compelled to confront the hidden truth head-on. We are not sure how they will respond to it; they may conceal the truth again or revise their false belief.

The underground man, by contrast, is much more conscious of his inner duality and self-deception. He tells the story from such an awareness. As he draws to the end of the philosophical ruminations that constitute the first part of the work, he states that he does not believe a word he has written, yet perhaps he does believe but cannot help suspecting that he is lying. Earlier he relates that he had once tried hard to fall in love and really suffered terribly but in his heart of hearts, of course, he did not believe that he was suffering. When disobedient to his father as a child, he would repeat how sorry he was and shed rivers of tears, of course deceiving himself but not pretending at all. This is important: deceiving himself but not pretending. He was not pretending, because he really did experience the emotions of unrequited love and remorse; but he was deceiving himself, because some part of him, his heart of hearts, did not believe in the emotions he really experienced. The underground man is conscious of his duality, his self-deception, throughout the story, but he has no means to escape it.

Let me at this point state again a tentative and provisional definition of self-deception: It is the condition of holding a belief about or image of oneself or of one's situation in reality that one really believes while knowing in another part of oneself that it is false. I should now like to explore several ways of understanding analytically the dynamics of believing something about ourselves that we know is not true. What is at stake? Why do we do it?

## REINHOLD NIEBUHR AND HONEST DISHONESTY

Our three literary examples of self-deception—centering on claims of knowledge, righteousness, and power—have a close relationship to Reinhold Niebuhr's classic theological analysis of human nature: pride is the fundamental sin, more basic than sensuality.[10] When we try to overcome insecurity by a will to power, we transgress the limits of creatureliness. We fall into pride when we try to raise our finite capacities to the absolute.[11] While pride can be categorized as *spiritual* when a person's absolutized finite capacities are explicitly thought to have divine sanction,[12] the inordinate self-assertions of human beings occur in the three specific realms of experience already mentioned—knowledge, morality, and power. But it should be observed, as our literary examples have shown, that these three areas of pride, and of self-deception, are not discrete but rather penetrate each other. In pride people claim more power, knowledge, or righteousness than they have or can have. Human beings make these assertions because they are simultaneously ignorant of their limitations and trying to overcome and obscure those limitations they do dimly perceive.[13]

Pride, then, for Niebuhr is closely connected to self-deception. But this dishonesty is not as much the basis as the concomitant of prideful self-love. In self-love people make inordinate claims for themselves, which they know are undeserved and which they can justify only by deceiving themselves. The pretensions of the self can be justified only by willful deception.[14] The dishonesty of self-deception is neither pure ignorance nor a conscious lie but rather a general state of confusion from which individual acts of deception arise.[15] The dynamic or motive of self-deception is the need to justify what is unjustifiable—claims of inordinate power, knowledge, and righteousness. I support my excessive claims by believing they are legitimate, and I achieve this by obscuring the dim knowledge that I am limited in all these areas and the claims are not legitimate. But human beings are honest enough about their limitations to have to commit the dishonesty of deceiving themselves about these limitations in order to justify their efforts to deny them. When I claim, for example, that I have more righteousness than I really have, I make myself believe this lie, because I am too honest to claim the righteousness if I know I do not have it. For Niebuhr, self-deception, as an organic constituent of sin, is rebellion; it is against God.[16]

### JEAN-PAUL SARTRE AND BAD FAITH

Jean-Paul Sartre has penetratingly discussed self-deception under the term "bad faith." For Sartre human existence precedes its essence. People *are,* before they are *anything.* Human being begins as undefined, as nothing, and then surges up and defines itself as something, as an essence. Since human being is not defined by anything outside itself, God is ruled out because God would be the definer of human existence.[17] Thus self-deception or bad faith is not against God but is simply the issue of the structure of human existence as Sartre understands it.

In his famous analysis of self-deception as bad faith Sartre defines the phenomenon simply as lying to oneself. Within the unity of a single consciousness and project I both know as deceiver and do not know as deceived. An idea and its opposite are held at the same time.[18]

Self-deception is grounded on the double property of human reality which for Sartre is the same thing as or is very closely related to being-for-itself and consciousness. This double property is that human reality is at once facticity and transcendence. Facticity for Sartre is the necessary connection that being-for-itself (human being) has with its own past and with being-in-itself, what is fixed. The pastness of human reality is fixed. Human reality also is defined in part by other phenomena that are fixed, that are essences having a specific definition, that are what they are as a house is a house or a rock is a rock. Transcendence, on the other hand, is the process whereby consciousness or human reality goes beyond the fixed given in a further project of itself. These two elements of facticity and transcendence are and ought to be capable of coordination. As facticity and transcendence, human reality or consciousness is a being that is not what it is and is what it is not. Not only is this its structure, it must be.[19] A person who is a waiter (facticity) is not a waiter in the sense a glass is a glass and not a table. He is separated from being a waiter by nothing (transcendence): He is not what he is. But in a sense he is a waiter, for otherwise he could just as well call himself a diplomat or a reporter. In being a waiter he is what he is not.[20]

Bad faith fails to coordinate facticity and transcendence. It rather seeks to affirm their identity while preserving their differences. Thanks to transcendence I am not subject to all that I am, thus I can flee myself if criticized. But in bad faith I separate the transcendence into which I flee from the facticity of my acts by denying and not seeing the qualities I possess. Then I affirm that I am my transcendence as if it were a thing. Only in this way can I feel that I escape the reproaches.[21] Here Sartre seems to be saying that I distinguish the two elements in that I separate my innocent transcendence from the faulty facticity. At the same time I identify facticity with transcendence, for I consider my transcendence to be a facticity—I *am* an innocent person. If a person is accused of being a thief because of acts of stealing, he says, "I am more than my acts; I *am* not a thief; I do not have the being of a thief; I am a not-thief." He separates his transcendence—being more than a thief—from his facticity—acts of theft. But then he turns his transcendence—not being a thief—into facticity—I am honest.

Evidently for Sartre *good* faith does coordinate facticity and transcendence. The homosexual (Sartre's own example) who recognizes his faults but struggles against the view that his mistakes constitute a destiny has recognized in himself the peculiar, irreducible character of human reality.[22] Such a person presumably has achieved the ideal of good faith. He acknowledges, keeps in view, both his faulty facticity and his transcendence without confusing them. But he may—or apparently does—fall into bad faith by taking his not being a homosexual (transcendence) to be a thing, a facticity, as a glass is a glass and not a table. Apparently not being a homosexual, which in good faith preserves a dimension of freedom and transcendence, becomes in bad faith being a heterosexual as a glass is a glass.

It may be worth observing again that for Sartre the transcendence that belongs to good faith is the nothing. It is a not-being something, not being a thing or a liar. I am these things in facticity, but I am always more than that, and they do not exhaust my being; thus I am not-they. The transcendence as a not-something is undefined; it is the possibility of being many things. In bad faith or self-deception, on the other hand, transcendence has been turned into the positive opposite of the undesirable traits. Transcendence by being defined has actually been reduced to facticity. It is no longer an open possibility but closes off the possibility of being other than what it is. Non-homosexuality becomes heterosexuality; non-foolishness becomes wisdom. The person who steals in bad faith separates his transcendence of stealing—I am not a thief—from the facticity of it—acts of theft—and turns the transcendence into a new facticity: I *am* an honest person. The ontological error made in this effort is that the openness of transcendence is changed into a fixed something, an honest person as a glass is a glass. But for Sartre the attempt cannot be carried out. I can assert that I am an honest person as a thing, but it is not really possible to escape the freedom that resides in the fact that I am an undefined, nonessential, existent resting on nothingness.[23] I finally cannot turn the freedom of transcendence into facticity, but by the effort to do so I do conceal from myself the character of my facticity; I hide the true nature of my past. I both believe and do not believe this lie.

For Sartre the dynamic of self-deception is the felt desire to escape the burden and anguish of freedom, to escape being "condemned to freedom," to flee from the need constantly to make my undefined existence, to turn my becoming someone through my choices into something already fixed.[24] If for Niebuhr self-deception is the necessary entailment of pride, the concomitant step that would justify the unjustifiable assertion of transcendence (claiming absolute righteousness), for Sartre self-deception seems to be the necessary first moment of recoil from the move into transcendence. The scope of unlimited possibilities which constitutes the freedom of transcendence is too much and must be neutralized by turning it into facticity.

According to Niebuhr, I conceal from myself my limitations because I cannot bear the pain of being caught in the visible, conscious dishonesty of claiming more knowledge, righteousness, or power than I have. In Sartre's view I conceal from myself my flaws, apparently, simply because I cannot bear to acknowledge my fault but also because I cannot bear the uncertainty of being more than my flaws. For Niebuhr I cannot tolerate the tension between what I am and what I claim to be; therefore I conceal what I am from myself. For Sartre I cannot tolerate the uncertain, open freedom that justifies my claiming to be more than my acts or roles; therefore I conceal this open freedom by turning it into a closed thing that is the opposite of my acts. And thus I also conceal my unacceptable acts from myself. Or is it that in order to conceal my acts (facticity) from myself I turn my transcendent freedom into a facticity that is the opposite of my acts?

It has been said that Sartre's rejection of Freud's interpretation of self-deception, which is based on Freud's conception of the unconscious,[25] is grounded on Sartre's dogma that all mental life is conscious.[26] And it has been denied, against Sartre, that all instances of self-deception must derive from the facticity-transcendence relationship. Furthermore, one could argue that while Sartre has successfully accounted for self-deception without appealing to a divided mind or to unconscious mental processes, his notion of disbelieving what one believes is not the same thing as knowing that what one believes is false while still believing it. For Sartre it is more a matter of "selective inattention." Self-deception in the strong sense requires positing a divided mind with some kind of partition between conscious and unconscious.[27]

In response to this criticism I would say that Sartre's bad faith is probably not as deeply rooted as self-deception is in some other descriptions of the latter. Yet Sartre does not think that all conscious phenomena are equally conscious, for he speaks of the truth that is *hidden* from the self as deceived.[28] Nevertheless, it seems to be the case that for Sartre the mask that conceals certain truths from me is not so much opaque as translucent. Or perhaps more accurately, the mask is toward the transparent end of the spectrum of possible translucencies. Those who consider the divisions of the mind less fixed than the Freudians do will view Sartre's position more favorably.

### HERBERT FINGARETTE AND
### PHILOSOPHICAL PSYCHOLOGY

Herbert Fingarette, in his book *Self-Deception* (originally published in 1969), has given an illuminating and comprehensive account of self-deception that has in view both psychoanalytical and moral concerns. The self-deceiver is a person who lies to himself and others and believes his own lie although he knows in his heart it is a lie.[29] As deceiver he is free, responsible, and insincere. As deceived he is an innocent victim. Fingarette tends throughout to emphasize the side of freedom and responsibility.[30] But occasionally he emphasizes victimization. In fact, at one point he seems to state as his own position that the self-deceiver does not have control over what he is doing, that his personal agency and moral capacity have been subverted to the point that we incline to see him as the victim of a mental breakdown. Fingarette is not as clear as we would like him to be as to whether self-deception is a universal human problem for which people can be held responsible or a limited instance of mental pathology for which one cannot be held responsible.[31] In faithfulness to the phenomenon of self-deception Fingarette maintains both sides of it, but he does not really deal in a focal way with the relationship between the two, perhaps because he thinks—mistakenly in my view—that he has escaped a paradoxical description of self-deception.[32]

One of Fingarette's main concerns is to transcend the view that self-deception is primarily a matter of holding two irreconcilable beliefs or contradictory concepts and to show that it is a matter of action, identity, and purposefulness. Therefore he is critical of Sartre. He wants to replace the "cognition-perception" interpretation of the phenomenon with a "volition-action" interpretation. Consciousness in his view is not a passive mirror and is not best grasped under the image of seeing but is rather the active skill of spelling out—of making something clear, explicit, and elaborated. It is more a matter of action than of knowledge.[33] I may spell something out to myself or not. In self-deception I do not spell out to myself, do not avow or acknowledge, certain of my life engagements, even though it is appropriate to do so. In fact, I disavow these engagements as a part of my identity.[34] Not only do I not spell out the unwelcome truth that I do not want to see (my attempt to undermine a colleague, my failure in a certain ambition), I also do not spell out that I have assessed the situation and seen this truth and that I have adopted the tactic of disavowing it. I avoid becoming explicitly conscious of the engagement and also avoid becoming explicitly conscious of this avoidance. Not only do I conceal the truth I have seen, I conceal that I have seen it and conceal that I have concealed it.[35] In self-deception a person does not simply make all of these denials; a person does so purposefully. The self-deceived person persuades herself to believe contrary to the evidence in order to evade somehow the unpleasant truth to which she has already seen the evidence point.[36] We see then that self-deception, according to Fingarette, turns more on the personal identity one accepts than on the beliefs one holds. Fingarette does, however, rightly acknowledge a connection between the dynamic and cognitive approaches to self-deception. The blindness or ignorance of the self-deceived person is generated by the absence of spelling out a life engagement.[37] It has been argued that Fingarette has not so much departed from a cognitive view of self-deception as he has shown that belief is less passive than it seemed.[38]

What, in Fingarette's view, is the motivation for self-deception? Why does a person not spell out to himself or herself certain engagements in the world? The crux is the engagement's unacceptability to the person. He or she cannot avow a particular engagement as his or hers because to do so would produce such disruptive and distressing consequences as to be unmanageably destructive. The unacknowledged engagement is incompatible with the synthesis of engagements the person currently avows.[39]

This same essential understanding of the motivation can be seen in a line that runs from Freud back through Pascal to Augustine (and obviously others could be placed in the line). People practice self-deception in order to avoid the inner pain of seeing the truth, particularly to escape seeing themselves in contradiction with their normative point of view.

As is well known, Freud divided the mind into three regions: conscious (attached to the ego), preconscious, and unconscious. The material in the preconscious is latent and can become conscious. The unconscious matter, on the other hand, is dynamically repressed and cannot of itself and without more ado become conscious. It is the ego that carries out repression in order to exclude certain trends in the mind from consciousness. It turns out then that there is an unconscious element in the ego. The ego is unconscious of the resisting force that carries out the repressions. And this unconscious element is not simply latent, as the preconscious is.[40] The essence of repression is simply turning something away from the conscious and keeping it at a distance. But what is repressed finds expression in consciousness in such concealed forms as neurotic symptoms. The motive and purpose of repression is nothing but the avoidance of unpleasure. One represses what would give pain, such as a hostile impulse against someone who is loved.[41] To bring the terminology of Fingarette and Freud together: To move an item from preconscious to conscious would be to avow it or spell it out; to leave it in the preconscious would be not to avow it; to push it into the unconscious (repress it) would be to disavow it.[42]

According to Pascal, self-love prompts us—all of us in varying degrees—to conceal the truth from ourselves. We want to think of ourselves as great, perfect, and happy, but we perceive that the opposite is the case. In order to relieve this embarrassment about our failures, we banish the truth about them, which we have seen, from our knowledge by hiding our faults from ourselves and others.[43] Similarly Augustine acknowledges that he had refused to see the wretched truth about himself—had deceived himself, put himself behind his back—because the truth was too painful to face.[44]

From the foregoing we may note that self-deception as a move against the evidence for the truth is an act or accomplishment that requires energy. It is thus more active than wishful thinking or impulsive forgetting.[45]

Stephen Crites sees Fingarette's central paradox as the view that self-deception is willed: I choose to deceive myself. But Crites believes that Fingarette has resolved the paradox by collapsing it. The responsibility side is lost through the assertion that the self-deceived is the neurotic victim of an emotional breakdown. The self-deceiver is not one of "us," but one of "them,"—a member of the class of people identified as neurotics. So victimized is she, it is difficult to see how she can be said to deceive herself at all.[46]

Crites's own view is that if personal agency is subverted, it is subverted by personal agency itself. Personal consciousness is set at cross-purposes within itself and is not simply broken down. The paradox is that deceiver and deceived are joined in one consciousness. The self-deceiver is both perpetrator and victim of his own deceits.[47]

Crites develops Fingarette's idea that in self-deception a person constructs a cover story to conceal the real story.[48] The real story, although not avowed, is the one actually believed and acted upon. The cover story, which must generally seem respectable, is devised to suppress the real story, which is unacceptable. It is so unflattering or heartbreaking that it cannot be faced. The negative real story is real in the sense that it generates one's action. But the cover story is put forward as a more acceptable explanation—rationalization—of one's action.[49] For example, a woman may act in a condescending way toward her lover because she really believes him to be a fool (real story). Her action reveals the real story. But being ashamed of being involved with a fool and not wanting to acknowledge that she is, she prevents herself from avowing his foolishness and instead avows his intelligence (cover story) to explain her being involved with him at all.[50]

While I do not disagree that the real story is likely to be revealed by action, I would want to add that it seems probable that a person would act on both the real and cover stories. A person who had concealed weakness (real story) with inordinate assertions of power (cover story) but was still aware at some level of the weakness would manifest both anxiety (reflective of the real weakness) and arrogance (reflective of the concealing power story).

A variation of the above formation is that the real story is suppressed because it is too positive rather than too negative. A person is unable to accept her strength or the nourishment that life offers; it seems too good to be true. A negative cover story is fabricated out of fear or distrust of what says yes. In a third type of self-deception, more prominent in Kierkegaard than the double-storied, the cover story is the only story. A pointless procession of gestures conceals the fact that there is no genuine project, no real story.[51]

I take up once more the paradoxical element in the concept of self-deception. As indicated above, the paradox is produced by modeling self-deception on interpersonal deception, in which one person, knowing the truth or believing a proposition, misleads someone else about it. When self-deception is seen in analogy to this, the same unitary self is simultaneously agent and victim, liar and lied to, knowing and ignorant, not believing and believing. These paradoxes pertain to both the process of becoming and the state of being self-deceived.[52]

We have also seen that many regard the paradoxical element as making self-deception a dubious or troubling concept.[53] One of the aspects that makes it most problematical is the claim that the self intentionally deceives itself.[54] A person voluntarily and intentionally misleads himself into believing what he believes to be false or into preventing himself from believing what he continues to believe is true.[55]

But it has also been argued that self-deception is not intentional. It is not initiated and directed by an agent for a specific reason or to serve a particular interest, but rather is subintentional or purposive. It persists because it serves the purpose of reducing anxiety, but it is not intentionally employed for that purpose.[56]

How is the dispute about intentionality to be resolved? Let us press a bit more closely the comparison between other-deception and self-deception. It may be argued that in other-deception the agent intends to mislead the victim, while in self-deception the deceiver misleads herself by means of rationalization[57] or evasion but not with deceitful intention.[58] How should we assess this distinction?

In *other-deception*—lying—the agent does intend to mislead the victim. But he also has the further goal of using that deception to manipulate the other for the sake of his own (the liar's) power or protection. Thus the deception itself is intended, but is also the means to a further intended goal. *Self-deception* is surely the means to a further goal—the overcoming of pain, embarrassment, self-contradiction. Can it also be thought of as intended itself? I would think that it can be, but in an ambiguous way. The self-deception (disavowing a belief or act: that my lover is a fool) is so closely and essentially tied to the intended goal (eliminating the tension between two beliefs: that my lover is a fool versus that I am an intelligent person and would not be involved with a fool) that the self-deception must also be regarded as intended—but ambiguously. I want (intend) to have the lie (my lover is intelligent); otherwise I cannot eliminate the tension. But I do not want to have it *as* a lie, that is, I do not with conscious intention subvert myself by depriving myself of the truth. With regard to the degree of consciousness the intention would seem to be neither fully conscious nor fully unconscious.

Obviously the intention to eliminate the offending belief or engagement and the attendant inner conflict does not succeed. The unwelcome items are merely concealed or camouflaged and manifest themselves in phenomena such as neurotic symptoms or Paul's obsessive zeal for the law.

Alfred Mele has suggested that in recent literature there have been three main ways of attacking the problem of the paradox—a paradox I want to maintain: (1) Self-deception is irreducibly paradoxical and is, therefore, to be regarded as impossible and unreal; (2) interpersonal deception is not to be taken in a strict way as the proper model for self-deception; (3) self-deception is to be accounted for by fragmenting or dividing the mind in various ways.[59]

The primary reason for denying the possibility of self-deception on the ground that the concept is incoherent is the belief that the self is essentially unified, or at least strongly integrated, capable of critical reflection, and oriented to truth. A person may fall into ignorance or error, but she cannot simultaneously believe and disbelieve the same thing.[60] She is too closely in touch with herself for that to happen. It may be said, for example, that the self-deceived person is only relatively, but not essentially, different from the hypocrite, who knows what his real position is but pretends something else.[61] But this may belong to the next category.

Mele suggests three ways in which self-deception can be conceived that would modify or abandon some aspect of the interpersonal model.[62] (1) The self-deceived person knows or believes the real story but does not really believe the cover story.[63] (2) He believes the cover story but not the real story. (3) He believes neither one of the stories but approximates both.

It should also be recognized that the questioning of intentionality is a way of qualifying the interpersonal model. Mark Johnston believes that the removal of intentionality is the way out of the paradox.[64] I have argued that intentionality cannot be removed.

It has also been maintained that dividing the mind dispels the paradox, that the same unitary self simultaneously believes and disbelieves the same thing. There is more than one mind—or system—at work here, each with its own beliefs, goals, plans, and strategies. This enables an explanation free of conceptual strains.[65] My question is, If the paradox is removed, can we still give an account of all the phenomena?

We have already viewed Freud's classic analysis of the divided mind. Stephen White gives a Freudian type of description while pointing out that this model is by no means restricted to Freudian theory but is common to recent theorizing in the cognitive sciences. It need not entail belief in a multiplicity of self-conscious subsystems or distinct persons. Subsystems $S_1$ and $S_2$ originally both believe the real story. $S_1$ causes $S_2$ to lose belief in the real story and possibly to believe the cover story while itself continuing to believe the real story. Subsequently $S_1$ tries to keep $S_2$ from acquiring evidence that the real story is true and also tries to conceal its own activity.[66]

An elucidative partition theory which is not committed to the Freudian unconscious has been put forward by Donald Davidson. According to Davidson, self-deception occurs when a person has evidence that the real story is true but against the evidence believes the opposing cover story. The person in fact simultaneously believes both: (1) I am bald (real story); (2) I am not bald (cover story). In fact, the first story is what motivates the second one. The real story causes the man to ignore the evidence for itself or to look for evidence for the cover story. Our self-deceived man accepts the evidence for the cover story (I am not bald) although he knows that the evidence for the real story is better; he induces this deception in himself intentionally.[67] The concept of self-deception demands that the person remain aware of the evidence for the unwelcome real story, for that is what motivates his effort to rid himself of the awareness of it.[68]

What needs explaining is how a belief can cause a contrary belief. The explanation for this is a cause that is not a reason. One is *caused* to ignore the evidence for the real story by the desire to avoid pain although this is not a *reason* that would justify the cover story.[69]

Davidson goes on to argue that it is possible to believe simultaneously two inconsistent propositions or stories but not to believe the conjunction of them when the inconsistency is obvious. To explain how a person can keep the two beliefs apart and avoid obvious inconsistency it is necessary to posit boundaries in the mind between separate but overlapping territories, although it is not necessary to say that one of the territories is closed to consciousness. The irrational step in self-deception is the drawing of the boundary that keeps the inconsistent beliefs apart.[70] Evidently for Davidson the boundary is erected by the cause (the desire to avoid the pain of believing one is going to fail an exam), which is not a reason, as it is against a reason for believing otherwise (evidence in hand that one will probably fail). The desire to avoid pain causes but does not justify the cover story that one will pass.

Brian McLaughlin has presented a position similar to Davidson's, except that his critique of the view that the unavowed content is unconscious is more explicit and focused. Self-deception does entail holding two contradictory beliefs simultaneously, but this is not to be explained on the ground that one of the beliefs is unconscious, for an unconscious belief may be too deeply buried to explain the tension in the conflict-ridden minds of most self-deceivers. Self-deception can, however, be explained on the basis of accessible and inaccessible beliefs, which distinction is not to be thought of as simply a replacement for the conscious-unconscious opposition.[71] The real story is believed, but inaccessibly. Fear, disappointment, regret, shame, and the like, engendered by the real story, produce a motive for believing the cover story. Belief in the real story is not eradicated but is rendered inaccessible.[72] "Inaccessible" might be taken to mean not so deeply buried as to require extreme measures but recoverable only with special scrutiny or outside help.[73] In order to articulate the different locations of the opposing beliefs one could also appropriate William James's distinction between the focus (clear perception) and margin (nebulous) of consciousness[74] or the distinction made by Michael Polanyi between focal and subsidiary attention or awareness.[75]

I am convinced that some kind of partition theory is necessary to account for the phenomenon of self-deception, but so must some degree of the mind's unity be preserved. This, it seems to me, is paradoxical; but if it is not, it still seems to be an accurate description. We can give up neither picture of the self. If the mind is thoroughly integrated and transparently in touch with itself, self-*deception* is impossible. But if the mind is so divided that the territories become autonomous or semi-self-conscious selves, the concept of *self*-deception is subverted. The identity of deceiver and deceived has been dissolved so that there is no self that deceives *itself*.[76]

The self must be regarded as to some degree unified and integrated in order to account for the fact that the disavowed belief or engagement is not totally inoperant but causes symptoms and certain kinds of behavior or may even itself be elusively glimpsed. The boundary separating the territories is not impermeable. On the other hand, the self must be regarded as in some degree divided with boundaries ranging somewhere between translucent and opaque in order to account for the fact that the unwelcome mental content and its concomitant pain can be camouflaged, though not eradicated.

It should also be recognized that while in some self-deception, including probably that portrayed in Paul and Matthew, the painful real story has been disavowed or repressed into the unconscious, in other cases of self-deception the nonconscious matter is only preconscious. There are degrees of self-deception. I will use the terms "unconscious" and "inaccessible" more or less interchangeably and use neither of them as having a hard or thoroughly precise focus.

# 2

## SELF-DECEPTION
## IN PAUL

If anyone thinks that she is something
though being nothing

In some significant sense self-deception surely is a modern concept. But although it is only in the last 150 years that the phenomenon of self-deception has become the subject of "uncommon attention,"[1] the problem nevertheless emerges in the thinking of much earlier times and is specifically addressed in the New Testament letters of Paul.

### PAUL'S OWN TERMS AND THE INTERPRETER'S

For if anyone thinks he is something, when he is nothing, he deceives himself [*phrenapata heauton*]. (Gal. 6:3)

Let no one deceive himself [*heauton exapatatō*]. (1 Cor. 3:18)

Beyond this succinct explicitness Paul develops the theme with a wealth of related motifs. Interpreting Pauline themes such as the law and wisdom under the rubric of self-deception reveals Paul's considerable anthropological reflection or analysis. In particular, Paul regards the pursuit of the law as wrong and injurious and the law itself as a destructive power, even though ambiguously so. What Paul calls the wisdom of the world (1 Cor. 1:20) is the condition of self-deception. Knowledge puffs up (1 Cor. 8:1); it deceives. The wisdom of the world leads one to imagine that she knows something when she does not know it (1 Cor. 8:2). God has shown that this wisdom of the world is foolishness (1 Cor. 1:20; 3:19). But those who stand outside the word of the cross do not know that (1 Cor. 1:18-25). Their misconstrued wisdom is the occasion for a self-glorying—a boasting (1 Cor. 1:29; 3:21)—which hides from them the fact that their asserted knowledge (1 Cor. 8:2) is really a not-knowing (1 Cor. 1:21).[2] It does not know God, whose way of dealing with human beings is for Paul the one thing really worth knowing (Phil. 3:7-11).

This condition of being deceived about what one knows—or is—grows out of an act of the person. The claim to have wisdom (Rom. 1:22) is the claim of a darkened mind (Rom. 1:21) which results from or is concomitant with a deliberate act. Knowledge of God is available to human beings in general through the things God has created (Rom. 1:19-20, 21), but this available knowledge has been rejected. People have suppressed the truth, have refused to honor or acknowledge God, and have exchanged the truth about God for a lie (Rom. 1:18, 21, 23, 28).

At the same time God's response to this is to give people up to the darkened mind that they have actualized, to a mind that cannot stand testing (Rom. 1:28). Thus the darkened mind turns out to be a fate as well as an act.[3] The ontic or actual situation of human beings is that they do not have the resources in themselves to know the truth (1 Cor. 2:10-14), and the possibility of knowing God through the creation turns out to be an ontological possibility or possibility in principle that is never realized—except through eschatological revelation that comes in Christ and the faith that responds to it.[4]

The point of view in 2 Thess. 2:9-12 is very similar. This letter, of course, may well not be a genuine letter of Paul (I shall assume that it is not), but the content of this particular passage is sufficiently akin to the Pauline point of view that it can be used to explicate Paul's position both by its likenesses to and differences from him. The thing that most obviously distinguishes it from the Romans texts we have been considering is that the vocabulary is more concrete and specific, more mythological. God's initiative in the delusion of human beings is thus more dramatically portrayed. Those who will perish are deceived because of a willful act on their part. They rejected the truth and took pleasure in unrighteousness. But at the same time they are victims of a strong delusion that God sends upon them to make them believe what is false.

One of the notable things about the 2 Thessalonians passage is the frankness with which God is made responsible for the delusion from which human beings suffer. It is also in Romans, but more implicitly. In 2 Cor. 4:3-4 we meet similarities with the 2 Thessalonians passage. In the latter, people perish because of a failure to receive the truth and in 2 Corinthians because of a failure to see the light (*apollymi* = "perish," in both cases). The striking difference is that in 2 Corinthians the failure occurs because not God but the god of this world has blinded the eyes of the unbelievers. We may consider "Paul's" shift of terminology here in the light of the narrative matrix of his thought. That there is a narrative matrix is seen in the fact that the "characters" in Paul's vision of the drama of salvation history are related to each other in the same dynamic way as the characters in a story. And these relationships manifest an underlying deep structure. In Paul's representation God is a sender or communicator who wills to communicate new life, light, justification (Rom. 3:21; 2 Cor. 4:1; 5:17-18) to human beings. God mandates Christ to be the subject or hero of the story who will carry out this intention (Rom. 5:8; 2 Cor. 5:19; Gal. 1:3-4; 4:4-5). God's project may be opposed by Satan or the god of this world, as it is in 2 Cor. 4:3-4. But in 2 Thess. 2:9-12 God is both sender or communicator and opponent. The literary critic Roland Barthes has observed that it is rare and paradoxical that the sender and opponent should be manifested in the same "character,"[5] in our case making God his own opponent. That is, the God who loves and calls people (2:13-17) is the one who also sends a delusion upon them in order that they cannot believe. Not only does the author of 2 Thessalonians give us that paradox, but when we juxtapose the Paul of 2 Corinthians to 2 Thessalonians the further paradox emerges that both God and Satan can occupy the opponent slot. They are correlatives of each other, belonging to the same paradigm, being elements in the same reservoir. This means that God and Satan stand in a metaphorical relationship to each other. Each is somehow seen as the other.[6]

Making use of this narrative model does not solve the theological problem involved. Perhaps it makes clearer what the problem is that constructive theology has to deal with. What does it mean that God and the god of this world can be substitutes for each other, that they can step in and out of the same role?

We may observe in passing that the language Paul uses of God that we have thus far considered might be mythological, depending on how one defines myth and interprets Paul. But that is not a point I wish to exploit here because I take myth to be a subcategory of metaphor. Paul's language is clearly metaphorical. Traits from a human modifier (vehicle) are attributed to a divine subject (tenor).[7] God sends a delusion, gives people up, makes the light shine, and so forth.

### Self-Deception and Deception by the Law

We may gain further access to Paul's understanding of self-deception by observing his metaphorical treatment of sin and the law. Paul deals with both of these as personified powers, and they interact with each other in the closest way. In 1 Cor. 15:56 he states very concisely that the law is the power of sin, and in Romans 7 he probes the relationship in an elaborate and subtle manner. James Hillman has noted that personifying is not something that we do but something that happens to us. It is given with the imagination. Personifying is the spontaneous experiencing and speaking of the configurations of existence—such as Fame, Night, Hope—as psychic presences, persons.[8] Let us see more specifically how Paul metaphorically views sin and the law as persons.

We will look first at sin, but this cannot be done in isolation from the law since Paul closely connects them. The law provokes sin as an act or attitude of coveting (Rom. 7:7). But sin is also metaphorically a personified power; it is the metaphorical subject to which are attributed predicates that lend it independent subjective existence. Sin is something that has dominion over us, enslaves us, and reigns in our bodies; and we are its obedient slaves (Rom. 6:6-7, 12-14, 16, 20). But it is also a power from which we can be set free (Rom. 6:7, 18, 22). Sin "finds opportunity" and works covetousness in Paul (Rom. 7:8). Paul applies the action pattern death-to-life to Christ (Rom. 4:24-25), to Christians (Rom. 6:4-6) in general, and to himself in particular (2 Cor. 4:10), that is, to persons, but he also applies the same pattern to sin. It lies dead and it revives (Rom. 7:8-9). Once aroused it deceives and kills (Rom. 7:11).

In the same metaphorical way the law also is personified, and as such it is not simply a splendor that has been superseded by a greater splendor but is a negative power. The law comes in (Rom. 5:20; 7:9), arouses sin (Rom. 7:5, 7), and holds us captive (Rom. 7:6). It promises life but reneges and serves up death (Rom. 7:10); that is, the law deceives. It cannot fulfill its promise because it has been weakened by the flesh (Rom. 8:3). Thus the law is portrayed as something—someone—evil and not just as a good that has been superseded by a better. The law's deception of me (Rom. 7:10) engenders an ignorance (Rom. 10:2-3), hardness of mind (2 Cor. 3:14), and blindness (2 Cor. 4:4) in which I mistakenly believe that my own righteousness of the law is the equivalent of the righteousness of God (Phil. 3:9) rather than its opposite. What else could Paul mean when he states that it is an unenlightened zeal for God that sends me in ignorant pursuit of a righteousness of my own?

### The Law: Intention and Result

I shall now look at Paul's understanding of the law in a somewhat more systematic way. It has been denied in recent years that Paul's concept of the law is consistent and unified.[9] There is a sense in which the charge of inconsistency is true, but I should like to pursue the question of the exact sense in which it is true. I begin with the issue of result rather than intention.

For Paul the result of the law's operation is to make human beings know sin as transgression (Rom. 3:20; 4:15; 5:13-14) and even to provoke sin (Rom. 7:5, 7). To know sin in Paul's view clearly means to do sin (Rom. 7:7-10). But Paul may also be attributing to the law a revelatory (making aware) role in the realm of knowledge. Without the law people may know that their deeds are wrong and destructive (see Rom. 1:24-32), but the law teaches them that the deeds are also against a transcendent power who wills human well-being.

If Paul in Rom. 5:20 and Gal. 3:19 suggests that the intention of the law is to provoke sin, he is probably just not paying careful attention to his own language, because in other places the intention of the law is to evoke faith and to bestow life (Rom. 9:31-32; 7:10; 8:3-4). In Rom. 9:31-32 Paul states that Israel, in pursuing the law, which affords righteousness, missed the law because they pursued it through works. This implies that the real intention of the law is faith (although its result is sin and death). Likewise the requirement of the law which is fulfilled in believers who walk according to the Spirit (Rom. 8:4, 7b) is the requirement to have faith (Rom. 3:31—4:9; 10:6-8). In Rom. 7:10 the law promised life, and again in that chapter it seems to be an impulse toward life (7:14a, 16b, 22-23). Similarly 2 Cor. 3:12-16 implies that Israel's failure to recognize the significance of Jesus was at one with their failure to perceive the real meaning of the law. Hence Jesus and the law must have intended the same thing.[10] The law's intention is nullified because human beings as flesh assert themselves against God and try to make themselves secure through a righteousness of their own (Rom. 8:3, 7; Phil. 3:4, 9-10). Thus, because of flesh— the drive of fallen humanity to establish its own security—the law that promised life (Rom. 7:10) cannot give life (Gal. 3:21).

It might be argued that when Paul holds the intention of the law to have been faith and life, he is contradicting his more frequently expressed view that salvation rests on God's promise, that the law came in later and that law and promise are antithetical (Gal. 3:15-18; Rom. 4:13-17; 5:20; 9:7-13). Such an argument, however, would fail to reckon with the fact that Paul knew Adam to have been under the law in principle (Rom. 5:13-14; 7:7-12) and knew the Gentiles to have been under the law written on the heart (Rom. 2:14-15). Moreover, the Gentiles' being under the "elements" is existentially equivalent to the Jews' being under the law (Gal. 3:23—4:7).[11] For Paul the law has always been an instrument of God's dealing with the world. Jew and Gentile are in the same kind of situation

(Rom. 3:9-20), but Paul forgot that when he wrote about humankind between Adam and Moses being without the law (Rom. 5:13-14).

What could Paul have meant when he said that sin is not "counted" when there is no law (between Adam and Moses)? Räisänen seems to be right in holding that sin's not counting (*ellogeō*) is a kind of heavenly bookkeeping that is extremely inconsequential, seeing as how people still suffered death—the wages of sin—while there was (allegedly) no law.[12] Paul's suggestions that the law has always been operative do not allow any substantive content to the idea that there was a period without the law when sin did not count. There has always been law, and the reality of death as the wages of sin shows that sin has always counted.

I have said enough to indicate that I do not believe that Paul rejected the law (Rom. 3:20, 28; 10:4-6; Gal. 3:21; Phil. 3:9) *because* he thought that salvation by the law would exclude the Gentiles.[13] On the contrary, he believed that the Gentiles had always been in principle under the law, although he probably saw them as more prone to boast of their wisdom (1 Cor. 1:22, 26-31; 4:7-10; 8:1) than of their righteousness. The law represents finite achievements that can be ultimately trusted.

Nor did Paul criticize the law because of a dogmatic view that salvation was by faith in Christ.[14] The law was not rejected thus by *definition* (because of not being faith in Christ) but because, despite the positive side we have seen in Paul's understanding of the law, there was for Paul a material, substantive, existential difference—opposition—between obedience to the law as he understood it and faith in Christ. It may well be that Paul's experience and interpretation of the law was at variance with the way most first-century Jews experienced the law, but his view is still an interpretation that stands on its own feet. More attention needs to be given now to Paul's view of the interaction between law and flesh.

The righteousness of faith is not merely relatively better than the righteousness of the law but is rather its antithesis (Phil. 3:8-9). It is qualitatively different. The negative value Paul gives to a righteousness of my own, based on the law, should be allowed to have the full force it has in the text (Rom. 9:30—10:4; Phil. 3:3-9). The fault with the law is not that it gives Israel a special status (which it does not) but that it offers the opportunity for a righteousness of one's own and leads away from God's righteousness. In fact, the law is sin's power (1 Cor. 15:56), all of this even before we consider Romans 7. What is wrong with the righteousness of the law is that it asserts itself rather than receiving from God, as faith does. Those who are seeking to establish their own righteousness by the law do not submit (*hypotassō*, in the passive) to God's righteousness (Rom.

10:3). Thus the pursuit of the righteousness of the law is a form of living according to the flesh. It is an expression of the mind of the flesh, which does not and cannot submit (*hypotassō*, in the passive) to God's law (Rom. 8:7-8).[15] The parallelism between Rom. 8:7-8 and 10:3 shows that the pursuit of the righteousness of the law is a hostility to God that refuses to submit to God. Therefore the *zeal* for God and the law that Paul claims for himself and attributes to his fellow Jews, and the *gain* of the blameless righteousness of the law that he acquired through that zeal, should be understood ironically. The zeal seems good and the gain, real gain when people are unenlightened and ignorant (Rom. 10:2-3), when they exist in a not-knowing (*agnoountes*) self-deception.

As we have seen, it is the flesh that subverts the law's original intention to call forth faith (Rom. 7:5; 8:3, 7) and causes it to produce sin (Rom. 7:22-23). Since all are in the flesh and sinful (Rom. 3:10, 23), all are provoked by the law to enmity against God. We have seen that Paul regards a righteousness of one's own based on the law in a very critical way. That it is the law itself which provokes the self-deceptive effort to establish myself on the basis of my own righteousness comes most explicitly to expression in Romans 7. But it is a very short step from the material we have been considering to that chapter. Note again that the law's original intention is redemptive. This intention is subverted by the flesh (Rom. 7:5; 8:3, 6-8), and the law becomes the instrument of sin, which we have seen is also a personified power (Rom. 7:8, 11, 13). Sin uses the law. But so closely tied is the law as instrument to sin, the initiating agent, that the law can also appear as the agent. Sin employs the law, but the law is the power (1 Cor. 15:56) that brings latent sin to active life (Rom. 7:9). Therefore, the law itself can be spoken of as the provoker that causes sin (Rom. 7:7) and that, installed in the flesh, works against God's redemptive intention (Rom. 7:22-23).

What kind of sin does the law provoke? The plain sense of Rom. 7:5, 7-8 suggests sin as attitudes and acts of disobedience to the law. This is supported by the plural "passions" in 7:5 and the reference to "every desire" in 7:8. Moreover, the references to members of the body and fruit for death in 7:5 point back to 6:19, 21, where we find the same terminology and where sin is acts of rebellion (*anomia*). In addition, the probable allusion to Adam here suggests sin as transgression of commands.[16] Paul coveted *because* the law commanded him not to covet, and he coveted in various ways.

But if Paul has in mind here sin as acts of overt disobedience (and if he at least includes himself in the human phenomenon he is describing), how can he have said in Phil. 3:4-9 that he was blameless regarding the righteousness of the law? Bultmann's famous answer is that Phil. 3:4-9 expresses Paul's consciousness as a Jew, while the sinning and internal conflict in Rom. 7:7-25 portray what Paul saw his pre-Christian situation to have been when he looks back on it from the standpoint of Christian faith. Moreover, the "desire"—sin—engendered by the commandment against covetousness is not so much coveting as the desire—unenlightened zeal (Rom. 10:2)—to establish oneself with God by one's obedience to the law, one's own righteousness. The conflict then is not primarily seeking to do the morally good but failing and doing wrong. That which is in view is not the moral flaw of committing acts of coveting.

The contradiction is rather seeking to provide life by my own righteousness while bringing about death.[17] The law provokes sin by seducing me into believing that I can create life for myself by my own righteousness. Gerd Theissen has convincingly brought these two types of sinning together by arguing that prior to 7:9 Paul is talking about sin in the sense of antinomian transgression, but in 7:9-11 he makes a transition to sin as zeal to fulfill the law.[18] The flesh, as the drive of fallen humankind to provide its own security, turns the law's intention to elicit faith into its seduction of people into the attempt to ground their life on their obedience to the law.

I basically accept the position just stated, and this obviously entails holding that the conflict Paul describes in Rom. 7:14-24—between the desire for life and the accomplishment of death—is unconscious.[19] It also means that the conflict pertains to Paul's pre-Christian life. Would he have spoken of redeemed humanity in such pessimistic terms?[20] However, it has always been a problem for this interpretation that the past tenses that Paul has been using in 7:7 and following are replaced by the present tense when he actually begins to describe the internal tension at 7:15. Must we not at least say that having become aware of the self-division on the basis of Christian revelation he presents the unconscious conflict of his past pre-Christian life *as if* it were conscious and present? Must we not in fact say more? I uphold the view that Paul is talking about his pre-Christian past. But the use of the present tense extends the self-dividedness of Rom. 7:14-25 into the present of Paul and his readers. Moreover, believers are only in the process of being renewed (2 Cor. 3:18; 4:16). As long as they bear the image of the old Adam (1 Cor. 15:39) and do not have Christ fully formed in them (Gal. 4:19), which means as long as time lasts (Phil. 3:10-11), all that pertains to self-dividedness and self-deception is still the struggle of believers.

We still need to refine the issue and to explore how unconscious or inaccessible was the failure that Paul describes in Romans 7 in light of the whole picture he presents and in light of psychological insight. The moral fault and the failure to achieve life through obedience (Romans 7) must have been to some degree inaccessible to him in order to account for his good conscience (blamelessness) in Phil. 3:4-9. But it must also have been to some degree conscious in order to account for the anxious zeal with which he continued to pursue the righteousness of the law (Phil. 3:4-6; Gal. 1:13-14; Rom. 10:2). The failure also needs to be regarded as partially conscious in order to explain why one would have reason to turn to the offer of salvation in the gospel.[21] How could or why would one respond to a new possibility if the old life seemed to be unproblematic?[22] Paul both believes and disbelieves the cover story that he is blameless. He both disbelieves and believes the real story that his own righteousness is refuse (Phil. 3:8) and that he does evil (Rom. 7:18-19).

The moral side of the sin attested in Rom. 7:5, 7-8 (largely ignored by Bultmann), that is, breaking the law by every kind of coveting, should not be lost sight of. It is there, and that means that the conflict in 7:14-25 is moral (willing to do good but doing evil) as well as existential (willing life but accomplishing death). Paul tries to create life by his moral obedience, but he fails both to be moral and to establish life, for the effort takes him away from the righteousness of God (Rom. 10:3) in which life resides (Rom. 3:21-26; 5:18, 21). The dual (moral and existential) failure is concealed beneath the cover story of blameless righteousness of the law. But it is not completely concealed, for the dim awareness of this failure is what drives him to the continuing anxious zeal for the law, urged on by the hope of overcoming both failures—and/or of concealing them.

These considerations point us to the motive or dynamic for self-deception suggested by Paul. We conceal the truth from ourselves, do not spell it out, because we want to be blameless in our own eyes, want to be justified, on the basis of an effort that is our own (Rom. 10:2-3; Phil. 3:3-9). It has been suggested that the anxious desire to be what we want to be disposes us to believe that we actually are: this is simply the way the human mind works.[23] Paul would qualify this by adding, No, this is the way the fallen mind, the mind of the flesh, works.

We have seen that for Paul the law has been a part of God's dealing with humankind from the beginning. By confronting people with a limit (You shall not covet) the law makes them aware of their finitude and should point them to a power beyond themselves. Law was to have been a vehicle of the promise of salvation. But human beings—as flesh—rebel against the limit (Rom. 7:7; 8:7). Once they have rebelled, the law in its concreteness makes them aware of themselves as sinners, although only dimly. If they do not turn to grace, they may—again as flesh—try to use obedience to the law as a means of self-salvation. When Paul speaks positively about the law (evoking faith and promising life) he is speaking about it ontologically, what it is in principle, in God's creative intention. The ontological is possibility in principle. When he speaks about the law negatively (as provoking sin) he is talking about it ontically, what it is under the actual conditions of fallen existence. The ontic is actual possibility. It is in this second (ontic) sense that the law came in after the promise and is antithetical to it. Christ is the *telos* (termination) of the law in its ontic sense and the *telos* (goal) of the law in its ontological sense (Rom. 10:4). When Paul suggests that the law cannot give life, he is speaking about it in the ontic sense. It is precisely because it cannot give life that it is not against—in competition with—the promise, whose function *is* to give life (Gal. 3:21). Had Paul been speaking of the law ontologically, if he were consistent with his usual position, he would have said that the law could give life, but as a means to faith rather than as an alternative to faith. Thus it would still not be against the promise.[24]

My distinguishing an ontological and ontic sense of the law in Paul would probably come under Räisänen's stricture as being a modern expedient that is overprecise where no precision is possible.[25] Interpreters, however, always bring presuppositions to the text, and they are justified to the extent to which they help to clarify the text. I believe that the distinction under discussion here is useful. Paul himself does not distinguish two aspects of the law in his text, and we do not know to what extent he may have been presupposing such a distinction. Paul's statements about the law simply seem to contradict each other, and at the textual level they do contradict each other. The value of the ontological-ontic distinction as an interpretive device is that it enables us to show that Paul's view of the law is largely coherent. It helps us to bridge a gap in the text. Paul is seen not to be saying opposing things about the law within the same aspect but to be grasping the law in two aspects, at two different levels, under two categories. And the two categories have a meaningful relationship to each other. Paul is not making contradictory statements about apples but is describing and relating apples and oranges.

Most of the conflicts in Paul's statements about the law are dissipated if we sort his statements out into the ontological and ontic categories. The two aspects cohere if they are seen as mediated by Paul's anthropological reflections. Succinctly, again: The law intends faith and life, but humankind as flesh subverts this intention so that the result of the law is sin. The ontological-ontic distinction makes this construct conceptually more precise.

We have also seen that there are elements of contradiction that will not fit into this scheme. Paul's assertions are not totally consistent. Against the dominant tendency to say that the purpose of the law is faith (ontological) while the result is sin (ontic), Paul can also say that the purpose is sin. And having put all (including Gentiles) under the law in Romans 2, and having closely connected the law, sin, and death, he can deny in Rom. 5:13-14 that human beings were under the law between Adam and Moses even though they die. But these are marginal tensions working against a coherent center. In my judgment one of the implications of such a phenomenon for interpretation theory is that radical deconstruction is wrong in holding that language—or writing—generally and texts in particular have no center or form that would give coherence and would place some limit on the absolutely free play of meaning. Deconstruction maintains that discourse always undermines the position it asserts. Discourses undo themselves by drawing inside an opposing, disconfirming outside.[26] But observe from Paul that the presence of tensions or contradictions is not in itself proof that there is no center. There can be both an informing, coherent center and elements in conflict with it. Nevertheless, deconstruction can be heuristically helpful in alerting us to look for tensions and to expect writers to deconstruct themselves, to disagree with themselves. I have tried to show that Paul's understanding of the law holds together in a fundamental way but that there are also elements that have not been assimilated to the center position. Yet I am inclined to believe that what I have called the dominant tendency or center actually is basic, because the contradictory elements could easily be modified and integrally connected to the center.

## THE TWO TYPES OF DOUBLE-STORIED SELF-DECEPTION IN PAUL

We turn now to a brief look at the tension between a cognitive and dynamic interpretation of self-deception and then move to consider Paul in light of the two-story construct. Paul can certainly speak of self-deception in cognitive terms. The world did not know God through wisdom (1 Cor. 1:21); if one imagines that she knows, she does not (1 Cor. 8:2); the god of this world has blinded the mind (2 Cor. 4:4); they believe not the truth but what is false (2 Thess. 2:11-12). But for Paul it is not simply a cognitive matter; that is, what one does not know is oneself as a being who wills. In 2 Thessalonians refusing the truth (2:10, 12) is coincident with taking pleasure in unrighteousness (2:12). And in Paul the not-knowing is ignorance or lack of understanding about oneself in relation to God, righteousness, law, and evil, and is based on the act of the whole self in rejecting the truth (Rom. 1:21-28; 7:10-11, 15; 10:2-3; 1 Cor. 1:21-23, 29; 2 Cor. 3:6, 14-15).

One needs to be aware that in Paul self-deception comprises two paradoxes. (1) The first is that a person deceives herself or himself (Gal. 6:3). This is paradoxical in that the knowing I who deceives is the same person as the not-knowing I who is deceived. (2) The second paradox is that the knowing I who deceives is deceived by God, Satan, the law, sin. That is, I am not only deceived after I deceive myself but am already deceived before I deceive myself. Yet Paul wants to maintain that I do deceive myself (Gal. 6:3).

The organic connection between self-deception and deception by the law—and other powers—needs to be carefully noted. I deceive myself into believing that I am righteous when I am not because the law deceives me into believing that obedience to it gives life (Rom. 7:10). Self-deception is entangled with deception by the law in the closest way. Therefore self-deception is not a posture that is simply freely chosen but is a condition into which also I am seduced by a personified transcendent power—the law. What I am seeking to integrate is the relationship Paul implies between the claims that human beings deceive themselves (Gal. 6:3) and are deceived by the law (Rom. 7:10)—and sin (Rom. 7:11). The law deceives me in and through my deception of myself. Thus the theme of deception by the law bears directly on the theme of self-deception.

If Herbert Fingarette at some point denies that the self-deceiver is responsible and free and sees him solely as victimized, it is because he maintains only one side of Paul's second paradox: that one is simply overcome by delusion. Stephen Crites, in apparently making self-deception exhaustively something that I visit on myself, affirms only Paul's first paradox, or the first side of the second one. That I am also deceived by a power outside myself is lost sight of. In order to take account of the moving temporality of human historicity, both of Paul's paradoxes need to be maintained fully. The moment in which I deceive myself is not detached but is part of a flowing stream of events and meanings in which I am already deceived.[27]

For Paul both types of double-storied self-deception that Crites mentions are operative at the same time. A person uses the positive cover story of boasting (Rom. 3:27-28; 1 Cor. 1:29; 3:18-21) or confidence in the flesh (Phil. 3:3-6), that is, confidence in one's own righteousness and wisdom, to conceal the negative real story that the wisdom of the world is foolishness (1 Cor. 1:20, 21, 25; 3:19), that no one has the righteousness of God (Rom. 3:10, 20, 23), and that one's own righteousness of the law is refuse (Phil. 3:6, 8-9). But the negative real story engenders, so to speak, a negative underside for the positive cover story in which we take boastful confidence. That is, the positive cover story that I am righteous is unstable or ambiguous. It is unstable in that the pursuit of a righteousness or wisdom of my own is generated by fear and anxiety about myself (Rom. 8:15; 1 Cor. 7:32; Phil. 4:6),[28] an anxiety that propels me into a zeal to secure my existence by my own righteousness or wisdom (Rom. 10:2-3; 1 Cor. 1:20-22; Gal. 1:13-14; Phil. 3:4-6, 8-9). This anxious zeal, this uncertainty about the righteousness I claim, is the negative cover story. This pursuit of the righteousness of the law (Rom. 9:31-32) is directly opposed to God's intention to save us apart from human striving. Therefore, it carries death within itself (Rom. 7:10, 15, 18-19, 21-24). Wisdom similarly turns out to be folly (1 Cor. 1:20-21; 3:19). The pursuit of one's own righteousness or wisdom is an ignorant not-knowing (Rom. 10:2-3) that conceals the positive real story that the righteousness of God (10:3) comes apart from the law (3:21); it is the gratuitous event (3:24) that God justifies the ungodly (4:5). Moreover, God gives to the justified the power and competence to achieve good things (1 Cor. 15:9-10; 2 Cor. 3:4-5; 4:6-7). This comprehensive event and gift is the too-good-to-be-true real story that is concealed by the negative cover story that I must achieve salvation by my own accomplishments even though it destroys me.

Paul's observations on the old covenant in 2 Cor. 3:6-15 cast light on this discussion. It is interesting to note that the veil over the face of Moses is the same as the veil over the Israelites' reading of the Scripture.[29] What is concealed by the veil—the veil being, in our terms, cover story—is the fact that the law is being abolished (3:7, 11, 13).[30] In verse 7 it is the splendor[31] of the old covenant that is being annulled, but in 3:11, 13 it is the whole ministry of the old covenant, symbolized by Moses, that is being abolished.[32] We see in 3:7, 11, 13 that, according to Paul's view, the splendor of the law was already being abolished in Moses' time. The law has always been flawed. Its annulment is grounded in the fact that it causes death (3:6-7). What the veil has concealed from Israel, then, is not just the abolition of the law but the reason for the abolition, the law's killing power. In psychoanalytic terms the aggressivity of the internalized norm was veiled.[33] The positive cover story that I have a righteousness of my own based on the law conceals all three of the other stories.

The last observation prompts us to consider the placement of the cover and real stories in relation to the conscious and the unconscious. Paul holds that the hidden purposes of the heart can be brought to light only by eschatological revelation (1 Cor. 4:5; 14:25) (to be discussed further in the next chapter). This suggests that we are not merely talking about degrees of consciousness and that "unconscious" might be more appropriate than "inaccessible," depending on how those terms are defined. In any case the secrets of the heart are not available without more ado.

The negative real story must be regarded as unconscious enough to account for the reduction of tension or dissonance caused by the unfavorable evidence. The unpleasant real story generates fear, shame, and embarrassment, all of which motivate believing the untrue cover story.[34] If the untrue cover story were not believed and the real story concealed, the pain could not be eliminated. The fact that Paul consciously believed himself blameless prior to faith (Phil. 3:6) rendered unconscious the unpleasant truth that his righteousness was refuse (Phil. 3:8) and his efforts a failure (Rom. 7:15, 18-19). Yet the unconscious real story is not so unconscious as to be inoperant because we must account for the fact that the tension is not totally eliminated. The negative real story generates the anxious zeal for the law that contains death. The positive real story must also be regarded as in some degree accessible, in order to account for the fact that Paul holds people responsible to God for their beliefs and actions. Because God has—positively—made knowledge of himself available in creation (Rom. 1:20), people are without excuse despite the fact that their minds have been darkened (Rom. 1:21, 28; 2 Cor. 4:4).

I propose, then, the following arrangement as doing justice to Paul's material: (1) The more conscious cover story is the positive one that the person is righteous and wise. (2) The less conscious cover story is the negative one that righteousness and wisdom must nevertheless be relentlessly pursued. (3) The less unconscious real story is the negative one that the person is unrighteous and foolish. (4) The more unconscious real story is the positive one that God graciously accepts people without regard for their righteousness or wisdom. In Paul's picture the person apart from faith is conscious of being in a justified position on the basis of his or her own achievements. But not far beneath the surface is the troubling need to keep pursuing achievements. This is engendered by the unconscious but operant knowledge that the person is not righteous. The most inaccessible truth, which becomes available only from outside by eschatological revelation, is the good news of God's free gift. But this recent disclosure was not totally inaccessible because it is in continuity with the subverted ontological intention of the law to evoke faith (Rom. 9:31-33) and with God's revelation of God's self in creation (Rom. 1:20), which goes back into God's eternal redemptive intention (1 Cor. 2:7-10).

## PAUL AND SARTRE ON THE TRANSCENDENCE OF FACTICITY

Sartre implies that *good* faith would be the situation in which a person acknowledges both one's flawed facticity and one's transcendence of it without eliminating either one of these or turning transcendence into a fixed thing.[35] Paul, given his view of the human situation, would regard this good faith as a possibility in principle and not as an ontic possibility— an actual possibility in fact—apart from the faith which belongs to justification. Without the faith that God gives through grace (Gal. 3:23-26; Phil. 1:29) I would turn my transcendence of disobedient acts into the facticity of a righteousness of my own based on the law.

It may indeed be the case that Sartre also regards good faith as possible only in principle and not in fact. Does he not tend to suggest that no one really attains it?[36] It may be that for Sartre I cannot escape being the freedom that is my true existence, but neither can I escape trying to escape it.[37] It does seem that in his view there is an inescapable fall into trying to escape from freedom into thingness, facticity, or in-itself, because the existence of the other person, which I cannot escape, confers on me an outside, a nature, a fixedness.[38] For Sartre, if good faith is given at all, it is given with existence. But for Paul, good faith is given only by the grace of the Christ event.

In 1 Cor. 7:29-32 Paul counsels that those who marry, experience emotions, buy and deal with the world, and so on should do so "as though not" (*hōs mē*). Paul's "as though not" may sound like Sartre's transcendence toward nothing, but it is not. Sartre's transcendence belongs to the grace of existence, what Paul would call creation, while Paul's "as though not" is a consequence of eschatological revelation.

Paul presupposes the same distinction Sartre makes between facticity and transcendence and related ideas in the very fact that a person can deceive himself. I can deny that actual foolish acts create a fixed destiny: I commit the foolish acts, but I am not foolish. However, I turn this negative transcendence—my not-foolishness—into a facticity, something fixed: I am wise. This move belongs to created existence that, under the conditions of life in the flesh, cannot help identifying transcendence with facticity. The contention that human beings turn negative transcendence—not-foolishness—understood as a fixed fact into a positive fixed fact—I am wise—is probably only implied in Sartre but is explicit in Paul.

But if, on the other hand, I let transcendence be transcendence and do not identify it with facticity, it will be because of the manifestation of God's wisdom and righteousness in the saving event of revelation. Now I am able to surpass ignorance and foolishness, not into my wisdom but into the not-foolishness that is God's wise foolishness or foolish wisdom (1 Cor. 1:21-25). Similarly, if I transcend wickedness, it will not be into my righteousness but into the not-wickedness that is God's unjust justice, God's justifying the ungodly (Rom. 4:5).

## METAPHOR IN PAUL'S LANGUAGE
## ABOUT SELF-DECEPTION

When Paul talks about self-deception he uses two levels of metaphorical language. On the first level, metaphor is an element *in* the process of self-deception. Self-deception occurs because a metaphor is misinterpreted. On the second level, Paul uses metaphors *to describe* the process of self-deception. Or to put it another way, on the first level, Paul says that metaphor has a role in *what* people do to become self-deceived. The images are there as misinterpretable. But, on the second level, he uses metaphor himself in his interpretive explanation of *how* the process of self-deception occurs. These two levels, however, are not sealed off from each other but rather interpenetrate. The descriptive metaphors of the second level, especially, operate also on the first. For example, Paul speaks of the law metaphorically in describing what happens in self-deception (law is described as a person), but in doing so he attributes to the law, metaphorically described, a central role in the lives of the self-deceived: The law is misinterpreted by them, or prompts them to misinterpret itself. Evidently Paul must speak of the law (a code of commandments) as a person—a metaphorical utterance—in order to describe what happens in people's encounter with the law which leads to self-deception. They mistakenly believe that obedience to it will bring life (Rom. 7:10; 10:1-3; Phil. 3:4-9).

### The Nature of Metaphor

Let me now present a fuller statement of my use of the term *metaphor*. Philip Wheelwright makes a basic distinction between two complementary uses of language. "Steno-language" intends to designate clearly. Its meanings have a fixed relationship to words and are the same for all who use the words correctly so that they can be publicly and exactly shared. Steno-language is closed.[39] "Tensive language" intends to express with maximum fullness. It gives voice to the ceaseless tensions and struggles between opposing forces in life. Tensive language arises from the fact that the particular imagery and perspective of the poet are in conflict with ordinary channels of thought. Tensive language is open.[40]

For Wheelwright metaphor is the most revealing unit of tensive language or thought, and he divides metaphors into two classes. (1) An epiphoric metaphor states a comparison between something strange and something familiar. The similarity should not be obvious in order that the comparison might come as a shock and yet as a shock of recognition. (2) A diaphoric metaphor does not depend on comparison but produces new meaning by juxtaposition alone. Pure diaphor is found only in nonimitative music and in the most abstract painting. The majority of interesting and effective metaphors will combine epiphor and diaphor in some way.[41] What constitutes the metaphor is the semantic tension between the relatively well known modifier (or vehicle) and the less well known subject (or tenor). The motion required to negotiate the distance between these two unex-pectedly combined elements evokes a sense of similarity in the dissimilar and thus gives a new vision of reality.[42] Wheelwright[43] and many others[44] take it that meaning passes from the modifier to the subject, but James Hillman is probably right that the meaning moves in both directions, that both elements are seen in a new light.[45] It should be observed that Wheel-wright at least hints or implies that there is some steno-element, some degree of precise reference to the world, in metaphor.[46]

Frank Burch Brown's appropriation and critique of Wheelwright is useful to the biblical scholar or theologian who wants to take seriously both the metaphorical nature of religious language and its potential for generating conceptual reflection. Brown wants to moderate any overly sharp separation between steno-language and tensive or depth language. For him the proper approach is to see steno-language (absolute conceptual clarity with determinate truth and meaning) and verbal music (tensive meaning felt rather than conceived) as two purely hypothetical poles. All actual discourse falls on a continuum between the two poles so that there are no absolute distinctions between usages of steno- and tensive language, but rather every use of language manifests both of the poles, varying in each instance in the degree to which each pole is present. This would mean that steno-language has a marginal degree of ambiguity and polysemy, for it is a basic quality of the human mind to see something as something else.[47]

Brown wants to exploit more fully the epiphoric (comparative) element in metaphor without neglecting the diaphoric. This entails attending more carefully to the steno-, conceptual, and paraphrasable component that metaphor has in virtue of its being epiphor. Because metaphor has an element of comparison (discernible if surprising likeness), it can to a degree be conceptually explicated. The meaning of the comparison can be articulated in thought. As the union of epiphor and diaphor, metaphor is the strategy for maximizing in one semantic situation, one utterance, the dialogue always present in thought between conceptualization and imaginative fabrication.[48]

Paul Ricoeur's understanding of metaphor has some similarities with the preceding but also has its own emphases. First of all, according to Ricoeur metaphor is not a matter of words, not a transfer of meaning from one noun to another, nor a substitution of one word for another. Neither is metaphor mere ornamentation.[49] Rather, the primary unit of metaphoric meaning is the sentence. In a metaphorical sentence meanings from one semantic field are predicated of words in another field that had hitherto been separated from the first. A meaning is wrenched from its normal anchorage and cast into a new field of reference. Therefore, several things are specified at the same time, creating semantic ambiguity or tension. One thing is seen as another.[50] A good example is David Tracy's "Jesus as the supreme fiction" cited by Mary Gerhart and Allan Russell. Fiction—from the field of literary criticism—is predicated of the Jesus of Christian experience so that the resulting clash challenges both fields. Jesus is no longer seen as securely fixed by history or dogma, and fiction is no longer "merely" a story but rather is the opening up of new possibilities of being.[51] Janet Martin Soskice is probably right in pointing out that the predication in metaphor is logical and not necessarily syntactic. Metaphor displays no one syntactic form, for its criteria are semantic and pragmatic and not just syntactic. She goes on to point out that the context required for constituting a metaphorical utterance may be less or more than a sentence. The metaphor is semantically established as soon as it is clear that one thing is being spoken of in terms suggestive of another.[52]

Ricoeur sees three tensions at work in metaphorical utterance. The first is that metaphor results from tension between two terms in the metaphorical utterance. But, second, metaphor really resides in the tension between two opposing interpretations of the utterance.[53] The literal interpretation of the metaphor self-destructs or abolishes itself because the metaphor at the literal level is absurd or contradictory. The literal level of interpretation employs not alleged primitive or original meanings but meanings established by use and enshrined in the dictionary.[54] The failure of the literal interpretation opens up the way for a new interpretation—the metaphorical interpretation—based on a twist in the literal meanings. Metaphor thus has split reference. Reference is suspended at the literal or descriptive level, but this negative condition engenders a new referential design, a new kind of referent constituted by the metaphor's surplus of meaning.[55]

The cancellation of the descriptive reference to the public world, then, is not the end of reference. In fact, for Ricoeur metaphor redescribes the world. It describes the world that might be, a world of existential possibilities that could be our own, the project of a new way of being in the world.[56] This brings us to the third metaphorical tension. Although the new view of reality does not tell us how things literally are, it does tell us what they are like. Being like involves a tension between "is" and "is not." This is a tension in the reference of the metaphor to reality, and it pertains to the ontological status of the reality imaged in the metaphor. Jesus both is and is not the supreme fiction. Both aspects must be allowed to stand. It is ontologically naive to ignore the implicit "is not" in the "is." But it is also inadequate to let the "is not" reduce the "is" to "as if."[57]

The metaphorical redescription of reality generates new conceptualizations or thought. The apprehension of the metaphor is not, however, simply a matter of the intellect. In being carried along from one level of meaning to the other, the person is assimilated existentially to the level of symbolic meaning. Metaphorical utterance moves us to the experience of the redescribed reality.[58] The metaphor carries us over into the new world described and enables us to experience it. It is often claimed that metaphor creates a world so radically new that we can grasp it only through metaphor.[59] Thus, to express doubt about whether Paul really thought of sin, for example, as a personal power at all because his language may be metaphorical[60] is to miss the significance of metaphor: The metaphor creates a real world that would not have been available otherwise.

We should note that the metaphor creates both disparities and similarities between the terms in it. Both old and strange new meanings are present. The disparity warns us that it is not the words that change in the metaphor but the concepts involved. The lack of change in the meaning of the words explains why metaphors can retain their power over the centuries: The unchanging meanings of the words maintain the tension with the new ideas.[61] On the other hand, the continuing tension and power could be explained by proposing instead that over the years words both keep old meanings and gain new ones.[62] In either case the unfamiliar view of the subject effected by the metaphor may produce a permanent change in the *thought* of the reader although the meaning—or some of the meanings—of the contributing words remains stable and unchanged. Metaphor is a moment in thought understood as a dynamic process to reformulate itself in unanticipated ways. Metaphor does transform what we know and offers new perspectives on our experience.[63]

In the light of these reflections we can understand that the term *law* for Paul, and for the exegetical tradition, continued to denote a body of commandments. But Paul's metaphorical treatment of the word has accomplished an enlarged understanding of how law functions, of its scope and extensions, of human existence vis-à-vis law.

### Metaphorical Existence

Having discussed metaphorical utterance and thought, I turn now to metaphorical existence or experience. James Hillman treats the archetypes of Carl Jung as metaphors. According to Jung, archetypes are primordial symbols that reside in the collective unconscious of the human race. An archetype does not have a specific, definite content but is the form or open possibility for any and every role, action, thought, and emotion we can have. There is an archetype for being a father, being a wife, experiencing despair, getting a new idea, and so on indeterminately.[64] According to Hillman, these archetypes are metaphors that are not events that happen but are likenesses to events, perspectives that make events intelligible. For him human actions enact ideas, and ideas in turn rest on myths or root metaphors. We become genuine souls or selves by seeing through the actions to the ideas they enact and penetrating through the ideas to the underlying metaphors or archetypes. Metaphor so understood is not simply a way of speaking but is a way of perceiving, feeling, and existing.[65] We see that for Hillman action or experience, thought, and metaphor belong to an unbroken continuum. And we may speak not only of metaphorical expression and perception but also of metaphorical experience and existence. If metaphor makes the world look strange, unfamiliar, and ambiguous, then metaphorical existence is the experience of the ambiguity of reality.

A person deceives herself when she thinks that she has wisdom or righteousness when she does not (1 Cor. 3:18-19; 8:1-2; Rom. 10:3; Gal. 6:3). This is the metaphorical experience of misinterpreting one's ambiguous existence. The possibility of transcending my folly by participation in God's not-foolishness, that is, God's wise foolishness, is misinterpreted as wisdom; and the possibility of transcending my wickedness in God's not-wickedness, that is, God's just injustice, is misinterpreted as my righteousness. Confronting the metaphorical juxtaposition of my own foolishness and unrighteousness to the possibility of transcending these faults, I misinterpret the nature of the relationship between the two elements. One possibility—lost by fallen humanity but recovered through Christ—is that transcendence (a right relationship with God, or faith) is predicated of my flawed facticity. I am both sinful and rightly related to God in faith. In this situation I do not dispose of transcendence, am not the basis of my own existence, but my existence is open to the possibilities of God since God is the giver of faith. Because I am sinful, however, I acknowledge neither the fault in my actual existence nor the gift of transcendence; rather, I reverse the metaphorical situation and predicate facticity of transcendence. God's transcendence—the just injustice or justification by grace—is reduced to the facticity of my righteousness (Rom. 10:3). I now do dispose of transcendence by my obedience to the law (Phil. 3:6, 9); that is, I tell God that I have done enough to obligate God to save me, and this conceals from me the fact that I really lack the righteousness of God. In sum, one possibility is to let God be the metaphor maker. God predicates God's transcendence of my facticity. But what we do as sinful is to make ourselves the metaphor makers who predicate our facticity of God's transcendence. The price I pay is that instead of having my facticity opened into God's surpassing possibilities, the latter are bound by my facticity, the righteousness of the law which is mine. I have been lured into self-deception by an ambiguous, misinterpretable situation. In deceiving myself I construct the metaphor of existence in the wrong way. Instead of letting God predicate God's transcendence of my flawed facticity, I predicate my facticity of God's transcendence. Existence is ambiguous with regard to how flawed facticity and transcendence should be related, and I am prompted to interpret it wrongly because of this ambiguity and because existence is shaped in significant part by the law as an ambiguous power. It promises life but invites, or compels, a response that produces death.

Metaphor is ambiguous, polyvalent, and subject to different interpretations, and this fact helps and even stimulates the will to self-deception. We deceive ourselves because we want to conceal our flaws and achieve self-justification. This is the dynamic of self-deception for Paul. It is generated by our zeal to have a righteousness of our own (Rom. 10:1-3). This for Paul is the equivalent of the idolatrous worship of the creature rather than the creator (Rom. 1:24-25). We want to interpret the world as if we were the gods. We are more concerned to have an interpretation of our life engagements that is favorable to ourselves than to have one that is true. The ambiguity and pliable misinterpretability of metaphor readily gives itself to our will to have the wrong interpretation. The law personified is such a metaphor: It invites misinterpretation.

We have seen that self-deception in Paul results from a free act of the human being, but it is also a fate, and the fated aspect can be expressed in at least three different ways by Paul: (1) It comes from God's giving people up to a base mind; (2) it is the result of blinding by the god of this world; (3) it issues from the fact that the law, along with sin, deceives us (Rom. 7:10). And we will consider still further the law as a metaphor or archetype that engenders and governs the experience of self-deception. According to Hillman, the archetypes or root metaphors are the personifications of the configurations of existence, the structures of the psyche, such as Fame, Night, and Hope. These structures confront us not just as patterns or modes of experience but also as persons. This tensiveness means that they are metaphors, or are grasped metaphorically. They are numinous borderline personalities that govern our perspectives on ourselves and the world. Thus they are gods.[66]

The law appears to function as such a metaphorical archetype in Paul. As we have seen, the law for Paul is a code of commandments (Rom. 7:7; 2 Cor. 3:3, 6). The law is also a custodian, a *paidagōgos*. In antiquity the pedagogue was not a teacher but a slave who accompanied the schoolboy to school and carried his books. He had supervision over the child and was to protect him and teach him good manners. The public generally did not have much respect for the pedagogue.[67] To be confined under the law-as-pedagogue, then (Gal. 3:23, 25; 4:3-5), is to be the slave of a slave. Since the law holds us captive and deceives us (Rom. 7:6, 10), personal agency is predicated of the law. But the law is not an ordinary person; it is a cosmic or supernatural person. The latter claim requires considering the law in relation to the elements—*stoicheia*—and in relation to the principalities and powers.

To be under the law (Gal. 3:23-29) is for Paul clearly the same thing as to be under the enslaving elements (*stoicheia*) of the universe (Gal. 4:1-4). What then are the *stoicheia?* In the ancient world the term *stoicheion* acquired several connotations, but evidently the root meaning was the primary, basic, irreducible constituent of any substance, entity, or system. Thus the letters of the alphabet were the stoicheia of words; numbers were the irreducible constituents for arithmetic; notes were for the musical scale; physical elements were for matter. Stoicheia could also mean elementary ideas and at some point came to mean spiritual bodies or star spirits.[68]

What does stoicheia mean in Paul? We shall see that neither the history-of-religions nor the internal evidence is unambiguous.

Let us begin with the former. Hans Dieter Betz has argued that in the syncretism of time the four or five elements of the cosmos (earth, water, air, fire, and ether) were not simply material substances but demonic entities of cosmic proportions and astral powers that were hostile to humankind. People were oppressed by these personal demonic forces. That is what the stoicheia are in Paul. These powers work on human beings from inside since they make up the body and from outside as Fate.[69]

But Eduard Schweizer has observed that throughout the first century A.D. the "stoicheia of the cosmos" meant simply the four or five cosmic elements and did not take astral spirits into its meaning until the second or third century.[70] For Schweizer this means that in Paul the stoicheia are the elements of the world—earth, water, and so on—which imprison the soul in their ceaseless rotation.[71] It has also been argued that the stoicheia are not demonic spirits but rather the elementary ideas and cultic practices of both Jewish and Gentile religion.[72] Yet Schweizer concedes that Paul might have anticipated the second- and third-century usage, though he regards this as improbable. I would suggest, however, that the claim that Paul meant demonic spirits becomes at least plausible in view of Schweizer's acknowledgement that even Empedocles speaks of the power of these elements and personifies them. And Schweizer quotes Philo to the effect that some people revere the elements under divine names, though, says Philo, the elements themselves are lifeless matter (*Vit. Cont.* 3–4).[73]

The Pauline textual evidence does not take us closer to certainty. It could be argued that the analogy between the stoicheia and the guardians and managers of Gal. 4:2 suggests that the former are lordly beings.[74] The parallelism in 4:8-9 is also significant. Beings that by nature are not gods are parallel to the weak and contemptible elements. This suggests that the elements were what some people regarded as divine. They are like the demons who are not gods (though many people take them to be) in 1 Cor. 10:19-20. On the other hand, if the parallelism is seen as loose (which it probably is) rather than tight, then the stoicheia could be something associated with rather than identical to the beings who are not gods.

The last point is perhaps supported by the fact that the stoicheia are introduced (Gal. 4:3) in a context framed by a discussion of the law (3:23-26; 4:4-5) and are thus seen as analogous to the law in some way. In any case both the law (3:23-26; 4:1-2, 5a) and the elements (4:3, 9) have the same impact on human existence—slavery. The stoicheia, then, seem not to be identified with the unreal gods of 4:8 but to be the means whereby these gods enslave (4:9-10).

Why should we try to fix one determinate meaning rather than appropriate and exploit the several meanings at play in Paul's juxtaposing the law to the pedagogue and to the stoicheia? In this juxtaposition Paul predicates of the law personal agency, cosmic power, and an affinity with the rudiments of religions generally as well as with the elemental physicality of the universe. If the law is as inescapable as our physical facticity, the latter is somehow like law. The attribution of these various dimensions to the elements of the cosmos means that the universe is not unlike human beings, who exist in various aspects—flesh, body, soul, spirit. To the extent that—or if it is the case that—the elements are in some part demonic spirits they are more or less identical with the principalities and powers.

I begin the consideration of the latter also with the history-of-religions background. The use of terms like "principality" (*archē*), "ruler" (*archōn*), "authority" (*exousia*), and "power" (*dynamis*) in an angelic or supernatural sense seems to have been largely the contribution of Paul.[75] But what exactly is the conceptual background, and how did Paul appropriate it? It has been argued that no sources from the first century A.D. or earlier—Jewish or Greco-Roman—attest a strong sense of the reality of hostile cosmic powers from which human beings need to be delivered.[76] It is then held, accordingly, that Paul bears witness to no belief in demonic cosmic forces. When he uses the terminology of principalities and powers, his normal meaning is the angelic heavenly host who worship Yahweh, though he may sometimes refer to human rulers.[77] A much more probable reading of the evidence is that sources such as Daniel, the oldest section of 1 Enoch, Jubilees, and Qumran give abundant testimony to a belief in evil powers and the need to be delivered from them.[78] In accord with this, Walter Wink's interpretation of the principalities and powers in Paul is convincing. He argues that Paul uses these terms to refer to any manifestation of power—in its inner and outer, spiritual and institutional, heavenly and earthly, divine and human dimensions. The two sides are distinguishable though not separable; however, in any given context one or another aspect may be foregrounded. The powers in Paul are both good and evil.[79]

Paul had plentiful material from which to construct his myth of the powers. A particularly interesting strand is the way in which the Old Testament dealt with the pagan gods so as to make them subordinate to Yahweh (Exod. 15:11; Ps. 29:1) but also to install them as members of his heavenly council (Ps. 89:5-7). The stars were also included in God's retinue (Judg. 5:20; Job 38:7). In Deuteronomy the gods are the angelic rulers of the nations other than Israel, who have delegated authority to rule under Yahweh's sovereignty (Deut. 32:8-9). If these gods get out of line and do not act justly, God will destroy them as if they were human (Psalm 82). Thus when the Israelites confronted the astral deities from the East, they had a scheme to which they could accommodate these gods. These ideas carry over into Judaism and are the background for Paul's understanding of the principalities and powers.[80]

I begin my discussion of the demonic powers in Paul with Eph. 6:12 because this text is the most definite and the least subject to variant interpretations, and then I move back to Paul. Although I do not take Ephesians to be by Paul, I assume that it is reliable evidence for him in this particular case because on the subject of the principalities and powers, as far as the general idea is concerned, we are not dealing with the reflections of a discrete author but with the presuppositions and worldview of an entire era. Moreover, the various terms for the principalities and powers are imprecise and interchangeable, and they can represent each other.[81]

Ephesians 6:12 piles up a number of terms to represent the powers, among them being "principality" (*archē*) and "authority" (*exousia*), which are unambiguously personal, transcendent or supernatural (heavenly), and evil (at war with human beings). We should expect these basic characteristics to carry over to Rom. 8:38 and 1 Cor. 15:24, which are similar in point of view and vocabulary. Among the terms in Rom. 8:38 are "principality" (*archē*) and power (*dynamis*), and these are regarded as hostile because they might, if left to themselves, separate believers from the love of God. Similarly in 1 Cor. 15:24 we have principality (*archē*), authority (*exousia*), and power (*dynamis*), which are specifically categorized as enemies of Christ, and implicitly as enemies of humankind, enemies who must be destroyed or subjected. This understanding of the powers as transcendent hostile forces is quite in agreement with Paul's belief that human beings are victimized by other personalized powers—sin, law, flesh—as well as by the consequences of Adam's sin (Romans 5).

Finally, and briefly, the law is organically connected to sin and death (1 Cor. 15:56), and death is similarly connected to the cosmic powers (1 Cor. 15:24-26; Rom. 8:38). The law and the powers belong to the same gestalt; they are metaphorical equivalents of each other. Paul's understanding of the law gives us the existential meaning of the principalities and powers; the powers reveal the grounding of the law.[82]

Paul would not consciously and intentionally have said that the law is a god, but as a personified cosmic power—a demonic "being that is by nature not a god" (Gal. 4:8)—it functions as Hillman says the gods do: They govern our perspectives on ourselves and the world. The law is a metaphor for a mode of experience. Or, perhaps more accurately, it is a metaphor for the transcendent ground or cause of a mode of experience. Through his metaphorical portrayal of the law Paul claims that the kind of experience we have been describing (self-deception) does have a transcendent ground. The law is a power that entices me into misinterpreting itself and thus into misinterpreting the nature of my existence.

We have seen that the law for Paul is the metaphorical equivalent of the cosmic powers while the latter are descended from the heavenly host or divine council of Yahweh which is descended from the pagan gods. The law as it appears in Paul, as a ground for self-deception, is a functional equivalent of the gods; and as a part of the configuration of principalities and powers it is a history-of-religions descendent of the pagan gods, who are given authority by God, who oppose God, and who will ultimately be overcome. Self-deception, then, governed by such a phenomenon as the law—a god (demon) functioning contrary to its purpose—is not just a mistake that can be avoided but is a power from which I must be delivered.

## THE IMPACT OF SELF-DECEPTION ON THE MORAL LIFE

In self-deception I cover the real story with a false one. I think that I am something when I am nothing. And this injures the moral life in at least three ways according to Paul.

First, I mistakenly believe that the law demands works rather than faith (Rom. 9:30—10:3) and that my obedience to it—ethical performance—makes me right with God (Phil. 3:4-6; Rom. 3:27). Therefore, the moral life is understood (misunderstood) as a means or condition for salvation.

Second, the real story—that my righteousness does not make me right with God—is not completely concealed. I know at some level, although I do not spell it out to myself, that I actually am at odds with God. Thus I feel compelled to do more, but since it is impossible to do enough to achieve what only God can accomplish, the futile effort to overcome the conflict with God by obedience to the law produces an inner conflict of self with self (Rom. 7:14-23). This I experience as an anguished living death (7:24). The situation Paul describes has been dramatically grasped in William Styron's *Set This House on Fire*. The character Cass Kinsolving wants to overcome the inner consequences of a racist past and make himself endurable in his own eyes by taking on the moral project of restoring an old Italian peasant to health. But because his goal is the impossible one of self-justification, he experiences his effort as something like a panic and a paranoid obsession. The obsessiveness is the evidence that I still do in fact sense the fault that I have refused to acknowledge.

Third, because people in self-deception believe that they are righteous but half-know that they are not, they reduce the moral requirement to which they feel obligated; they make it less demanding in order to feel that they do in fact live up to it. If little is asked of me, I will be able to meet the obligation. This would seem to explain much of what Paul says in Romans 2. The Jews as Paul describes them are relying on the false security that they know the will of God and have a relationship with him but are disavowing the awareness that the law calls for action, which they have not rendered. They steal, commit adultery, and rob temples (Rom. 2:17-24). In Rom. 2:28-29 Paul seems to move into the slightly different point that they mistakenly believe that external obedience is enough when God really requires the obedience of the heart. Thus we see that for Paul we are not only deceived about the religious dimension of our righteousness, mistaken in believing that it makes us right with God (Rom. 10:1-3). We are also deceived about the moral nature of our obedience: It is neither enough nor the right kind. Remember that in Phil. 3:6 Paul claimed that as a Jew he was blameless regarding the righteousness of the law. But in Romans 2 he asserts that his fellow Jews were less obedient than they thought. And in 1 Cor. 4:4 Paul acknowledges that even when he is a believer, God may have something against him even though he does not know of anything against himself. Given his awareness of the human propensity to self-deception, should Paul have said in Phil. 3:6 that he mistakenly believed that he was blameless before the law?[83]

# 3

## THE RECOVERY OF WHOLENESS IN PAUL

Freedom to believe
and to act

For Paul the gospel—the word of the cross—brings salvation effectively into the present as God's power (Rom. 1:16-17; 1 Cor. 1:18). This word accomplishes (1) justification, which deals with willful rebellion, and (2) deliverance or liberation, which deals with human victimization under demonic powers. These two motifs interact upon and interpenetrate each other in Paul's writings.[1] The subjective side of salvation from the powers (the law, the god of this world, and others), but not an exhaustive interpretation of it, is the disclosing of the secrets of the heart (1 Cor. 4:5; 14:25)—the bringing of the unconscious to consciousness. For Paul, as we have seen, the real stories that have been concealed and repressed are one's own unrighteousness and foolishness and the too-good-to-be-true story of God's unconditional acceptance. These are what can now be consciously apprehended. One can face one's own fault nondefensively and noncompulsively, freed from the need to conceal it and from the attempt to overcome it on one's own, because one knows that one is accepted by God without regard for achievement.

This restitution of wholeness confers a new freedom that is freedom for the totality of reality (1 Cor. 3:21-23), but this freedom is dialectically limited because one is also freed for love, freed for obedience (Rom. 6:16-23), freed to dispose oneself toward the human world in love, which disposition is both a gift and a demand. The capacity to love is given by the Spirit (Rom. 5:5; 1 Cor. 12:1, 31; 13:1-13; 14:1; Gal. 5:22) or can be spoken of as the means by which faith (a gift) is put in motion (Gal. 5:6). But love is also an obligation (Gal. 5:14; Rom. 13:8). This freedom, for everything and for love, is the consequence of not being compelled to the impossible task of establishing one's own righteousness. In Galatians love is specifically represented as the vehicle by which freedom actualizes itself (Gal. 5:1, 13). Note that while love is the central norm, one of the central warrants for love (regard for the other) is the well-being—wholeness—of the moral agent, oneself. The believer is to love the other with the intention of achieving her own wholeness. We will take a fuller look at the word of the cross, wholeness, freedom, love, and the justification of ethical norms. Especially will we explore the justification that appeals to self-actualization, which is the well-being of the self as wholeness.

## THE WORD OF THE CROSS DISCLOSES
## THE SECRETS OF THE HEART

For Paul the deliverance from self-deception occurs through the cross. The cross continues to occur in the event of preaching (1 Cor. 1:18; Rom. 1:16-17), which is a clarification of the human situation. The word of the cross is an event of such surprise and ambiguity that it explodes and rearranges the makeup of the self in self-deception. The wisdom of God occurs in what both Jews and Greeks take to be foolish (1 Cor. 1:21-23, 25); the power of God occurs in what is regarded as weakness (1 Cor. 1:24-25); the blessing of God occurs in one defined by Scripture as cursed (Gal. 3:13-14). God manifests himself where least expected, and God's purpose in so doing (1 Cor. 1:29) is to undermine boasting (Rom. 3:27), the self-deceived confidence in one's own resources (Gal. 6:3). The un-expected combination of power and weakness, wisdom and foolishness, blessing and curse, in the cross shows that things are not what they seem. Thus God brings those who think that they are something to nothing (1 Cor. 1:27-28). But those brought to nothing have their lives reconstituted on something, a sustaining reality from beyond themselves—the righteous-ness and wisdom of Christ (1 Cor. 1:30; Rom. 4:17).[2]

The gospel has power to bring light (2 Cor. 4:6) and knowledge (Phil. 3:8a) and thus to dispel self-deception; and Paul refers to this illu-mination as the disclosing of the secrets and purposes of the heart (1 Cor. 4:5; 14:25). Those things about myself that had been hidden from me (1 Cor. 4:5; 14:25) are now brought to knowledge (Phil. 3:8-11). Thus a unifying wholeness of the self is achieved.

For Paul the dark purposes of the heart cannot be brought to con-sciousness, as Freud put it, without more ado. That the god of this world blinds the minds of unbelievers (2 Cor. 4:4) means in psychological terms that consciousness resists the revealing of the unconscious and the con-comitant movement of the boundary between conscious and unconscious.[3]

That is, the conscious pursuit of a righteousness of one's own prevents grasping the truth that righteousness is freely given by God. In terms of human hermeneutical judgments what gives the gospel the needed power to break into the recesses of the heart—the "more ado"—is the radical content of the word of the cross, which overturns all normal evaluations.

Paul gives a confessional theological interpretation of the disclosing of the concealed secrets by attributing the power to effect the change both to Christ and to the Spirit. Christ is in us (Gal. 2:20; 2 Cor. 4:7-12) as the light of God's glory (2 Cor. 4:6) which reveals our hidden selves to us (1 Cor. 4:4; 14:25). For Paul the Spirit is the source of life (Rom. 8:11); it is in fact both the giver (2 Cor. 3:6) and the result (3:15-17) of the life being given in the precise sense of freedom from the veil that conceals the truth. Hans Dieter Betz suggests that the ecstatic experiences caused by the Spirit would be required to shake up the inner self so that it could be grasped by and grasp the meaning of Christ's death as liberation.[4] The Lord and the Spirit (they are functionally identified in 2 Cor. 3:17) are the power of the word (2 Cor. 3:3) to illumine the heart, to bring the hidden to light and create wholeness. This power enables the avowal of the hidden real stories because it makes God's acceptance of people without regard to their merits (Rom. 3:21-31) a living reality in the heart (2 Cor. 3:3, 6).

The hidden purposes of the heart will be revealed only at the eschatological judgment, according to 1 Cor. 4:5, and it is the Lord who will bring these things from darkness to light.[5] Paul says, I do not know anything against myself, but I am not thereby acquitted (justified) because it is the Lord who judges me (1 Cor. 4:4). The first "I" in this statement is the "I" of conscience, the "I" that judges itself in relation to an independent standard. But the second "I" transcends conscience. It knows that conscience may be wrong. As we shall see, it is functionally equivalent to the human spirit. Paul forbids human beings to anticipate the judgment of the Lord by pronouncing judgment on each other "before the time." At least he enjoins the Corinthians from judging him. But Paul also believed that the intelligible preaching of the church—prophesying—had the power to convict unbelievers and disclose the secrets of the heart. Thus prophetic preaching does anticipate the eschatological judgment (1 Cor. 14:25). Perhaps Paul's theological rationale for attributing this power to preaching is that preaching is an action given and produced by the Spirit (1 Cor. 12:4-11; 14:1-5), the same Spirit that has the power to give life by removing the veil of self-deception (2 Cor. 3:6, 16-17).

## THE RECOVERING OF WHOLENESS AS A PROCESS

This revealing of the heart's secrets means in relation to self-deception that the positive cover story that claimed righteousness and wisdom is rent (1 Cor. 1:17; Phil. 3:6-7) to reveal the negative real story, which is that my self-alleged accomplishments are nothing (1 Cor. 1:28b) or, alternatively, are refuse or dung (Phil. 3:8). But the positive too-good-to-be-true real story now also brought to light is that God gives me a right relationship with himself—accepts me—quite apart from any achievement of mine (Phil. 3:9-11; Rom. 3:21-22). This shatters the negative cover story in which my anxious effort to claim righteousness was a futile attempt that produced inner division and the dissolution of the self, what Paul calls the body of death (Rom. 7:9-11, 15-25). So in the new self-understanding given with faith I am able openly to acknowledge both my flawed facticity or concrete existence and the transcendence of it by God's action without turning transcendence into a righteousness of my own as a fixed thing.

The psychological credibility of Paul's position is seen by reference to the statement of the psychoanalyst Heinz Kohut that when acceptance by another—one's mother or analyst, for instance—is internalized, a person acquires self-generated self-acceptance. He or she can shed the defensive cover stories by which the flawed or impaired self was protected.[6] What distinguishes Paul is that he is speaking from a faith standpoint; therefore, it is God's acceptance, rather than that of another human being, that is and needs to be internalized. The divine action is necessary because for Paul the human heart, or spirit, is a dimension of such depth that only the divine spirit can reach it. The human spirit and divine Spirit are correlatives but are not ontologically identical. Since human beings are deformed in their being by self-deception even at the depth which is their openness to God—the human spirit[7]—only God can remove the defensive cover story. Paul envisions the meeting of the divine Spirit and human spirit as being at a mysterious depth where the interaction cannot be articulated in words (Rom. 8:16, 26-27).

The new wholeness achieved by the disclosing of the heart's hidden purposes is the first moment in a process of becoming whole (2 Cor. 3:18; 4:16), a process in which wholeness is progressively realized by moral action. The purpose of the first moment of redemption is that we might walk in newness of life, act in a new way (Rom. 6:4). If we live by the Spirit, if our life has its source in the Spirit (Gal. 5:25a, and the first-class condition indicates that we do), we are to walk by the Spirit (Gal. 5:25b). The reason for the ethical walk is that one's way of being engaged in the world should correspond to the inner renewal by the Spirit. Thus, while under self-deception the purpose of ethical action was to provide the necessary condition for salv tion, now in the life in the Spirit the purpose is to realize more fully the wholeness, that is, salvation, that is already achieved. The quest for wholeness has both a backward and forward look, that is, it is both motive and intention. It looks back to the renewal that occurred at baptism (Rom. 6:4-6) and in the gift of the Spirit (Rom. 5:5; Gal. 5:25a), and this in turn enables the look forward to the future in the hope that full actualization of one's possibilities—resurrection—will occur (Phil. 3:10-16).

I should like to probe a bit further the ontological nature of the process of becoming whole, the relationship in lived human existence between moral achievement and new life. How is *walking* in the Spirit (Gal. 5:25b) and *acting* obediently (Rom. 6:17)—the ethical imperative—related to the *being* of new creation (2 Cor. 5:17) or new life (Rom. 6:23) which is given by God's saving action (Rom. 5:17-18)—the soteriological indicative? In my judgment Victor P. Furnish connects the moral achievement and new life too closely. He states that they are not identified, but it seems to me that in fact he identifies them. The new life in his view is not just a possibility but an actuality; therefore, moral obedience is not the result of the new life but rather constitutes it.[8] Ernst Käsemann takes virtually the same position when he holds that the moral obligation and the gift of new life coincide and that the Lord is no longer Lord for those who do not serve him obediently.[9]

I believe that Bultmann is right in holding that the moral imperative is the result of the reality of new life.[10] In Gal. 5:25 living by the Spirit is a fact, stated in the indicative mood. But walking by the Spirit is a hortatory subjunctive and is, therefore, distanced from the fact of new life, as a result of it, and is projected into the future, by however slight a degree. Similarly in 1 Cor. 5:7 Christ as our passover sacrifice is the cause (indicated grammatically by *gar*) for the result that we are to cleanse out the old leaven from our lives. If moral obedience and new life through justification are virtually identified, then if one is disobedient she loses her justification and is removed from the lordship of Christ. But that would contradict Paul's view that it is the ungodly whom God justifies (Rom. 4:5) and that nothing can separate us from the justifying love of God in Christ (Rom. 8:33-34, 37-39). In Paul's theology new life and moral obedience are organically connected, and the latter should follow upon the former, but they are not identical. Their relationship is paradoxical. The new life given in justification is an actuality and not just a possibility. But the very existence of the imperative—become what you actually are in Christ—shows that the new life is also a possibility. The new creation is an unrealized, or an only incipiently realized, reality. It is in the process of being realized by moral action.

For Paul new life or salvation is apprehended by faith (Rom. 3:25, 26; 4:3; 10:6-9; Gal. 3:1-6), and the coming of salvation can even be spoken of as the coming of faith (Gal. 3:23-26). Since faith is a new self-understanding (Rom. 10:5-21; Gal. 2:20; Phil. 3:7-11), the progressive interaction between life = faith and moral conduct is an interplay between understanding and action. The psychological pertinence of this can, again, be seen in light of Kohut's claim that a patient in therapy is well and ready to terminate when he or she has acquired both self-acceptance and a moral ideal and has achieved a new structure of the self, in which insight can be productively enacted.[11]

It may be that for Paul salvation, so far as it pertains to the individual, is most comprehensively understood as the recovery of wholeness or the reunification of the self. Consider two exemplary texts. That salvation resides in wholeness is presupposed in Paul's discussion of conscience in 1 Corinthians 8 and 10. The idea of conscience had emerged centuries before in popular Greek wisdom and probably achieved its place in the Corinthian correspondence because of its use by the Corinthians. According to the understanding current in Paul's time, conscience may be defined as a human being judging himself or herself in light of a standard independent of conscience itself. This judgment may have reference to past actions or future contemplated actions (1 Cor. 4:4; 8:10; 10:25-27). Conscience was held to be a universal human phenomenon, belonging to human beings as human, and its normal function was pain. The latter could be spoken of in terms of (1) being pain, (2) inflicting pain, or (3) feeling pain.[12] Paul is trying to educate the strong in the Corinthian church to be sensitive to the conscience of the weak—or to the weak as conscience. Conscience is the same in structure whether it is weak or strong: painful accusation of oneself on the basis of violating a norm outside of conscience. Paul wants the strong not to entice a weak brother into painful conflict in his own (the weak brother's) conscience.

In discussing the problem of whether one should eat food that had been sacrificed to idols, Paul seems to have held that conscience can be weak in two senses. First, it is weak in that it regards as wrong something that objectively is not wrong, and it does this because it lacks knowledge. The weak at Corinth will have a painful conscience if they eat food sacrificed to idols because they do not really feel the force of the knowledge that there is only one God and that an idol, therefore, is nothing (1 Cor. 8:1, 4, 7).

Second, conscience is weak in the sense that it cannot prevent one's going against what one believes one's norm requires even though the act will cause pain. The weak person could be enticed by the example of the strong—in eating meat offered to idols—to do the same thing (8:10-12). First Corinthians 8:10 may be Paul's ironic paraphrase of a sentence from the letter of the Corinthians to him. The conscience of the weak person is built up or strengthened (*oikodomeō*), but the positive sense of "built up" is ironically reduced by the fact that the conscience is "built up" to eat food offered to idols.[13] In giving the provocative example, the strong sins against his weak brother. The action of the strong beats or strikes (*typtō*) the weak conscience (entices the weak brother to act against his conscience). Since one function of conscience according to current usage was to feel pain; to beat the weak conscience is to make it feel pain.[14] This pain is the destruction of the weak brother (8:11). It is the tension caused by going against what one believes is right, the pain of self-division, of violating wholeness. Clearly Paul believes that conscience should not be violated even if it is not properly informed by knowledge. To hold that inner division is a destructive beating is to presuppose that well-being resides in wholeness.

The second text that presupposes that salvation is wholeness or the unification of the self is Romans 6, where Paul is dealing with the question of why believers should not sin. Given the fact that salvation is by grace and ethical works do not count toward it, does Paul really have an argument to support his contention that those saved by grace should not go on in sin? Some would say no. John Knox, for example, argues that while Paul repudiated the notion that justification by grace does not require ethical living, he nevertheless had no logical reason for why the believer ought to be ethical. In Paul's view it is not that the believer ought to be ethical but that in the nature of the case she must be.[15]

But how does Paul in fact argue? In dealing with this issue I want to touch on the conceptual or logical relationship of wholeness as an ethical warrant to the moral imperatives or norms. If Paul had maintained that ethical obedience was a necessity given with the new life, his ethical imperatives would have been logically superfluous. But the very fact that ethical imperatives are so prominent in Paul, and often in the very contexts where the affirmation of new life is made (as in Romans 6), shows that Paul does not intend to say that ethical obedience is a must but that it is rather a possibility and ought to be enacted (6:11-13). Yet why should the believer act obediently? Paul tells the Roman Christians that they should not sin because in baptism they have shared in Jesus' death and potentially in his resurrection. Jesus' death was a victory over sin (6:10); therefore, our baptismal participation in his death frees us from sin (6:6-7). We ought not to sin in our everyday engagements in the world because we have been freed from sin in baptism. Our ethical lives should correspond to our sacramental lives. This is an appeal to enablement—do not sin because baptism has freed you from it—and is not a direct appeal to a motive, as is 1 Cor. 8:11-12. In the latter passage Paul explicitly states a motive for his prohibition: Do not sin against your brother *because* Christ died for him and *because* to sin against him is to sin against Christ. But enablement is an implicit motive. To say, "Do what you have been enabled to do, liberated to do," is to say, "Enact what you have become in baptism; be at one with yourself." The believer should not sin because it undermines the wholeness of the self in which ultimate well-being resides.

We have seen that the recovery of wholeness by the dispelling of self-deception gives to the moral life a new power and motivation. At the same time the actualization of wholeness through the exercise of the moral life prevents the self-dividedness in which self-deception grows. Salvation for Paul involves the unification of the poles of a number of polar relationships. I mention several of them, some of which I express in Pauline terminology and some with interpretive categories: conscious and unconscious, facticity and transcendence, life (or faith) and obedient action, sacramental life and moral life, body and spirit. These are not identical but overlap each other in varying degrees. Unity or separation in any of these polar relationships has an impact on the others.

### FREEDOM

Wholeness engenders freedom. While the term "freedom" (*eleutheria* and its cognates) has a central and unique importance in Paul among New Testament writers,[16] the theme of liberation is prominent in the Old Testament and in the Synoptic tradition: liberation from political and economic oppression, from punishment and guilt, from illness and the demons, from social marginalization, and from religious alienation.[17] Paul's doctrine of salvation can be understood as a concept of freedom. Christ represents freedom (2 Cor. 3:17) by having enacted it for us (Phil. 2:6-7; 2 Cor. 8:9), and his death and resurrection constitute a liberating event (Gal. 1:4; 2:19-21; 3:13-14, 26-28; 5:1, 13; Rom. 6:6-8; 8:2-11) that confers freedom upon us: freedom from the law, sin, flesh, death, the god of this world, the consequences of Adam's disobedience; freedom for love and the totality of reality—but dialectically.[18] Apart from this deliverance by Christ freedom is not possible for human beings.[19]

I should now like to paraphrase closely five key passages from Paul and comment on their interrelationships. Two other related texts will then be discussed somewhat more fully.

1.a. Everything is permitted to me, b. but I will not be put under the power of anything (1 Cor. 6:12).
2.a. Christ set us free for freedom; b. do not be subject again to slavery (Gal 5:1).
3.a. You were called to freedom; b. only do not use the freedom as an opportunity for the flesh (Gal. 5:13).
4.a. Though being free from all, b. I made myself a slave of all (1 Cor. 9:19).
5.a. All is yours, b. and you are Christ's, and Christ is God's (1 Cor. 3:21-23).

The first part (a) of each of these two-part passages affirms the virtually limitless freedom of the believer, while the second part (b) suggests some possible qualification of this freedom. Numbers 1 and 2 say approximately the same thing in both of their parts. The believer is free (1.a and 2.a), but the warning or exhortation regarding slavery (1.b and 2.b) shows that the freedom of the Christian can be lost.[20] Number 3.b explains how this loss might take place—by using freedom as an occasion for the flesh. That is, if one affirms something in this finite world—righteousness, wisdom, marriage, business, whatever—without limit and makes it one's ultimate security or god (Phil. 3:19), one will be enslaved by it (Rom. 1:22-25).[21] The text in 5.b (You are Christ's) provides the grounding for the freedom affirmed in all the a parts and explains why 4.b (I made myself a slave to all) does not undermine this freedom. Belonging to Christ gives me a grounding in transcendence. This slavery to the one who through his resurrection belongs to and with God, who is above all things, affords me a standing above all things. All things then—people, the world, the present and future (1 Cor. 3:21-22)—are openly available to me for my engagement, as long as I do not idolize them. Belonging to the transcendent one makes it possible not to idolize them: I know that my ultimate well-being does not lie with them. Here we have Paul's paradox that only slavery to Christ gives freedom for the world. Because I belong to Christ, I need not be enslaved to the law and cosmic powers that he is defeating. And because of that belonging, my slavery to other people (1 Cor. 9:19) is not real slavery. That is, it is qualitatively different from the helpless victimization that characterizes one's subjection under the powers, which I am not free to escape on my own. Slavery to other people is freely chosen and for their sake. I can critically assess it and withdraw from it if the situation changes. Belonging to Christ guarantees this freedom.[22]

I turn now to a discussion of 1 Cor. 7:29-35 and especially 7:29-31, where freedom for the world has an eschatological grounding as compared with the christological grounding given in 1 Cor. 3:21-23. Having all of reality available to one because one belongs to Christ is essentially similar in meaning to living in the world as though not (*hōs mē*) because the time is short and the world is passing away. One passage expresses the stance positively and the other negatively, but the meanings agree. To be free for the world by living in it as though not (7:29-31) is to be free for it by living in it as belonging to Christ (3:21-23). Belonging to Christ expresses positively the meaning of "not."

Our text appears in a chapter in which Paul is concerned to advise the Corinthians not to be anxious to change their status (as from circumcised to uncircumcised or vice versa). They should not think that such changes will give them a higher form of spiritual existence. Vincent Wimbush points out that 1 Cor. 7:29-35 is the only place where Paul self-consciously provides both a model for Christian existence in the world and a theological rationale for it. Here Paul clarifies his position on why the Corinthians should not want to change their status.[23]

A skeletal outline for 7:29-31 may be presented as follows: (1) proclamation of the imminence of the end (7:29a); (2) parenesis (7:29b-31a); (3) proclamation of the imminence of the end (7:31b).[24] What is the relationship between the two terminal parts of the passage: the time has been shortened (29a) and the form of the world is passing away (31b)? It could be that 31b is less eschatological than 29a and comes from a different source.[25] However that may be, Paul has tied the two terminal parts closely together to form an eschatological inclusio for a tightly cohering poetic piece. Beginning and end together form the ground and horizon of meaning for the passage. The key terms in the two parts are "time" (*kairos*, 29a) and "world" (*kosmos*, 31b). They are closely connected phonetically in that both are two-syllable nouns that begin with *k* and end with *s*. Beginning (*kairos*) and end (*kosmos*) also are strongly bound together conceptually, for *kairos* and *kosmos* represent two fundamental coordinates of human existence—time and space—and both are portrayed as of limited value. Time is limited by its shortness and space by its ephemerality. The limited value of the time-space continuum is the negative reason for living in the world as though not. One should be detached from the world because of its limited value. But the "not" is highly dialectical. It is negative because it expresses detachment from something of limited value. But it is also positive because the detachment is the transcendence of the world that derives from belonging to Christ. The imminent eschaton reflects back on the present and makes the present also the eschatological time (2 Cor. 6:1-2). Thus the present posture of being "in the world as though not" is Paul's way of expressing the coincidence of time and eschatological salvation. One can be truly engaged in the world without losing one's freedom to it because of being also in the eschatological "not."[26]

The whole of the parenetic middle of the passage is an imperative. Those who have wives, who rejoice and mourn, who buy and deal with the world are (ought) to do these things as not.[27] But it is a soteriological rather than an ethical imperative and so is an elaboration of the "work out your own salvation" of Phil. 2:12. It is a call to actualize the eschatological transcendence that surrounds the world of human relationships and allows one to live in them without being submerged in them. Paul here gives his rationale for his counsel against changing one's cultural status. What counts with God is not one's state in culture (7:18, 20, 24) but keeping the commandments of God (7:19). And the close context suggests, if it does not require, that one prominent commandment of God is the imperative in 7:29-31. Thus salvation depends not on having this rather than that status but on living in one's status as though not.

Paul's "as though not" is a posture of the whole self toward the world and its varied relationships. It is a stance of detached involvement, of being in the world and not in the world at the same time. The exhortation to live "as though not" in the middle of 7:29-31 is a demythologizing of the eschatological inclusio. In this posture the wholeness of the self is maintained because there is a balance of facticity (in the world) and transcendence (not).

Now what is the relationship of 7:29-31 to 7:32-35 (marriage and anxiety)? It may be that Paul intended the latter to be an interpretive extension of the former and, naturally, thereby to be in agreement with it.[28] If, however, that was Paul's intention, I am inclined to think that he did not accomplish it, but rather brought about in 7:32-35 a fairly severe deconstruction (pulling the opposing outside in) of 7:29-31. In 7:32-35 marriage does not just participate in the transience of the world but is a source of anxiety which is in direct competition with devotion to the Lord.

In 7:32 Paul states that he wants the Corinthians to be without anxiety. This turns out to mean that he actually wants them to be anxious about or to care about the Lord (7:32, 34), that is, to be devoted to the Lord without distraction (7:35). This is impossible for married believers because they will be anxious about the Lord but also about how to please their spouses and thus they are divided (7:32-34) and not devoted without distraction (7:35). Paul clearly opposes the Lord and the world as good and bad (and identifies wanting to please the spouse with anxiety about the world). Thus being anxious about the Lord is positive and being anxious about or showing care for one's spouse is negative.[29] Being anxious about the things of the Lord is a slightly ironic equivalent of undistracted devotion to the Lord. In other places Paul does seem to take the view that marriage is good for some people and bad for others, but the universalizing tone of 7:32-35 does not leave much—or any—room for thinking that marriage is advantageous for anyone.

In 7:29-31 living in the world as though not is a relationship to eschatological salvation that allows one to be involved in the world without being absorbed in it. There is no sense here that a life of involvement is incompatible with genuine faith, unless one breaks the dialectic of in and not in. The relationship to God's eschatological dealings does not demand renunciation of the world. But in 7:32-35 the relationship with the Lord is inherently in competition with involvement in the world (marriage). In 7:29-31 faith holds God and the world together so that one can be properly related to both. But 7:32-35 implicitly denies that one can have a particular involvement in the world without being inordinately entangled in it. Here faith in God is in principle opposed to life in the world. Faith has only to do with God and not with holding God and the world together. Paul synthesizes being related to God and to the world in 7:29-31 in the "as though not," which is positively evaluated. But in 7:32-35 being related to both is a matter of self-division, which is negatively evaluated. Thus the two contiguous paragraphs evaluate the same stance in opposite ways. If there were marriage within the requirements of 7:32-35 it would have to be marriage without care and evidently without the passion assumed in 7:1-7, 36-38. Verses 32-35 call not for a yes and no involvement in the world but for a renunciation of it. Parallel to the two views of life in the world and of faith are two understandings of God: God as the transcendent depth of the world (7:29-31) and God as the furthest extension of the world (7:32-35).

I take 1 Cor. 7:29-31 to be Paul's central or "normative" position even though it is in some tension with other Pauline texts.[30] The dialectic of in the world but as though not accords with the Jewish affirmation of the goodness of the created world. And it also is consistent with Paul's dual eschatology. The end has not come (so live in the world, 1 Cor. 5:9-10) but has come (so live in it as though not). The tension between this and other texts arises when a change of context prompts Paul to modify his position in such a way as to reduce the dialectic.[31] When Paul confronts a situation in which a believer seems to be deifying the world (Phil. 3:19), he tells his readers that their commonwealth is in heaven, not on earth (Phil. 3:20).[32] But when he addresses a situation where there seems to be no danger of idolizing the world, he can exhort his readers to rejoice with the joyous, to weep with the distressed, and to live in harmony with one another (Rom. 12:15-16)—with no "as though not" expressed (contrast 1 Cor. 7:30). The yes to the world is missing in Phil. 3:20 and the no, in Rom. 12:15-16. But the continuity of these two texts with the combination of yes and no in 1 Cor. 7:29-31 is also clearly visible.

The text of 1 Cor. 9:20-23 extends one of the freedom passages we have already discussed (9:19), has a terminological and conceptual relationship to 7:29-31, and provides a transition to the consideration of love in the next section. In 9:19 Paul states that he enslaved himself to all, and 9:20-23 unfolds the sense in which he has done that: He has become all things to all people. In 7:29-31 Paul issues a soteriological imperative to his readers: actualize the eschatological freedom that has been offered you. In 9:20-23 he speaks of his own sense of being under an ethical imperative to be a Jew to Jews, a Gentile to Gentiles, a weak person to the weak. The imperatival element is not grammatically expressed but is indicated by the context. Paul does not say that he *ought* to have become a slave by becoming all things to all people but simply states that he did it. But he did it because he is under obligation—necessity (9:16-17)—to preach the gospel and win converts (9:20, 21, 22).

Thus becoming all things to all is the means to a mandated end and is thereby itself an obligation. It is for the sake of making the gospel effective. The eschatological freedom that the readers are summoned to realize in 7:29-31 is assumed as the basis for the ethical imperative that Paul describes in 9:19-23. Paul is called upon to rely on that freedom and to trust that if he becomes the slave of another, he will still be free. We recall that choosing to become the slave of others is qualitatively different from being a slave of the law or the cosmic powers. One can choose to withdraw from it.

First Corinthians 9:20-23 is also akin to 7:29-31 in the employment of the as though not motif, although Paul has slightly changed his diction. In the earlier passage the "as" and the "not" occur in the same clause: have a wife or deal with the world, *as* though *not*. However, in 9:20-23 he has put the two words in different clauses: I became to those under the law *as* one under the law, though I am *not* under the law. I became to those without the law *as* one without the law, though I am *not* without the law of Christ.[33] Paul regarded it as his duty for the sake of winning people to the gospel to assume the position of various kinds of people whom he hoped to win, even though their position was not his own. That he could assume their position shows that he was detached from his own. But that their position was still not his demonstrates that he was involved in his own position.

The topic of freedom is introduced at the beginning of 1 Corinthians 9 apparently as a part of Paul's defense against opponents who charge that because he works for a living (9:6) he is not free and not really an apostle (9:1). The opponents evidently believe that the command of the Lord that those who proclaim the gospel should get their living from it (9:14) means that apostles should not have another job. They have the duty to accept support from those to whom they preach so that they can be free from secular work and free for their mission. The opponents could have seen Paul's renunciation of support from the churches and his insistence on working as a lack of trust in God. But Paul has reinterpreted the command of the Lord as a privilege or right rather than as a duty. It is a right that he has renounced (9:12, 15) in order to labor as a leather worker.[34] And Paul has a different angle on freedom. He wants to work in order to be free from all people so that he can be a slave of all in order to win more. With no financial obligation to anyone he is free to identify himself with the position of any and all.[35] Paul and his opponents agree on the goal of winning people to the gospel. They disagree on how one can best do this: by freedom from secular work (opponents) or by freedom from obligation to any group (Paul).

For Paul it is belonging to Christ (1 Cor. 3:23) that grounds the freedom of the believer. To belong to Christ is to be his slave. Paul can refer either to himself (Rom. 1:1) or to other believers (1 Cor. 7:22) as slaves of Christ. He can in a similar fashion also refer to believers as slaves of God (Rom. 6:22), of righteousness (6:18), of correct teaching (6:17), or of obedience (6:16). Clearly what defines slavery for Paul is obedience (Rom. 6:16-17). The slave is the utterly obedient one. What gives to the themes of freedom and slavery in Paul both their meaning and power is the highly tensive way Paul combines them. We saw this tendency to associate them in the first five passages discussed in this section. We see it in 1 Cor. 7:22 and in Romans 6. To be the slave of God and righteousness is to be freed from sin (6:14, 18, 22) and given to life (6:13, 22-23). Only complete obedience to the source of life confers freedom in the sense in which Paul understands it. Nothing less enables one to have free access to the whole of reality without being enslaved by the latter. The widespread tendency to connect freedom and slavery in this tensive and paradoxical way shows that Paul does understand each in light of the other. And if the obedience element is weakened, both freedom and slavery suffer a reduction in meaning. It is precisely the paradox that gives the dual theme its power.[36]

## LOVE: SEEKING THE ADVANTAGE OF THE OTHER

Given the centrality that Paul bestows upon the love commandment, this imperative—to seek the advantage of the other—is the primary way in which one expresses ethically (in relationship to other people and their needs) one's appropriate detachment from one's own involvements in the world. Living toward my wife as though not means existentially (in faith) that I do not make the idolatrous mistake of overvaluing the marriage by believing that it can save me. It means ethically that I prefer her interests to mine. Living in the world as though means that I prefer her interests ethically. Living in the world as though not means that I do not idolize her.

I shall turn first to the famous 1 Corinthians 13, although I am not sure that it is Paul's most instructive statement about love. In 1 Cor. 13:1-3 Paul contrasts love (*agapē*) both with spiritual experience (speaking in tongues, having prophetic powers, understanding mysteries and knowledge, having all faith) and with deeds (giving away one's possessions and giving one's body to be burned). Paul can make this dual contrast without changing the meaning he attributes to love. Spiritual experience without love does not count for anything, and neither do deeds without love count for anything. Since love is contrasted both with acts and with spiritual experience it must be an inner disposition (not deeds) that is ethical[37] (not spiritual). What is the content of that disposition?

That, I think, is best indicated by the frequency with which Paul exhorts his readers to seek the good of the other. This is a persistent theme that Paul can state with a variety of terminology. Paul states that he does not seek (*zēteō*) his own advantage (*symphoron*) but that of the many (1 Cor. 10:33). In 1 Thess. 5:15 he exhorts his readers to pursue (*diōkō*) the good (*agathos*) toward one another. No one is to seek his own "thing" (*to*—singular neuter definite article) but that of the other (1 Cor. 10:24). They are not to look out for (*skopeō*) their own things (*ta*—plural neuter definite article) but those of others (Phil. 2:4). Believers ought not to please (*areskō*) themselves but the neighbor for her good (Rom. 15:1-2; 1 Cor.

10:33). Love does not seek its own things (1 Cor. 13:5). Clearly Paul's central ethical norm—to seek the advantage of the other—is formal and open. What the good of the other is has to be determined in context.

Love then in 1 Corinthians 13 is the disposition to seek the good of the other. That it is an inner disposition is shown by the fact that it is contrasted with deeds.[38] One can both have religious experience and perform deeds for others without having this ethical disposition, without really seeking the advantage of the other. Paul then defines love in 1 Corinthians 13 as a disposition, and his concern is to say that religious experiences and ethical acts lack wholeness without it.

In 2 Cor. 8:8-12 Paul's conceptual position is essentially the same, although his definition of love has changed somewhat. It is still his purpose to affirm that the ethical responsibility of the believer includes both will or disposition and action. In urging the Corinthians to complete their collection for the Jerusalem Christians, he tells them that their intention should be matched by their deeds. But now the word "love" (8:8)—if love is to be genuine—includes both the readiness to will (*prothymia tou thelein*) and the carrying out of the action. Love here is no longer defined as the disposition.[39] We see that for Paul the believer is to extend love to all and not just to the Christian community (1 Thess. 3:12; 5:15; Gal. 6:10).

Krister Stendahl appropriately sees Paul as interpreting the love command in his exhortation to the strong in Corinth to forgo their freedom so as not to entice the weak into a conflict of conscience by their example of eating meat offered to idols. Paul himself carried this willingness to accommodate to the position of others to the point of becoming all things to all people: a Jew to the Jews, a Gentile to the Gentiles, weak to the weak (1 Cor. 9:19-23).[40]

Before continuing Stendahl's interpretation we might pause for a moment to ask in what sense the weak of 1 Cor. 9:22 were weak and in what sense Paul became weak for them. According to Dale Martin, Paul has the socially weak in mind, and he became weak in the social sense of working at a demeaning manual trade.[41] This may well be part of the meaning but can hardly be an exhaustive interpretation, for "weak" in the Pauline context is more than a social term. In 1 Cor. 8:7-13 it is a weak conscience that is in view, and in Rom. 14:1-4 weakness pertains to faith. And in 1 Cor. 9:19-23 since Jew and Gentile are defined by the law or lack of it—a religious-ethical phenomenon—and therefore cannot be regarded as purely social categories, neither can the weak in the same context be regarded as purely social. Clearly in 1 Cor. 4:10 Paul identifies himself as weak in the sense in which he understands the cross to be weak: It is the place of weakness and foolishness at which the power and wisdom of God come to expression (1:18-30). Precisely because Paul identified himself with the weakness of the cross, he can endure (4:12)—and more (Rom. 5:1-5). In weakness he has power to relinquish his own interests and to identify with those who are weak in conscience, faith, and social standing.

Stendahl makes the provocative claim that Paul in his becoming all things to all people established love rather than integrity as his central norm.[42] Stendahl does not give an explicit definition of integrity, but he implies that integrity would be living and acting in accordance with one's own freedom and convictions. Love in this context is living according to the convictions of the other. Somewhat surprisingly Stendahl then says that if becoming all things to all people were made into a general principle, it would be abhorrent and certainly without integrity.[43] But why, on Stendahl's terms, would a lack of integrity be abhorrent or a problem at all since the norm is love which calls for a relinquishment of integrity? Stendahl does not make himself clear. But I think that we can explain why Paul, if asked, would probably have said that one should not always renounce her own convictions and live by the judgments of another person's conscience. Adopting the position of the other should not be a general rule because the basic norm is to seek the good of the other, and there may be cases when the other's good—love for him or her—requires that I live by my convictions, maintain my integrity, rather than act in conformity with her convictions.

Although we do not find Paul actually drawing this conclusion in 1 Corinthians 8–10, the imperative to seek the good of the other logically implies or allows that there may be cases where the other is better served by trying to help him overcome his convictions than by our acquiescing in them. Paul speaks of love in Rom. 12:21 as active rather than passive. Evil is to be conquered or prevailed over (*nikaō*), not just accepted.[44] To cite Paul in that way implies that the believer as moral agent is sometimes justified in interpreting the convictions of the other as evil. Paul supports that conclusion.

In Gal. 2:11-21 Paul shows himself as unwilling to live by or support the convictions of the Jerusalem Christians who believed that Jewish Christians should not eat with gentile Christians (2:12, 14), although the Jerusalem group must have believed sincerely that open eating violated God's revelation in the law. Paul felt that to comply with them would compromise justification by faith (Gal. 2:14-19). Thus sometimes it is necessary to insist on one's own position to the point of splitting the community in order to build up the community in the long run. For Paul, then, one must decide in individual cases whether love calls on one to relinquish one's integrity for the sake of the other or to insist on one's integrity for the sake of the other. It is not always simply love or integrity. It may be love and integrity.

Paul does not articulate a principle for deciding whether the situation calls for love rather than integrity (assuming the position of the other's convictions as in 1 Cor. 9:19-23) or love and integrity (maintaining one's own convictions, as in Gal. 2:11-21), but he may imply one. Apparently Paul was willing to accommodate to the beliefs of others—to make himself a slave of all—if that entailed relinquishing his own freedom, surrendering the fruit of the gospel in him. Love may call on one to actualize the freedom to give up his or her own freedom. But Paul was not willing to compromise what he understood as the gospel itself which is the ground of his freedom and the freedom of others (Gal. 2:11-21).[45]

## NORM AND JUSTIFICATION: PAUL'S SEXUAL ETHIC

We have seen that Paul rejects obedience to the law as a way to salvation and interprets the law, under the actual conditions of fallen human existence, as a demonic power that leads people astray. But the believer in the gospel now participates in the ontological intention of the law to elicit faith and in the ethical intention of the law to promote love. The law influences the content of Paul's norms. E. P. Sanders is right in suggesting that the law of Christ (Gal. 6:2) is the law of God (Moses) as fulfilled in love (Gal. 5:14).[46] Law as fulfilled equals love to the neighbor. This does not mean that love is the way in which the believer must still obey all the separate details of the Old Testament law. Rather, love is the one thing to be done because it expresses the intention of all the individual laws: to avoid doing wrong to the neighbor (Rom. 13:10). And love to the neighbor is the law of Christ, for Christ has defined what it means not to please oneself but rather the neighbor (Rom. 15:1-3; Gal. 2:20).

In 1 Cor. 7:19 Paul says that what counts is keeping the commandments of God. Since the latter are distinguished here from circumcision, they must not refer to cultic commandments. We have seen that in part the commandments contextually mean the imperative to live in the world as though not (1 Cor. 7:29-31). But the term "commandment" (*entolē*) is too closely associated with the Old Testament law by Paul (Rom. 7:7-12; 13:9) not to bring that also into the picture here as a source of moral commandments. Obviously the prohibition against fornication has a background in the Old Testament legal tradition (Exod. 22:16-17; Deut. 22:13-21, 28-29).[47] So the Old Testament not only provides the encompassing moral principle of love; it can also influence particular rules. Given the centrality of love, however, the other norms should be understood as ways of making love concrete[48] or of preventing freedom from becoming an occasion for the flesh (Gal. 5:13), which would subvert freedom.

It should also be observed that Paul rejects (although not with complete consistency) the idea of unexceptionable rules. Strong Christians ought not to engage in eating habits or other activities that would lead weak Christians into a conflict of conscience (1 Cor. 8:7-13; 10:23-30; Rom. 14:1-9). But "do not eat food offered to idols" is not a rule that always obtains. Contextual circumstances determine whether one should so eat. Would Paul not logically have had to have the same attitude toward Old Testament rules? We can say, then, that for Paul the law is a trace of God's will. It may express God's will but does not contain it in full.

Paul gives a variety of justifying reasons that would authorize the performance of an action.[49] He can appeal (in deontological fashion) to the *authority* of various sources of his norms. He appeals to the will of God (Rom. 12:2) or to God's glory (1 Cor. 10:31). And he can say "Do it" because (*gar*) it fulfills the law (Rom. 13:8). Or he can invoke the authority of the word (1 Cor. 7:10-11) or example (Phil. 2:5; 1 Cor. 11:1; Rom. 15:1-3) of Christ. And he appeals to the authority of his own role as father (1 Cor. 4:15; Phil. 4:9) and the authority of his example (1 Cor. 4:16; 11:1). In addition Paul invokes what nature teaches (1 Cor. 11:14) and what the churches of God recognize (1 Cor. 11:16). Again he appeals (deontologically) to the *inherent rightness* of certain values and virtues. In Phil. 4:8-9 he calls on his readers to enact a number of moral qualities: what is true, honorable, excellent, worthy of praise (*epainos*), and so forth. These are terms from popular moral philosophy, none of which is specifically Christian, whose use shows that Paul acknowledged moral discernment among the pagans.[50] The employment of these terms might be an appeal to the authority of the popular philosophical tradition, or even to the reward of being praised. But I would judge that particularly the term "worthy of praise" invokes the inherent rightness of these virtues.

In addition, Paul can justify (in consequentialist fashion) moral behavior by appealing to the *consequences* for the other. In 1 Cor. 9:19, 21, 22 he behaves in a certain way—assumes the alien position of others—for the express purpose of achieving a specific consequence, that is, the salvation of those people. Similarly in 1 Cor. 10:31-33 he seeks to please others and relinquishes his own advantage in order that the many may be saved. In 1 Cor. 8:9-13 and 10:24-30 the good of the sister is both the norm to be pursued and the reason for pursuing it. The ethical imperatives of 1 Thess. 4:9-11 are to be carried out in order to achieve the consequence of walking becomingly toward outsiders (4:12). This is an appeal to an effect on others, but one that will at the same time enhance the social well-being of the believers.

I would judge that the most fundamental justification for ethical norms and for obedience to them in Paul is the appeal to the wholeness of the ethical agent, the believer. We have already had occasion to discuss this theme, and it comes to expression again in 1 Cor. 6:12-20. This, I believe, is the justification most integral to Paul's total position, and certainly it is the one most integral to the aspect of his theology and ethics which I am here studying: Do it—or refrain from doing it—in order to be a whole person.[51]

Finally Paul can appeal to eschatological consequences for the ethical agent: Do it in order not to lose out on inheriting the kingdom of God (1 Cor. 6:9-11; Rom. 14:12; 2 Cor. 5:10). But this turns out to be an externalized version of the appeal to wholeness or self-realization, for the invocation of reward and punishment means that in ethical action the self that one is to become is at stake.[52]

## 1 Corinthians 6:12-20

Although Paul does not explicitly employ the mutual responsibility that husbands and wives have toward each other in marriage as an argument against fornication, he does, nevertheless, maintain that mutuality, at least in the realm of sexuality. And however much he may have failed to draw out the full implications of sexual mutuality for the full equality for women, he did make a significant beginning of a task we are still engaged in. Each spouse is to render to the other his or her sexual due (1 Cor. 7:3), for each has authority (*exousiazō*) over the body of the other (7:4). The equal place of the woman would have been novel—perhaps shockingly so—in Paul's day.[53] The contrast with current custom can be epitomized by observing that in Gen. 3:16 the woman's desire or turning (*apostrophē*) is toward her husband and he will lord it over (*kyrieuō*) her,[54] but nothing is said here about the man's desire or the woman's rule. And clearly Paul recognized the reality and legitimacy of sexual desire and maintained that in marriage it should not be denied except for brief periods of prayer (7:5). Paul in fact regarded the satisfaction of desire as a legitimate reason for getting married.[55] If Paul believed that marriage was a second best alternative to celibacy, as he did (7:1-2, 7-8, 28b, 32-33), he still believed that it was preferable not only to immorality but to burning with unsatisfied passion (7:9).[56] While Paul did not join with Plutarch in praising a wife's erotic passion toward her husband,[57] he was certainly a long way from the first century A.D. Stoic Musonius Rufus, who held that sexual intercourse was justified only in marriage and only then for procreation and not for pleasure.[58]

Paul's discussion of fornication (*porneia*) in 1 Cor. 6:12-20 introduces a section on rights (*exousia*) and freedom (*eleutheria*) which extends to 11:1.[59] Paul is opposing a libertine group—of whatever degree of enthusiasm—that does not believe that sexual activity outside of marriage affects the essential self.[60] For this group nothing is forbidden. Paul opposes fornication, which in 6:12-20 means the use of a prostitute (*pornē*),[61] but in 7:2 may refer to sexual relationships outside of marriage more broadly. I will try to show that Paul's argument against fornication in 6:12-20 applies logically against all forms of nonmarital sex.

It is unambiguously clear that Paul is against fornication, but exactly what his argument is in support of this negative norm is not so transparently evident. Nor is it altogether unambiguous exactly what the fault is in fornication.

William Countryman in his provocative book has argued that Paul does not see certain sexual activities as wrong because they are unclean or impure but because they express the greed of the heart.[62] Paul identifies impurity with greed (1 Thess. 4:3-8). Uncleanness becomes overreaching to take sexual property that belongs to another, trying to get the better of someone else, competitive greed.[63] We may raise the question then of how sex with a prostitute would be greed in Paul's view since she is not the property of a husband, whereas in 1 Thess. 4:3-8 Paul does seem to have in mind taking someone else's wife. Had Paul forbade sex with a prostitute on property grounds he would have had to regard the prostitute as owner of her own sexual property. It would be wrong as the commercial use of the personal. Paul does not move in that direction, but he is very much concerned with the reason for fleeing fornication.

Paul states that the man who joins himself to a prostitute becomes one body with her (6:16). One of the difficulties of our passage is that having made that assertion, he then backs it up by quoting Gen. 2:24 which is a statement about marriage: the two shall become one flesh. What is the upshot of Paul's identifying the one body achieved with the prostitute with the one flesh achieved in marriage? (The parallelism makes body and flesh synonyms in this case.) One direction of meaning that the identification takes is to draw the marital relationship toward the illicit sexual relationship, to assimilate the former to the latter. The association of the marital union with the union with a prostitute inevitably puts marriage in a negative light. Comprehending both prostitute and wife in the same language—one body/

flesh—seems to say that it is the union with the woman, in marriage or outside of it, that is the fault. Paul, as we have seen, manifests some tendencies in this direction. Marriage is a second-best alternative to celibacy (1 Cor. 7:6-7) and causes anxiety that distracts one from undivided devotion to the Lord (7:32-35). But Paul does not draw the full consequences of this tendency; he states that marriage is better than fornication (7:1-2) and is not a sin (7:28, 36).

Another direction of meaning is that the quotation about the one flesh union in marriage in 6:16b simply confirms and underlines the oneness of body with the prostitute already affirmed in 6:16a. The connection draws the illicit sexual relationship toward the character of the marital relationship—one body/flesh. In this case the fault is not the sexual relationship itself (in or outside marriage) but is the fact that a human bodily union that belongs to one kind of relationship—marriage—has been achieved outside of the relationship that legitimates it. This creates a tension or self-dividedness which is the clue to the sin against the body in 6:18. To pursue that issue we must look further at Paul's understanding of the body and the human spirit. What I want to argue is that for Paul body and spirit belong integrally together, but fornication pulls them apart. It is a sin against the body in that it divides the self, violates wholeness. Paul has affirmed that the work of redemption unifies conscious and unconscious, understanding and action, sacramental self and moral self. The presupposition in 1 Cor. 6:15-20 seems to be that it also unifies body and spirit. Fornication sunders them. But because for Paul body is not just physical, this severance of body and spirit can be called simply an offense against the body, a denial of the body's spiritual dimension.

Since Paul hints that fornication will sever one from Christ, the intention not to be thus separated is suggested as the reason for not indulging in fornication. But Paul never actually says that illicit sex will separate from Christ. What he does say is that it is a sin against the body, and thus the warrant for the imperative to flee fornication is to avoid injuring the body, to preserve wholeness. Hence the only actual manifestation of severance from Christ that Paul brings to expression is the sin against the body, the violation of the wholeness of the self achieved in Christ.

The body has been given wholeness through the salvation wrought by Christ or the Spirit (1 Cor. 6:19-20; 4:5; 14:25; 2 Cor. 3:15-18; 4:6). It is the body—the temple of the Holy Spirit—that is sinned against. But the wholeness of the self is for Paul the ontological constitution of human beings as human, prior to redemption. The self in its essential nature is self-related, a harmonious relationship of communicating parts. The spirit of a person knows the things of that person (1 Cor. 2:11). The body is the object of one's own actions (1 Cor. 9:27). As conscience a person knows herself (1 Cor. 4:4; 2 Cor. 1:12), and for Paul and his contemporaries conscience belonged to all human beings as human.

What might appear to be a tension between two justifications for the norm—(1) the appeal to the unifying effect of salvation (do not undo your relationship with Christ and the Spirit) and (2) the appeal to the ontological constitution of human being as created (do not sin against your body)—turns out not to be a real tension because for Paul what God does in salvation is what he decided before the ages (1 Cor. 2:7) and must have acted upon in creation. God is re-creating the self-related wholeness that God effected in creation but that has been lost through sin. However, the tension, or contradiction, about the nature of the fault in fornication—the sexual relationship per se versus sex with a prostitute—remains. And this tension is related to the one we have already observed between 1 Cor. 7:29-31 and 7:32-35.

### Body and Human Spirit

As is well known, Bultmann interpreted body (*sōma*) in Paul as meaning the whole person. To be sure, Paul uses the word "body" to mean one's physical presence in the world (1 Thess. 5:23; 1 Cor. 12:12-26; 2 Cor. 10:10; Gal. 6:17; 1 Cor. 9:27; 13:3), but this shades off into Paul's characteristic usage, which is that the body is one's whole self, something one is rather than has (Rom. 6:12; 12:1). It is the whole person in the sense of the self that can be the object of one's own actions and intentions (Rom. 6:12-14; 12:1; 1 Cor. 9:27; 13:3; Phil. 1:20). The body thus stands for the person as ontologically self-related. Since one is self-related she can be either at one with herself or estranged from herself.[64]

It has also been argued that the term "body" in Paul calls attention to the physical body rather than to the whole person. There is no need to think that the association of the body with the Lord (1 Cor. 6:13) or with its own resurrection (1 Cor. 15:44) extends the meaning of body beyond the physical.[65] Robert Gundry, who takes this position, maintains that if the physical body were thought to represent the whole person figuratively, that would not satisfy the demands of a holistic definition, for the latter requires that body refer directly to the whole person.[66] I am not sure why that would need to be the case. But evidently Gundry's reason for denying that body can represent the whole person figuratively or metaphorically is his belief that if body were made to straddle both physical and spiritual senses the result would be confusion.[67] But, as we have seen and will come

of body to this reshaping of existence. The body is the concrete specificity in which the openness is structured.

### The Sin against the Body (1 Cor. 6:18)

We have seen that the body against which one sins is the whole self both given in creation and re-created through salvation. There is a problem in translating this verse. A more or less literal translation would say: "Flee fornication. Every sin that a man might commit is outside the body, but the fornicator sins into (*eis*)—that is, against—[73] his own body." To achieve a translation is to move toward an interpretation, and as I pursue that goal two questions will be in view: (1) What is the relationship of fornication to other sins, and (2) what is the nature of the sin against the body?

The translation problem is this: If every sin is outside the body, how can this one sin be into it? There are several possible solutions. One, taken by the RSV, is that Paul meant to say that every *other* sin is outside the body, but fornication is into it. Only fornication really injures the body-self. Another possibility is to take "body" in the first clause to mean the body of Christ, the church, and "body" in the second clause, one's own body, to mean the self. Thus Paul would be saying that every sin is alien to the Christian community,[74] but sexual sin also destroys one's selfhood. In either case Paul is making the point that there is something uniquely damaging about fornication.

Against this interpretation it has been argued that Paul in fact did not in any other place take the extreme position that fornication was qualitatively different from all other sins. Therefore, "every sin is outside the body" is understood as a slogan of the Corinthian opponents, and "but the fornicator sins against his own body" is taken to be Paul's rejoinder.[75] But C. K. Barrett has pointed out that there is no clear evidence that Paul rejects the "every sin is outside the body."[76] Moreover, Paul's claim, in view of his conception of the body, would have to be "but the fornicator sins against his very self." And in order for that assertion to have a real point the opponent would have to be saying "every sin is outside of, does *not* affect, the body"—in the sense of the whole or real self. It does not seem probable to me that Paul's Hellenistic opponents would have thus understood the body as significantly constitutive of the self.

I am therefore inclined to take "every sin is outside the body, does not affect the true self" as Paul's own and to understand him as not meaning to be taken literally. He is speaking relatively or comparatively.[77] Paul's "every sin is outside the body" is hyperbole, and his overall point in 6:18

is that no sin injures the wholeness of the self as much as fornication does, but not that other sins do not affect the self at all.

Paul does not say explicitly why marriage justifies sex nor does he expressly set forth the sense in which sexual relationships outside of marriage deform the person. We can surmise why Paul would have found a sexual relationship between a Corinthian believer and a nonbelieving prostitute—or mistress or lover—especially problematical. All sexual relationships create the one flesh union that characterizes marriage (1 Cor. 6:16), and in marriage the body of each partner is under the authority of the other (7:4), and body in some way includes the whole self. A believer involved in a sexual relationship with a nonbeliever would be caught in a tension between the authority of the Lord and the authority of the nonbelieving partner. For Paul this would also logically be a problem for a marriage between believer and nonbeliever. But for whatever reason Paul believed that marriage neutralized the tension. He tells Christians not to leave their non-Christian spouses, for their presence sanctifies the non-Christian spouse and the children (7:12-14). Perhaps Paul thought that the lordship of Christ extended through the believer to the whole family.[78] Again, why this should be so Paul does not clarify; possibly he was thinking in terms of corporate personality. But I think that we can infer what it is about marriage that justifies the sexual relationship as it cannot be justified outside of marriage. Paul's implicit belief that marriage contributes to the wholeness of the self may or may not have been part of his reason for believing that marriage might overcome the tension between believing and nonbelieving spouses.

Sex outside of marriage deforms the wholeness or unity of the self in which well-being resides. If body and spirit go together in one's relationship with Christ (6:15, 17), so must they in one's sexual relationship because the self in principle, in its ontological structure, as created, is unified. But in fornication body and spirit are pulled apart. Body and spirit go together in principle, but in fornication one says with one's body what one cannot say with one's spirit. Or, to put it another way, the spiritual dimension of the body is denied, sinned against. One says more with one's body, creating one self by creating one body-flesh, than one can mean in the spiritual dimension. The latter is the dimension in which one understands and interprets oneself, the world, and God; the dimension in which one can hold oneself responsible. Thus fornication is a sin against the body in the simple sense that it divides the self. One both commits and does not commit the whole self. One does what calls for ongoing responsibility in a situation where that is not possible. Because the body—*sōma*—is both physical body and more than physical, a physical union is always more than physical. However, outside of marriage the more than physical—the spiritual—is denied. That is, the body-spirit union is split or the body is sinned against. But in the ongoing mutual accountability of marriage the whole body-self can be committed. To preserve the wholeness of the person, the unity of body and spirit, is the reason to flee fornication.

Paul's argument does not stem from the view that illicit sex is unclean. We should also distinguish Paul from another canonical writer who seems to be similar but who is really quite different. The wisdom teacher in Proverbs 6 warns his readers that the adulterer is without sense and destroys himself (6:32). But the way in which he destroys himself is that he becomes the object of a jealous husband's furious revenge (6:34). The justification for the moral action is strongly prudential. But in Paul it is based on his understanding of human existence. Do not do it because it violates who you are.

I would judge that Paul's argument from the structure of human existence gives strong backing for his rule and thus that it would take very good reasons to override it. At the same time we should remember that whatever subjective inclinations Paul may have had on this issue, his text as a whole has a disinclination to assert unexceptionable rules. And the rule to flee fornication must be placed in the context of Paul's fundamental norm—to seek the advantage of the other. It must be asked in an open way whether the denial of sex outside of marriage is always and unexceptionably in the interest of the well-being of the other.

We have seen that Paul's argument for sex inside of marriage is drawn from his understanding of the whole person as given in both creation and redemption. Faithfulness to one partner sustains human beings as created, but human beings as created are prone to worship the creature rather than the creator (Rom. 1:25). Once God has been rejected, people turn to the creation for security, for a functional god, an idol. And a significant sexual relationship with one other person may be such a false god. D. H. Lawrence had a sense of that possibility, although he would not have given it such an explicitly theological interpretation. He was not an obscene writer who encouraged promiscuity. Rather, he valued all too highly a relationship with one woman. He hoped that it would save him. Or at least his spokesman, Rupert Birkin, does in the novel *Women in Love*. Rupert has told his friend, Gerald, that he wants the finality of love with one woman. "The old ideals are dead as nails," and life has no center, so all there is is a kind of ultimate marriage with one woman. Then Gerald questions him: "And you mean if there isn't the woman, there's nothing?" "Pretty well that," responds Rupert, "seeing there's no God." [79]

Paul's preference for marriage over fornication is based on his understanding of human beings as created and redeemed. But apart from salvation, which gives to the person a standing in transcendence, a standing beyond creation, the one woman, or man, becomes all too easily the center of the universe and also a tyrant. Salvation protects from the overvaluing or absolutizing of marriage. Paul obviously does not reflect that explicitly on the issue, but this is what he has in mind when in 1 Cor. 7:29-31 he exhorts those who have wives to be as not having them. We have seen that he does not mean to be married but without sex. Rather, he is talking about a basic posture toward the marital relationship as a whole—and also toward emotional involvements with friends, business connections, and whatever other relationships one has with the world. It is a posture of detached involvement. In faith a person is both engaged in the world and free from domination by it, both in it and not in it. The freedom to be involved in the world and detached from it at the same time, the freedom that enables ethical action, is also the freedom not to idolize the ethical project or its fruits.

Perhaps I should give a reminder of the reason for the long discussion of freedom and ethics: The wholeness achieved by the revealing of the secrets of the heart is progressively realized in moral life and action.

# 4

## SELF-DECEPTION
## IN MATTHEW

*Why do you not notice?*

Self-deception is the human phenomenon in which a person conceals the real story with a cover story that he or she really believes yet only half believes. The real story then becomes inaccessible without more ado, but is still operant. As such, self-deception is an instance of the violation of human wholeness, a rupture of the correspondence of the self with the self. We turn now to self-deception as it comes to expression in the Gospel of Matthew.

### THE TREE AND ITS FRUITS

The passage about the tree and its fruits in Matt. 7:15-20 begins with an exhortation to beware of false prophets, the wolves in sheep's clothing (v. 15).[1] The command is followed by a section framed (7:16a, 20) by the claim that you will know them by their fruits. The material inside this frame (7:16b-19) explains why or how you know them by their fruits: because tree (heart) and fruit (act) correspond; it is not possible to get bad fruit from a good tree or vice versa. The "they" who are known by their fruits are in part the false prophets, but the generality of the comments here as well as in the parallel section in 12:33-37 makes it clear that Matthew is talking about human being universally.

Now who are the false prophets in Matthew's situation? I believe that the sheep's clothing image suggests that they are Jewish Christians who practice an ethic of external obedience. But the fact that they confess Jesus as Lord (*kyrios*) and appeal to their prophesying and miracle working (7:21-22) may indicate that they are enthusiasts and antinomians.[2] Briefly stated, enthusiasts are people who put more store in having the Spirit than in belonging to the historical order with its moral responsibilities. Perhaps the historical author was faced with a theological battle on two fronts: He was in conflict with both legalists and antinomians. But for the implied author—the author as he is shaped by the writing of the text and who thus becomes the unifying principle of the text—the situation is somewhat different. (Generally when I use "Matthew" as the name of a person, I mean the implied author.) The pressure of the text fuses external obedience to the law (5:20; 7:15; 23:27-28) with opposition to God's will (7:21, 23) so that there results within Matthew's narrative world, as distinguished from his historical situation, only one opponent: people who are antinomian in that they obey the requirements of the law only externally.[3]

Now I can pose the exegetical problem: Since people, in principle, are known by their fruits and since the false prophets present the fruits of sheep, how does the author know that inwardly they are wolves? Daniel Patte answers that the sheep's clothes are only an attempted disguise. Their fruits show what they really are.[4] But we shall see that in view of certain distinctions—certain opposing pairs—that Matthew puts conceptually in parallel, the clothes are the fruits. These people really look like good sheep; the clothes are not just a disguise. They are the real acts—good acts—of these people, and there are no other acts to show what the wolves really are. Matthew has said that one can read a person's heart (tree) from his or her fruit. But can one? Does that accord with other things Matthew says?

Matthew affirms that fruit reveals the true nature of the tree because tree and fruit correspond (7:16-20; 12:34-35). It is impossible for them not to correspond, impossible for a tree to produce contrary to its nature (7:18; 12:35). The outside manifests the inside because the inside determines the quality of the outside (23:26). The unity of person and act is also implied in 5:14-16 since light (*one* image) is an image for both the person and her acts or the person in herself and the person as expressed in her acts.

But does Matthew really mean that the fruit reveals the tree, or in what sense can he mean it, since in at least three places he indicates that the outside can falsify, conceal, or misrepresent the inside? In our present text (7:15) people who are really wolves appear as sheep. In 12:33 Matthew puts the reader under the imperative to create correspondence between tree and fruit, which implies that the accord does not exist. The Pharisees are said to be clean, whitewashed, and apparently righteous on the outside, but within they are unclean and wicked (23:25, 27-28). Thus there is actual conflict rather than correspondence between the inside and the outside of a person.

What are we to make of this tension in the Gospel of Matthew? It appears that at the level of textual articulation the Gospel simply contradicts itself. Fruit reveals the true nature of the tree, and it does not. We might say that Matthew deconstructs himself. He has brought an opposing outside into the inside of his discourse. He says two conflicting things, and his meaning thus is undecidable. We could, however, relieve the contradiction in part by saying that the correspondence between inner (good tree) and outer (good fruit) belongs to the ontological level of reality, to unfallen creation or what is true for human beings in principle or latently. The contradiction between heart (bad) and action (good), on the other hand, belongs to the ontic level, to what is actually true for fallen human existence. At the same time the correspondence between bad heart and bad conduct (12:33b) would also seem to pertain to the situation of actual fallenness, although Matthew may imply that this consistent rottenness is less evil than the contradiction between good conduct and a wicked heart. Matthew's Jesus admonishes his hearers to be consistently either good or bad but not conflictingly both good and bad (12:33). So what is the force of the causal "for" (*gar*) introducing 12:33c and 12:34b? Make inside and outside both either good or bad, for (because) the tree is known by its fruit, the heart manifests itself in its words (12:33c, 34b). The causal clause expresses the ontological structure, the principle, of human being. Be consistently good or bad *because* correspondence between inner and outer (12:35) is your nature. In fact you cannot—it is not possible to—speak or do the good when you are evil (12:34). The words or deeds come from the heart, which qualifies the former (7:17-18; 12:33-35). There is a necessary correspondence between inner and outer. Perhaps this is why we have the allusive suggestion that bad fruit and bad tree are better than good fruit and bad tree. The former is closer to the structural principle of human being.

But, again, the correspondence belongs to the ontological. There is, as we have seen, actual noncorrespondence. This is Matthew's judgment about the seriousness and complexity of the human situation: In principle inner and outer match, but in actuality they do not. People do do what in principle they cannot do. Matthew's position is hard to pin down systematically because he is telling a story and because the issue will not conform to strict logic. Because people do what they cannot do, their actions are ambiguous. An act may be good in that it expresses the weightier matters of the law and can be seen to be good because it is evaluated by an external criterion, the law (to be discussed below). Matthew can speak of acts of obedience to the law quite positively (23:23). But acts that are externally good (the sheep's clothes represent such acts) may also be called false, the acts of false prophets (7:15), evil acts that bring about punishment (7:23). Evidently for Matthew the notion of "apparently" (*phainō*) good (23:27-28) mediates between good and not good. Acts that appear to be good are only apparently, not really, good (discussed further below).

The distinction between ontological and ontic helps us to sort out Matthew's ideas in part, but then we must ask ourselves what the hermeneutical status of the ontological/ontic distinction is. What is the locus of the distinction? Where does it come from? One option is to argue that while the implied author—the text's principle of unity—contradicts himself, the historical author presupposed the distinction. But how would we know that? The historical author may have, but we are not sure. So perhaps we should understand the text as an incomplete set of clues which has to be turned into a work by the pre-understanding of the reader.[5] Thus the interpreter completes the work by taking Matthew's contradiction into his own horizon, into his synthesis of the text and his own pre-understanding. That is, the interpreter in his work shows that Matthew's claim that tree and fruit correspond and his claim that they are in conflict do not really contradict each other because they belong to two different categoric situations, the ontological and the ontic.

We should note here in summary form that the correspondence of fruit and tree belongs to the ontological or latent level while the contradiction belongs to the ontic or actual situation of unbelief. It should also be pointed out that for Matthew the correspondence is re-created or actualized in the believing disciple. Understanding the gospel changes the heart and produces ethical fruit (13:14-15, 23). This is the new actual situation.

Although we can relieve Matthew's contradiction by bringing in the ontological/ontic distinction, we still have a problem: How does Matthew know under the conditions of fallen human existence that there is in fact a wolf underneath the sheep's clothing? How does he know that people are not what they appear to be? In believers there is correspondence between inside and outside, and in unbelievers there is contradiction—our provisional conclusion about Matthew's position. But Matthew also states that human beings are not capable of telling who is a believer, are not able to distinguish weeds from wheat (13:29). Only God can read the heart (6:4, 6, 18). The intention of the heart is the criterion of righteousness (5:22, 28), but actions may actually conceal one's true character or inside. On the other hand, Matt. 24:45 seems to assume that actions may in fact reveal what one really is on the inside. According to Patte, Matthew holds that it is difficult but essential to distinguish faithful and wicked disciples.[6]

The point I am developing is that however essential one side of Matthew thought distinguishing the good and the bad was, another side of him raised serious questions about the possibility of it. The human situation is thoroughly ambiguous, for actions may either conceal or reveal. So how does Matthew know that there is a wolf in there, that there is in fact a contradiction between inner and outer, that the righteousness of the false prophet is not real (5:20; 23:28)?

Perhaps Matthew would have been able to identify false righteousness if he had had an *external* criterion to test real righteousness, and it may appear that he did have one. The law, or the law as reinterpreted by Jesus seems to provide him with a general ethical principle if not precise rules. One's acts are evaluated by the law. The Pharisees are condemned as hypocrites who are not really righteous because they pay attention to the minutiae of the law (tithing) but do not really attend to the law's weighty matters of justice, mercy, and faith (23:23). Thus for Matthew an act is defined not only by its relationship to the heart (7:16-18; 12:34-35) but also by its conformity to the higher principles of an empirical code.

It seems that with Matthew the law applies in distinguishing cultic behavior (tithing) or petty morality from high morality (justice and mercy). Matthew also suggests that it applies in distinguishing high from higher morality. Loving the neighbor is high morality (5:43), but loving the enemy, Jesus' reinterpreted law, is higher (5:44). In the case of loving the enemy it is still a matter of reinterpreted law, for the command probably has more to do with the scope of responsibility than with the depth of obedience, though the latter is also there. In any case, the rule can be applied in the public arena to determine whether the scope of one's concern is appropriately inclusive. Law can decide whether your action is weighty and whether its scope is as inclusive as it should be.

The case is similar with regard to Matthew's position on divorce. In the divorce sections (5:31-32; 19:2-9) Matthew evidently means that physical unchastity (*porneia*) is the only ground for divorce. The contrast with the Jewish permission to divorce shows that he wants to limit divorce. If he understood *porneia* radically, so that the meaning would be that whoever divorces his wife except for *porneia in the heart* and marries another commits adultery or makes his wife an adulteress, then divorce in virtually every marriage would be justified. Since his limitation of divorce vis-à-vis Judaism shows that he does not want to do that, *porneia* must have reference to the physical act. And since this limitation of divorce is an ethical norm for Christians and is a rule governing deeds and not a demand for the correspondence of heart and action, these texts show that in some measure such rules are proper norms for the community of saved disciples. So to some degree for Matthew law (Jesus' interpretation of it) can distinguish between inadequate righteousness (unlimited legal divorce) and adequate righteousness (divorce only for *porneia*). But we must still consider later the issue of the righteousness that "exceeds" (5:20).

In the unfallen creation, then, or in the eschatologically renewed creation, heart and act would completely correspond. But even disciples who have believed and seen the truth and who have had their hearts renewed are still characterized by little faith (6:30; 8:26; 14:31; 16:8). The kingdom of heaven has both come (12:28; 13:17) and not come (13:36-43, 49-50; 24:14, 32-34); the heart is both renewed and not renewed. The disciples even in the presence of the resurrected and exalted Son of God both worshiped and doubted (28:17). If the heart of the believer is divided, her acts would have an ambiguous relationship to the heart. They may be better than the (unredeemed) heart (7:11) and worse than the (redeemed) heart (16:17-20, 23; 26:41). Thus, under the conditions of fallen existence even the believer's situation is ambiguous. The ambiguity may be seen by contrasting 7:11 with 12:34-35. A person who is evil may *do* better than he *is* (7:11); an evil person *cannot* do good (12:34-35). The opposition in 7:11 is between being evil and knowing how to give the good. This means that an evil person may yet be capable of evaluating what is good. It would be difficult to say in a clear way what the difference is between the addressees in 7:11 who do better than they are and the hypocrites of Matthew 6 and 23 who also apparently do better than they are. Certainly there is a difference in the tone of the descriptions. Perhaps Matthew does not attribute (as much) self-deception to the addressees in 7:11 as he does to the hypocrites in chapters 6 and 23. In order to do the will of God under the human condition of ambiguity two things are needed: (1) the enablement of a disposition to love, which results in continual renewal coming from the inside, the heart qualifying the act (23:26) and thus achieving wholeness (see the next chapter); (2) the (reinterpreted) law as a norm for righteousness, which is necessary as long as redemption is not complete. But as we shall see, the role of the law as an ethical norm, as an expression of the will of God, is qualitatively provisional.

Thus the law reinterpreted is a criterion for righteousness if we are defining the proper quality of *behavior*: It distinguishes the weighty from the superficial and even the weightier from the weighty. But Matthew also suggests a distinction between weighty or weightier behavior and real righteousness, the righteousness that exceeds (5:20). Real righteousness is the comprehensive wholeness of (1) a heart directed by love and (2) acts of caring (5:27, 43-48; 12:34-40; 18:35; 22:34-40; 25:31-46). Both are necessary. Now how does one tell that the weighty behavior is not real righteousness, that those who appear to be sheep are really wolves? We must look further both at the nature of real righteousness in Matthew and at the significance of the sheep's clothing.

### The Law and Righteousness

Let us begin with a brief and selective consideration of Matthew's understanding of the authority of the law, since it is closely related to righteousness. Matthew's Jesus has come to fulfill, not to abolish, the law and the prophets (5:17-20). In discussing this passage I will not pay attention to tradition and redaction, though such studies are interesting and important, but will rather try to give an interpretation that expresses Matthew's final meaning and is consistent with his theology as a whole.[7]

Jesus fulfills the prophets by bringing to actuality what the prophets predicted (the eschatological time), and he validates the law by disclosing and clarifying its true meaning. This clarification leads to the questioning of parts of the law in 5:21-48. The prohibition of oaths (5:34) abrogates the Old Testament's requirement that oaths be taken in certain circumstances (Exod. 22:10-11). The repudiation of eye-for-an-eye justice (5:38-39) rejects not just a permission but a requirement that was a basic principle of Israelite criminal justice (Exod. 21:24; Lev. 24:20; Deut. 19:21). Jesus' fulfillment of the law undermines the law as a formal authority. It is no longer authoritative by definition in all of its parts. Nor can the will of God be definitively or exhaustively stated in the law. The will of God goes beyond rules. Matthew, therefore, is not an ethical legalist.

In 5:18 it is maintained that the old law will "never" pass away until all is accomplished. But for Matthew all has been accomplished by Jesus' fulfillment of Scripture in his teaching, death, and resurrection. Therefore, "not one of the least of these commandments" (*entolōn*) is to be loosened, released, or broken (*luō*) (5:19). The commandments that are not to be broken are Jesus' commandments, his reinterpretation of the law or the law as reinterpreted by Jesus.

There are four reasons that support the view that the commandments refer to Jesus' teaching and not to the law of Moses per se. First, the criticism of breaking the commandments is inferentially connected to Jesus' accomplishment of all things (5:18) by "therefore" (*oun*). Jesus has fulfilled the eschatological hope, therefore do not loosen his commandments. Second, this interpretation brings 5:19 into accord with 5:21-48 where some parts of the law of Moses are in fact relaxed or set aside. It is also true that some of the antitheses intensify (5:21-30) rather than abrogate the law.

Third, to understand Jesus' teachings as "commandments" is consistent with the fact that there is a sense in which Matthew takes Jesus' imperatives as law. Matthew in my judgment is not an ethical legalist but is, at least to a significant degree, a theological legalist. That is, obedience to Jesus' commandments is a condition for salvation (6:15; 7:24-27; 16:27; 18:34-35). What one does is all-important. This becomes problematic when it is recognized that for Matthew the action—practice (16:27, *praxis*)—which is the condition for salvation includes not just deeds but a pure and forgiving heart (5:8; 18:35), an inner self free of anger and lust (5:22, 28). Law generically belongs to the public arena, and its requirements must be within human capacities.[8] The Old Testament legal tradition is aware of those conditions (Deut. 29:29; 30:11-14), and Matthew also seems to regard Jesus' commands as possible—doable (7:24-27; 11:28-30; 19:17-22; 23:23). We may question whether they are, but this problem must be further nuanced as the discussion of Matthew proceeds.

The fourth reason for taking the commandments as Jesus' commandments is that it allows the organic relationship between 5:19 and 5:20 required by the "for" (*gar*) that introduces verse 20. The connection established by the "for" suggests that the righteousness which exceeds that of the scribes and Pharisees (5:20) is keeping the commandments of 5:19. These are the means for attaining the superlative righteousness. If these commandments—means—were those of the Old Testament law, the righteousness of the disciples would not exceed that of the Pharisees, but if the commandments are those of Jesus' reinterpreted law, obedience to them would be the righteousness which exceeds.

This interpretation seems justified to me by both the text and the larger context of the Gospel. At the same time it is a reconstruction and is probably not that explicit in the text, which Matthew composed from several pieces of tradition. It may be that Matthew (or his tradition) consciously meant the law of Moses in 5:19. But if that was the case, the pressure of the context transformed it into the law of Jesus. Or to put it another way, the historical author may have thought of 5:19 as referring to the law of Moses and then have intended in 5:20, 21-48 to say that obeying the law of Moses is not enough. But for the implied author, the commandments became the commandments of Jesus.

Righteousness is a key term in Matthew, the noun (*dikaiosonē*) occurring some seven times (3:15; 5:6, 10, 20; 6:1, 33; 21:32) as compared with once elsewhere in the Synoptic Gospels (Luke 1:75). We have seen that the righteousness which exceeds is associated with the reinterpreted law by the close relationship between 5:19 and 5:20, and it is expounded in the antitheses of 5:21-48. I take righteousness in Matthew not to be God's righteous action toward human beings or the gift of a new covenant[9] but rather to be the conduct God requires of human beings.[10] While this is the case, I think that it is not true that the content of this righteousness is a quantitative, extremely meticulous observance of the law, as claimed by Przybylski.[11] For the latter Matthew does not radicalize the law but rather treats it in a way that is analogous to the rabbis' building a fence around the law. Do more than the law requires in order to be sure of avoiding a transgression of it. I think that Matthew does radicalize the law and in two senses: (1) In some instances the law is intensified so that it claims the inner person as well as actions (5:21-30). (2) In other cases the law is abrogated so that it is no longer a formal authority. People have to learn in individual situations what mercy requires (9:13; 12:7). This means that the righteousness which exceeds embraces intention or inner disposition and action in an organic wholeness,[12] as we have amply seen in the discussion of tree and fruit.

Given Matthew's concern about the inner person and hidden righteousness (6:1-18)—as well as about deeds—I find it puzzling that Leland White wishes to interpret Matthew's concept of righteousness in terms of the Mediterranean notion of honor. White intends to make the tacit meanings in the text explicit by relating them to an abstract model of human action and interaction.[13] I am not opposed to this in principle but wonder how successful this particular application is.

Honor in the Mediterranean world, according to White, was a matter of public esteem, worth ascribed to individuals or groups by others whose worth is beyond question. Honor is public recognition that is ascribed on the basis of one's associations more than it is individually earned.[14] White acknowledges that the noun "honor" does not appear in the Sermon on the Mount but believes that righteousness is Matthew's term for honor. Matthew's community needed to be compensated for the negative judgments of the surrounding society in a public forum where righteousness could be vindicated. Righteousness in Matthew is a matter of public acceptability before God and others.[15]

I believe, to the contrary, that for Matthew real righteousness is hidden and not public because what makes it real is the inner intention, or the union of inner and outer. But the outer alone is not real. In Matthew one does not gain well-being by public respect but by achieving the union of tree and fruit, heart and act. Matthew's Jesus calls on his hearers to act in secret and be rewarded by God who sees in secret (6:1-18). Moreover, righteousness in Matthew is enabled by God and earned by achievement, not ascribed by others. Matthew more nearly repudiates the honor concept than he interprets righteousness by means of it.[16] White's position is a deconstructed one because he concedes most of the points that tell against his view that Matthew interprets righteousness as honor: the forum in which Christians are vindicated is only quasi-public; righteousness is hidden; it is the kingdom of heaven which is the forum of vindication; righteousness is before God.[17]

The Joseph story (1:18-25) treats law and righteousness in a suggestive and curious manner. It is not that the law is directly criticized here but rather that the grounds that make law possible are questioned. Joseph was embarrassed, and out of the embarrassment of a righteous (*dikaios*) man (1:19) there unfolds a story that changes his and the reader's understanding of righteousness. There is a hint (1:20a) that Joseph hesitates between two responses to his own natural interpretation of Mary's pregnancy: Thinking her to have been unfaithful,[18] he hesitates between "legal" righteousness and "compassionate" righteousness, but once the angel has given the supernatural interpretation that the baby was conceived by the Holy Spirit, Joseph accepts it with unhesitating certainty.

By the dream itself Joseph is moved to accept the dream as a mode of revelation, to believe that the divine acts in his personal life in such a way as to complement the law but, apparently, not to supersede it. That is, Joseph is not overtly told to marry an adulteress, but the issue of the source of her condition is backgrounded in favor of the theological interpretation of it.[19] Joseph's natural interpretation of everyday reality is overturned. What appears as an immoral act on Mary's part is to be understood as an act of God for the salvation of God's people, and what is required of Joseph is to act toward Mary in this light. It may well be that in the story Joseph is not given to know that Mary was a virgin when the child was conceived in her by the Holy Spirit. He simply accepts that God was active in this pregnancy which occurred prior to marriage, however she got pregnant. There would be two main reasons supporting this suggestion. (1) In the Old Testament tradition God can be understood as intentionally active through the natural, nonmiraculous procreative process (Ps. 139:13-16; Isa. 49:1, 5; Jer. 1:5, 7). (2) In our text it is only the reader, not Joseph, who learns by means of the quotation from Isa. 7:14 that Mary was a virgin.[20]

We see then that Joseph cannot be righteous by obeying the law, which would have allowed or required him to divorce Mary, or even by following his compassionate impulses, but only by responding to a reality that is the opposite of what it appears to be on the ground that God is immediately present apart from the law—both to the moral subject (to Joseph in the dream) and in the reality to which the subject must respond (in Mary's pregnancy). Joseph performs a specific act—he accepts Mary and the child—grounded in a reorientation of his existential and moral self-understanding. To act in this way he must allow the law to be complemented, if not suspended, and must also relinquish his natural interpretation of everyday reality. He had eyes, did he not? He could see. This kind of obedience is inseparable from a world in which the divine sovereignty constantly overrules ordinary human perception and response.

Matthew's representation of Joseph's situation thus breaks the natural complicity between the law and everyday reality. A particular situation in reality to which particular laws seem to apply turns out to be a situation to which the law does not apply. This raises in principle the question whether, in view of the radical revisioning of reality, the law applies directly to any situation.

The institution of law or moral rule requires that situations be similar enough to be classified and that the law be generally or universally applied to all agents who come under the situations specified by the law or its context. A rule has no application to a unique case but only to acts that can be classified.[21] If a law is a possible demand, there must be a class of situations to which it applies. In the instance of Jewish laws requiring or allowing a man to divorce his betrothed if she had been unfaithful, pregnancy would generally be regarded as evidence of sexual activity and thus as a fault deserving disciplinary action. But in the case of Joseph and Mary the pregnancy is not regarded as a fault. Mary's situation is not to be brought within the generalizability of the laws. The law does not apply. Joseph's responsibility lies outside and beyond the law; God's intervening presence makes Mary's situation unique and other than what it appears to be. Since God is free to be present anywhere and to do the unexpected (recall the salvation-history roles of the "questionable" Tamar, Rahab, Ruth, and wife of Uriah [1:3-6]), God can make any situation unique and unclassifiable. That possibility raises the question whether there can be such a thing, from the standpoint of this text, as a rule or law, an action guide that applies to a class of situations. The possibility of law is undermined because God's transforming presence undoes one of its grounds—the classifiability of acts and situations. All situations are potentially unique and other than what they appear to be. This extends Matthew's thrust against ethical legalism. It does not directly affect his theological legalism, but it does affect it indirectly. If rules cannot state in advance exactly what one must do—because the classifiability of acts has become questionable and God lays claim on the heart—it becomes difficult to know how to calculate whether one has done enough to be saved. But that, nevertheless, did not keep Matthew from making salvation dependent on doing the reinterpreted law (5:20; 16:27).

Let me summarize my position on the law and righteousness. Matthew's concern is that the commandment (15:3, *entolē*) or word (15:6, *logos*) of God be done. The terms "commandment" and "word" would not in and of themselves be opposed to law, but in both of these cases they are contrasted with tradition or oral law and thus in context stand over against it and show that there is a norm other than law. More importantly Matthew gives a certain centrality to the will of God. He parallels Mark 3:35 in 12:50 and Luke 22:42 in 26:42 and adds three references to it (6:10; 7:21; 18:14). According to Przybylski, doing the will of God is Matthew's characteristic term for discipleship, and will of God is more comprehensive than righteousness because it includes God's saving intention (18:14) as well as his ethical intention.[22] And in the antitheses Jesus' own authority supersedes the law.

The law may express the will of God. The written law does in 5:17, 21, 27; 19:17b-19. And the oral law does in 23:2-3, 23. But the law may also be opposed to the will of God.[23] The written law is so opposed in 5:34, 38-39 and the oral law is opposed in 15:20. The law then, written and oral, is for Matthew a possible clue to the will of God, a trace left on Israel's religious culture by the will of God.[24] But the law is not a formal authority. It does not in and of itself say adequately and unequivocally what one must do to fulfill the will of God.

The righteousness which exceeds and qualifies one for the kingdom is Matthew's term for obedience to Jesus' reinterpreted law, when that reinterpretation takes law beyond the public observable realm and challenges law in principle (1:18-25; 5:22a, 28; 18:35b). But Jesus' reinterpretations do not always do that (5:31-32, 43-44; 19:3-9). Righteousness is probably a more limited term in Matthew than is often thought. As Przybylski has pointed out:[25] (1) righteousness does not contain Matthew's understanding of salvation as God's gift; (2) Matthew does not employ it in some of his pivotal sections on discipleship (12:46-50; 28:20). But neither is righteousness as provisional or as confined as Przybylski asserts. Because it includes both intention and act (5:20, 21-48), it is related conceptually to Matthew's other pairs (tree and fruit, and so forth), and thus it is part and parcel of Matthew's concern about wholeness. Moreover, as embracing both inside and outside, righteousness seems to be more encompassing than will of God is in 7:21, for there will of God is strongly oriented simply to doing (7:24-27). Will of God is probably a more fundamental category than righteousness. But Matthew is not rigorously consistent, and righteousness can be more inclusive (5:20, 21-48) than will of God (7:21).

## The Sheep's Clothes

We must now determine what the clothes of the sheep would actually be in the context of Matthew's Gospel. The evangelist distinguishes heart from act (5:21-22, 27-28), tree from fruit (7:17-18), heart from speaking (12:34), treasure from moral action (12:35), inside from outside (23:25-28), and inside from clothes (7:15). Given these parallel pairs, clothes must mean acts or fruit. But what kind of acts? These wolves exhibit the behavior of sheep, so who are the sheep in Matthew? Sheep in the Gospel may be a negative image—Israel in its lostness and in need of redemption (9:36; 10:6; 15:24). And it may also be a positive image—those who feed the hungry and visit the prisoners (25:33-36). In Matthew 7:15 the image of sheep is positive because it is contrasted with that of ravenous wolves. Thus the sheep in 7:15 are connected with those in 25:33-36, and their clothes then stand for acts of caring. These wolves in sheep's clothing feed the hungry, clothe the naked, visit the sick and imprisoned (25:35-36). This is weighty morality. But it is said to be in contradiction to their inner disposition (wolfishness). This contradiction makes them like the Pharisees, who are clean on the outside but unclean within (23:25-28). The reference to the Pharisees here makes a connection with Matt. 5:20, which also tells us about the righteousness of the Pharisees. It is not sufficient to enable one to enter the kingdom. But what is its content? This is indicated by the antitheses that follow (5:21-48), these statements of opposition between what the law requires and what Jesus requires. The context shows that the Pharisees do not do what Jesus demands, but they do fulfill the requirements of the law. Since 5:20 contrasts the righteousness of disciples with the righteousness of Pharisees, in the contrasts that follow in 5:21-48—contrasts between what the law requires and what Jesus requires—it may be assumed that the Pharisees obey the law while Jesus' disciples obey, or should obey, his reinterpretation of it. Therefore, the Pharisees are people who do not commit murder or adultery, who do not divorce without the proper document, who tell the truth under oath, who seek justice rather than unlimited vengeance, and who love their neighbors. This is also the behavior of the wolves in sheep's clothing, along with their feeding the hungry, clothing the naked, and so forth. Recall the linking of Pharisees and wolves in sheep's clothing mentioned above. But Matthew tells us that this righteousness does not meet the demands of Jesus to love from the heart (5:22-23, 28) and that it has only the outward appearance of righteousness (23:28). Beneath this apparent righteousness is the rapaciousness of wolves (7:15), the term for rapacious (*harpages*) being cognate in Greek with the greed (*harpagēs*) that Matthew attributes to the Pharisees in 23:25.

We are led to the conclusion that Matthew implicitly includes two gradations in his category Pharisees, and the law is useful in distinguishing them. There are Pharisees who concern themselves with such things as tithing (23:23a), but these are distinguished by the weightier matters of the law, such as justice and mercy, from those who do practice justice and mercy. We have seen that there are Pharisees who should be seen as obeying the theses of the antitheses (5:20-48). Also in this second gradation belong the wolves in sheep's clothing who care for the helpless and oppressed (25:31-46) and obey as well the commands in the theses of the antitheses. They, too, meet the law's demand for justice and mercy. But the law is seen as unable to generate or identify real righteousness, the righteousness which exceeds, in that these Pharisees/wolves-in-sheep's-clothing/false prophets obey the law but do not have real righteousness. This failure to generate real righteousness is why the law is finally only provisional. Because Matthew treats both the Pharisees outside the church and the false prophets/wolves in sheep's clothing inside the church as living a contradiction between inside and outside, he reduces the difference between these two groups virtually to zero.

Having considered at some length the wolves in sheep's clothing, I want to take a very brief look at the saved sheep of 25:31-46, who give to the wolves in sheep's clothing such positive aspect as they have.[26] This is also a point of contact with the next chapter. The sheep at the judgment are told that in serving the neighbor—the poor and wretched—they have served the Son of Man. But this should not be taken to mean that the religious requirement to respond to God's eschatological revelation in the Son of Man/Son of God has been exhaustively absorbed in the moral requirement to love the neighbor and enemy.

The Son of Man who makes himself identical with his sisters here has also identified with the exposure and danger of the human situation during his earthly ministry (8:20). But 25:31-46 probably goes beyond that. In 8:20 he is among the exposed while in 25:31-46 in some way he *is* the exposed. This Son of Man is also the apocalyptic judge from above (26:64) who has power to dispense final reward and punishment (16:27-28; 25:31-46). Thus the immanent Son of Man, identical with the poor and imprisoned, is the hidden, transcendent one. Those who have been disengaged from their anxious self-concern (6:19-34) so as to act for the poor have been encountered by the transcendent whether or not they know it. The Son of Man meets the nations in the oppressed and breaks through the self-centeredness of some of those among the nations.

The consequence of the Son of Man's presence as grace is that the sheep have been given the good hearts requisite for good acts. Our text, of course, does not say that, but it is implied in the Gospel text as a whole. The sheep inherit the kingdom of heaven, and in 5:20-48 the only kind of righteousness that can enter the kingdom is that which unites heart and act. For Matthew it is not possible to get good fruit from a bad tree (7:18b); the outside of a person (behavior) is qualified by the inside (23:26). According to Matthew, the sheep produce good fruit, so from his point of view it was necessary for them to have been given a new heart or inside.

But the fact remains that the sheep, the blessed ones, do not know that they have met the Son of Man and received the grace that enables action. They are aware only of having performed acts of care for whomever. They do not know what Matthew normally maintains that a disciple must know. To be a disciple one must do the will of God (7:21; 12:50) and understand the gospel of the kingdom (13:11, 16-17, 23, 51). This entails receiving the revelation that Jesus is the Christ, the Son of God (14:33; 16:16-18). The importance of theological confession perhaps rests on Matthew's belief that one must be justified by *words* from the heart (12:34-37) as well as by deeds from the heart (7:16-20). The actualization of the whole self requires the articulation in language of the understanding in the heart. There must be actualization of the correspondence between the inner core (heart) and both words and deeds. Thus we see the incompleteness of the sheep's response. Wholeness, or one of its dimensions, requires seeing and being able to articulate what is going on in the inside (23:25-28) and on what that is grounded.

The reader of the Gospel is given the responsibility of discovering how to shape the position constituted by the tension between (1) the full knowledge about Jesus and the kingdom—including the promise of reward—which he or she has attained by reading the Gospel and (2) the innocence of the sheep who have acted in love without calculating any benefits, divine or human, for themselves but who do not know the how or all the whys of their action. The reader is called on to enact the non-calculating love demonstrated by the sheep. But he or she knows that the Son of Man is present in his disciples and brothers and promises reward (10:40-42).

Matthew urges his readers to be on their guard against the false prophets, who are wolves in sheep's clothing (7:15). Their righteousness is not real, for it does not correspond to the heart, the inner disposition (7:15b; 23:27-28). These people live in violation of the wholeness that constitutes well-being. But how does Matthew know that the false prophets' hearts are evil since it is also his position that acts can either disclose or conceal the heart and only God really knows what is on the inside (6:4, 6, 18)? The truth is that he cannot know. His theological portrayal of the human condition makes it impossible for him to know whether acts in any particular situation really reveal or conceal the heart. Matthew urges the reader to discern the falsity of the false prophets, but since that is in the final analysis impossible, the imperative is turned back on the reader. Beware of the false prophet in you. Are you the ravenous wolf hiding in sheep's clothing, who appears to be righteous but within is full of rebellion? Only about yourself—and not perfectly then—can you discern whether the act was for God's glory and in order to be God's child or was for the sake of human praise.

## HYPOCRISY AS SELF-DECEPTION

We have seen that for Matthew the structure of human being in principle and then again in faith is the correspondence of self with self, or wholeness. But the actual situation in unredeemed historical existence is that heart and act have fallen apart. Outside and inside are in contradiction and lack organic wholeness. The depth of this self-division is seen more specifically in Matthew's understanding of hypocrisy. The conflict in 7:15-20 recalls the hypocrite in 6:1-18.[27] The condition of the lost person is that he or she has become blind to the alienation of act from heart or character, and the external act is taken to fulfill the will of God. The division has been deepened into a blindness to the existence of the gap and even into a lack of awareness that there is an inside. Hypocrisy in Matthew is self-deception, the intentional not-knowing the truth about oneself. Or so I will argue.

In classical Greek the word group associated with the noun *hypokritēs* and the verb *hypokrinomai* was used primarily of one who interpreted or recited poetry or drama, and only secondarily did it carry the sense of consciously playing a part.[28] The term "hypocrite" did not in and of itself have a negative connotation,[29] but Ulrich Wilckens holds that in the classical and Hellenistic periods it could take on a transferred negative meaning. The stage could be seen negatively as a sham world and actors as deceivers (Plato and the Stoics). "Hypocrisy" then takes on the sense of pretense.[30] In the LXX and other Hellenistic Jewish literature it acquired a strongly pejorative meaning but not always with exactly the same connotation. When "hypocrisy" represents the Hebrew *hanef* it seems to have the general sense of "wicked" (Job 34:30; 36:13).[31] But it may also take on the more specific connotation of pretending or deceiving (2 Macc. 5:25; Sir. 1:28-30). By the first century A.D. *hypokritēs* was the ordinary word for actor,[32] and it could also mean either a conscious deceiver or one who is self-deceived.[33]

What then does hypocrite mean in Matthew? According to David Garland's instructive study, it may have several senses. In 6:2, 5, 6 and 23:3-10 hypocrisy is a disparity between outward appearance and inner reality in which one consciously pretends to be more than one is.[34] (It should be noted that in 6:2, 5, 6 and 23:25, 27-28 the contradiction is between external action and internal being, while in 23:3 it is between saying and doing.) But in the woes of 23:13-36 the clash is not between act and being or saying and doing but between what the hypocrites do and the will of God. In discussing the latter part of 23:13-29 Garland seems to lean to the view that hypocrisy there is self-deception or a lack of self-knowledge, as also in 7:1-5. This rather than the conscious deception of others is probably the dominant meaning in Matthew.[35] Finally, as at Qumran, hypocrisy probably included the false interpretation of the law.[36]

It may well be that there are different meanings of hypocrisy in Matthew, but this is not a necessary interpretation, especially if we interpret the hypocrisy texts in light of each other. Once the sense of self-deception—really believing but also not believing what is false—is seen to be present in some passages, the other passages are compatible with it. The clearest evidence for self-deception is 7:3-5 and 23:25-28. The hypocrite depicted there does not notice certain things about himself. The blindness to his inner self, the lack of consciousness of his real story, is explicit. But nothing in 6:2, 5, 16 or 23:3-10 requires that the people described there are conscious of the contradiction between inner and outer. This is unspecified. Therefore, given the explicitness of the not-seeing or unconsciousness in 7:1-5 and 23:25-28, it is perfectly possible to interpret the neutral or unspecified contradiction in 16:1-18 and 23:3-10 as also unconscious. Moreover, the contradiction between the hypocrites' action and the will of God in 23:13-24 need not be conscious. In fact, the frequent use of the epithet "blind" in 23:16-17, 19, 24 suggests that the hypocrites there are unconscious of not doing the will of God. Self-deception is not just a matter of being unconscious of one's inner self but also includes false beliefs about one's relationship to one's world. Along the same line of argument the hypocrites here would also be blind to their false (from Matthew's viewpoint) interpretation of the law. One fails to interpret the law correctly because one intends not to see how much is really required of one.

Robert Guelich denies that any notion of pretense, intention to deceive, or conscious lack of integrity attaches to hypocrisy in Matthew's usage. The hypocrite in Matthew believes that he or she is righteous before God and other human beings on the ground of obedience to the law and fails to realize that he or she is really alienated from God. The belief that acceptance by human beings guarantees acceptance by God is based on the view that both God and human beings uphold the law as the expression of God's will.[37]

I think that Guelich is right that Matthew's hypocrite is self-deceived rather than a pretender, but I argue that Matthew does hold such a person responsible and culpable in part. If the hypocrite is not consciously and cynically pretending, he is still responsible for being unconscious of the dichotomy between self-image and reality. The hypocrite may not intend to deceive others, but he does lack integrity, correspondence between inner and outer, and is responsible for the deficiency because he has concealed the true nature of the inner person from himself.

Matthew seems to suggest that there are two related strands of self-deception in the hypocrisy he describes. In the first one the hypocrite wants to be right with God or rewarded by God. This intention is indicated by the assertion that it is the divine reward that has been lost (6:1b) or the kingdom of heaven that has not been entered (23:13). The reason for the failure to enter the kingdom is the false belief that external acts of piety or morality performed to be seen by others will gain one a reward with God (6:2b, 5b, 16b). One is deceived about the appropriate means toward the end of divine reward.

In the other strand the proper end or goal of life has itself been eclipsed. The goal has become human approval. In the discussion of hypocrisy in 6:1-18 Matthew use dramatic images that appeal to the senses of sight and hearing to portray behavior as public evidence—sounding the trumpet, praying on the street corners, disfiguring the face. The fact that the acts described here are ostentatious does not mean that the perpetrators are not deceived into thinking that that is enough. In 6:2, 5, 16 and 23:5-7 Matthew uses grammatical constructions that explicitly express that the purpose of the behavior is to get glorification and praise from humans. It is not that the hypocrites want human praise as a means to or assurance of divine reward but rather as a substitute for it. So enticed have they become by the security of public acceptance that they have lost sight of the divine. This confusion about the proper goal of life is a secondary self-deception in Matthew, while the primary one is the false belief that external behavior will gain reward from God. And these two strands have been interwoven.

This concern about how we stand with others reveals the social dimension of self-deception. What others think about us reinforces our beliefs about ourselves. Bruce Wilshire speaks of the phenomenon as "mimetic engulfment." The intention to mislead oneself works through the intention to lose oneself in others. We obscure ourselves from ourselves, conceal our own intentions from ourselves, by refusing to recognize our mimetic engulfment with others.[38] Matthew can help us to clarify this a bit. We can accomplish hiding ourselves from ourselves by believing that we are what others believe us to be, by becoming engulfed in their opinions about us. We convince others by pious acts that we are righteous, and their belief about us reinforces our belief that we are righteous. Our false belief about ourselves imitates the others' belief about us, but we do not acknowledge this imitation. We believe that our false belief is true.

The hypocrites really believe that they are in the right: Have we not confessed Jesus as Lord and worked miracles (7:21-22)? When did we fail to care for the Son of Man (25:41-44)? They do not realize that the human approval is all that they are going to get (6:5). They have been paid in full and are alien to the divine reward (6:1b). That Jesus explicitly tells the hypocrites that they have already received their reward and will get no other implies that they believe they still have an additional reward to receive from God. Hypocrisy is not pretending consciously to be more righteous than one is but really believing erroneously that one is righteous, that one has met the divine requirements. The hypocrite actually does not see the flaw in herself (7:1-3). Five times in 23:16-26 Matthew states that the hypocrite is blind to her self-division. The theme in 23:25-28 is the contradiction between inside and outside. If the Pharisees are described as blind but as knowing or believing that they are righteous on the outside, the blindness must pertain to the inside. Since they have a conscious belief about the outside, what they are blind to, unconscious of, is the inside. The hypocrite is blind to the fact that the only thing that meets the divine requirement is the correspondence between inner and outer cleanness.

The hypocrite as blind and self-deceived will not spell out her true condition to herself: That external morality, however weighty, is not enough; that the inside is rebellious, ravenous, unclean. The dynamic generating this failure to avow is the hypocrite's desire to be right with God (6:1b) and to have life but also to have this on her own terms, to have life by taking the wide gate and easy way (7:13-14). In order to believe that she can have life by taking the easy way, she must convince herself of the lie that that way is enough.

As a failure to see the truth, hypocrisy is for Matthew the same thing as the fattened heart (13:14-15), for the function of the heart, the seat of understanding, can be referred to as seeing (13:13-16). In Matthew, then, hypocrisy is a term for the human condition and not just a word for a few especially vicious people. The words about the fattened heart are said about the crowd generally (13:1-2, 10), and they are words from Isaiah spoken about Israel as a whole (6:9-10). Apart from revelation, the failure to understand the kingdom and oneself is inescapable (11:25; 13:11-15), and yet people are responsible for their incomprehension and are culpable. The many imperatives in the Gospel, including the imperative to see the truth (7:5), show that people are capable of action and insight; and they are guilty if they have not acted and understood. There has been ample manifestation of God's kingdom, but Israel has refused to respond (11:20-24), has shut its eyes (13:15c), has blinded or deceived itself. The blindness of hypocrisy in Matthew 23 is condemned in a very accusatory way.

In terms of cover story and real story the hypocrite uses the positive cover story that he is righteous because he is praised by humans (6:2; 23:28) to conceal the negative real story that he is alienated from God (6:1b) and corrupt within (23:25-28). Matthew 23:28 describes the Pharisees, hypocrites (23:27), as full of hypocrisy and "inquity" (*anomia*) on the inside. *Anomia,* often translated "lawlessness," does not have a strictly legal background, for in the LXX it is often used to mean not disobedience to specific commandments but a fundamental rebellion against God's will. It may have meant especially the wickedness of the eschatological time (Matt. 24:12; 2 Thess. 2:3; *Did.* 16:4).[39] Since for Matthew the Pharisees, or some of them, are obedient to the law but do not have their fruit connected to a good tree or inside, this obedience that is composed only of deeds is rebellion—*anomia.* The term "hypocrisy" in 23:28b is paired with *anomia* and refers simply to the quality of the inside rather than to the discordant relationship between outside and inside (as in 23:25, 26, 27). Therefore, hypocrisy in 23:28b means simply wickedness. What the hypocrite fails to spell out to herself is the very reality of depth, the inside, the heart, in its corruption. In concealing the uncleanness within, she conceals the very dimension of the heart or the within, from which can come either love and forgiveness or anger, hatred, lust, and so forth (5:22, 28; 12:34-35; 15:18-20; 18:35). The hypocrite is blind to her own depth because she does not want to give her whole heart, her depth. It is two sides of the same reality that the hypocrite conceals both the radicalness of the divine requirement and the depth of her own heart on which that demand lays claim.

In Matthew as in Paul, though more elusively in the former, there is recognition that the cover story is not completely believed and the real story, not completely concealed. We see an indication in the Gospel that in the self-deceived hypocrite there is a veiled awareness of the rebellion within (negative real story) that disturbs the tranquillity of believing oneself righteous (positive cover story). This awareness generates a negative cover story, less conscious than the sense of righteousness, which is seen in the zeal of the self-deceived to win converts (23:15). This zeal expresses anxiety.

My interpretation is suggested by John Gager's discussion of the role of cognitive dissonance in early Christianity. The dissonance or conflict between a belief and disconfirming evidence for the belief produces pressure to eliminate the dissonance. One way to reduce the conflict is to win converts to the threatened belief on the assumption that if more and more people can be persuaded to accept it, it must be correct after all. Gager uses this theory as an explanation for the Christian missionary impulse. Christian belief in the finality of Jesus was threatened both by his death and by the delay of his return.[40] The cognitive dissonance explanation, however, may be applicable to any missionary effort. On the basis of this argument, then, a mission hotly pursued—traversing sea and land to win one convert (23:15)—would be evidence that the missionary had doubts about his consciously held position, in our case, doubts that righteousness seen by human beings is enough. The negative real story (wickedness), concealed but still operant, challenges the positive cover story (righteousness) and generates the negative cover story (anxious zeal to win proselytes).

The positive real story would be the good news of the Gospel, concealed apart from the eschatological revelation in Jesus (11:25-27; 13:11). This would be the most unconscious story. Russell Pregeant has argued provocatively in effect that the gospel story in Matthew is relatively accessible. Jesus is a symbol and reminder of the life of faith and righteousness which is universally available to humankind, both in principle and in fact.[41] I have argued that in Matthew the possibility of faith and righteousness becomes actual only through a disruptive intervention.[42] The self-understanding contained in the gospel is not accessible without considerably more ado, and it is unconscious. But it is not totally unconscious, for it is attested in nature (5:45; 6:26-30). It is also attested in historical experience in that 25:31-46 assumes that people can be brought to relinquish self-interest in order to help the poor and oppressed simply by being confronted with the latter. But Christology is not abandoned; rather, the poor are christologically interpreted. The sheep who respond to the poor do so simply because they see the need that is there. But what enables them to do this is the hidden presence of the eschatological Son of Man in the poor. The sheep experience the effects of the Son of Man's presence without understanding what elicited these effects. This is related to the theme of grace as enablement or power in Matthew, which will be developed in the next chapter. And finally the gospel is not totally inaccessible in human beings because, as will again be discussed in the next chapter, the wholeness of human being which the gospel intends was God's creative intention from the beginning and thus has been to some degree latent in humankind.

In final summary, there are four levels of story in Matthew that are quite comparable to Paul's four: (1) the more conscious (positive) cover story—righteousness; (2) the less conscious (negative) cover story—anxious zeal to promote the positive story by means of converts; (3) the less unconscious (negative) real story—rebellion; (4) the more unconscious (positive) real story—the good news.

# 5

## THE RECOVERY OF WHOLENESS IN MATTHEW

*"And he went about . . . preaching
the gospel of the kingdom."*

$S$elf-deception is cured by the gospel or the word (13:19) of the kingdom which gives understanding and insight, which is to say that the gospel reforms the fattened or uncomprehending heart. This transformation then produces ethical fruit (13:23). Matthew uses the term "gospel of the kingdom" for the message of Jesus (4:23; 9:35) and also for the comprehensive message of the church (24:14; 26:13), which includes both Jesus' message and his story. In addition, Matthew can use Jesus' expression "these words of mine" to refer to Jesus' teachings as demands that must be obeyed in order for one to be saved (7:24-27). But my topic here will be the word or gospel of the kingdom as the event of grace or power. What is required of human beings by God is also enabled by God.

### THE WORKING OF THE WORD

The theme of the power of the word is spread throughout the Gospel. Both Jesus' ethical teaching (7:28) and his miracles (9:26, 31) become widely known. As a result, people come to Jesus (8:5) with the request for healing (8:5-6; 9:18; 15:22),and this coming with expectation is interpreted as faith (8:13; 9:29; 15:28). So the circulating word about Jesus brings people to faith. And Jesus' own word has power to heal (8:8, 13; 9:2, 6b-7), to shape human commitments (9:9), and to control nature (8:26).

### The Word in Matthew 13:
### Why Does Jesus Speak in Parables?

One could reasonably argue that Matt. 13:1-53 is the center of the Gospel both formally and conceptually.[1] To note simply the most immediate context, 11:2—12:45 is dominated by Jesus' conflict with Israel, and then in 12:46–50 the disciples are identified as those who do God's will. Following 13:1-53, in 13:54—17:27 the opposition from Israel continues while the response of the disciples to Jesus becomes more explicit: They confess him as Son of God and Christ (14:33; 16:16). The pivotal section in between (13:1-53) is related to these developments in that we see in it Jesus' dismissal and condemnation of Israel and his turning more directly to the disciples.[2] At the center, in Matt. 13:1-53, is the Gospel's discourse on the word, both its content and its way of working. The context on either side develops two different responses to Jesus, while the parabolic discourse in the middle presents the cause for this division and difference. The cause is the functioning of the word. I now want to turn my attention primarily to two sections of this discourse—Jesus' reason for speaking in parables (13:10-17) and the interpretation of the parable of the sower (13:18-23)—where Matthew's interest in the word of the kingdom is most explicit and concentrated. The crowd is put in the foreground as the audience of this discourse (13:2), but Matthew also regards the disciples as being there (13:10, 18, 36).

Why does Jesus speak in parables? In the Gospel of Mark the vague, indirect question of the disciples about the parables (4:10) is taken to have two meanings, as the answers of Jesus show. The first meaning is why do you speak in parables (4:11-12), and the second is what is the meaning of the sower (4:13). But Matthew clearly states the question as having one meaning: Why do you speak to them in parables (13:10). And the disciples do not ask just why do you speak in parables but why do you speak *to them* in parables. The "them" are distinguished from the disciples. Jesus answers that he speaks to them in parables because it has been given to you disciples to know the mysteries of the kingdom but it has not been given to them.

The Greek word *hoti* in 13:11b should be translated as "because" and not understood as a quotation mark (recitative *hoti*).[3] The primary argument for this is the structure of the passage. There is a tight parallelism in 13:10b, 11, 13 constructed from causal *dia* and *hoti:*

*dia ti . . . hoti . . .*
*dia touto . . . hoti . . .*

Why or because of what (*dia ti*) do you speak to them in parables (13:10b)? Because (*hoti*) it has not been given (13:11b). Because of this (*dia touto*) I speak to them in parables (13:13a), because (*hoti*) seeing they do not see (13:13b). The second *hoti* is clearly causal; therefore, in view of the close parallelism, the first *hoti* also should be translated "because." Jesus speaks to "them" in parables because it has not been given to them to know—they are not to know—the mysteries of the kingdom; therefore, the parables are represented as a means of keeping them from understanding these mysteries. There is a further causal element introduced in 13:12, this time by *gar.* The mysteries are given to the disciples but not to the crowd because things are given to those who already have, but those who have not have even what they have (not) taken from them. The disciples already have a call (4:18-22; 8:18-27), ethical instruction (5-7) and authority for a mission (10:1-8); therefore, they are given the mysteries of the kingdom.[4] The crowd does not have anything; therefore, it will lose even the nothing it has. The hermeneutical circle—one must have understanding in order to get understanding—seems to work in a harsh way. The parabolic word causes nonunderstanding.

On the other hand, the meaning of 13:10-12 could be that the crowd hears the parables as riddles[5] because they have not been given the key to interpret them; that is, they have not been given the mysteries of the kingdom. This shift of interpretation would change our estimate of Matthew's understanding of the parables. They do not function in a *causal* sense as enigmas that are to prevent understanding. Rather, they function *consequentially* as riddles, as a result of the fact that the crowd has not been given what it needs to interpret them. But this shift would not change our estimate of Matthew's comprehensive view of revelation. The clue to understanding has been given to some (disciples) but not to others. There is negative causality in God's dealing with Israel.

It is hard to say which of the two interpretations of 13:10-12 is better. The view that the parabolic word is itself the cause of its own incomprehensibility may be slightly favored by the fact that the whole issue is not put as a question about why the crowd hears in a defective way but about why Jesus speaks in a certain way.

Now I move on to 13:13-15. The second possible interpretation I gave for 13:10-12 is more probable for 13:13-15 than for 13:10-12 despite the fact that the issue as explicitly put is, again, not why the crowd hears the wrong way but why Jesus speaks in parables (riddles) (13:13a). However, the theme is immediately shifted to hearing by the allusion to Isa. 6:9-10—because seeing they do not see and hearing they neither hear nor understand (13:13b). Jesus' speech sounds like riddles to the crowd because they cannot understand what they hear. It is well known that at this point Matthew has "because"(*hoti*) where Mark has "in order that" (*hina*) (Mark

4:12). In Mark Jesus speaks in parables in order to make the outsiders misunderstand, while in Matthew he does so because they cannot understand. This is often taken to mean that Matthew softens Mark's harsh intentionality.[6] Matthew pulls back from saying that Jesus actually intended to make the crowd misunderstand.

There is, however, really no substantive difference between Mark and Matthew on this issue. In both Gospels the situation of the nondisciples is heavily fate-laden. In Mark they do not understand because Jesus intends for the parables to harden them. We have seen that in Matt. 13:10-12 the crowd does not understand because they have not been given to know the mysteries; the parables are a means to prevent them from knowing these secrets. The riddling word prevents comprehension, or the crowd hears in riddles because God has withheld the interpretive key. Matthew 13:13-15 essentially reinforces this position, although there is a slightly different nuance. True, the crowd hears enigmas because it does not understand what it hears. But it does not understand because (*gar*) its heart was hardened by God. Note the divine passive (13:15). Paradoxically the people have also shut their own eyes (13:15). Furthermore, the negative purpose (*mēpote*) clause in the second half of 13:15 qualifies the action of the people. That is, they have shut their eyes *in order that* they might not perceive, hear, and understand, thus illustrating the intentional character of self-deception. This element of human initiative and responsibility, however, does not mean that God has not at the same time rendered them incapable of understanding. The situation of those who do not receive the word of the kingdom is complexly drawn. Three different possible motifs for expressing the fate-laden side of the failure play upon each other: (1) the parables as riddles cause their own incomprehensibility; (2) God has not given the interpretive key; (3) God has hardened the heart. At the same time the crowd has shut its eyes.

The basic point of view of 13:10-15 is extended in 13:34-35. That Jesus speaks to the crowd in parables is presented as a fulfillment of Ps. 78:2. The psalm itself seems to make the point that what has been hidden in the darkness of parable is now going to be brought to light. But for Matthew, in context, the expression in parable is still hidden expression[7] for all of the reasons we have seen that the crowd does not understand. Jesus simply utters hidden things; he does not clarify them.

Let us consider a bit further the idea of concealed revelation in Matthew, as it appears outside of 13:10-23. The "messianic secret" is attenuated in Matthew in comparison with the programmatic centrality it has in Mark, but it is nonetheless present. We have seen that the stories about Jesus' miracle-working power circulate openly, among the crowd, and in some cases this news effectively brings people to faith. Moreover, miracles have been worked in public and should have been attended to (11:20-24). But knowledge about Jesus' miracles (8:4; 9:30; 12:15-16) and also about his identity (16:20; 17:9) is withheld, and it is withheld both by Jesus (8:4; 9:30; 12:15-16; 16:20; 17:9) and by God (11:25). Everything has been delivered to Jesus by God (11:27) and in context all things seem to include both Jesus' miracle-working power (11:20-24) and his identity as Son (11:27b-28). Only the Son can reveal what has been delivered to him (11:27b), but we saw above that he seems quite reticent about letting this knowledge out. Moreover, lack of understanding can be attributed to the work of the devil. In the parable of the tares and its interpretation (13:24-30, 37-43) the sons of the kingdom are the work of the Son of Man and the tares are the work of the evil one. The devil has sown them as weeds into the field (13:38b-39a). The devil is the cause of their plight. The devil's act can also be portrayed as the consequence of the nondisciples' lack of understanding (13:19). In Mark 4:15 Satan seems to be the cause of not understanding, but in Matt. 13:19 his action seems more nearly the result.

We have in Matthew the paradox of hidden revelation. Disclosure is concealed at the source, concealed at the point where it is given, and this is concisely portrayed in 9:30-31. Power does occur in the healing, yet Jesus orders the healed blind men not to let anyone know that he has restored their sight (9:30); but they report it anyway (9:31), and the word is spread through the district. However, this apparent violation of Jesus' command of silence is rendered ironical by the fact that Jesus' command, intended to prevent knowledge of him, wins out. What he does and says is in fact not apprehended by the crowd (11:20-24; 27:22-26). The fatedness of concealed revelation logically moderates the responsibility of the uncomprehending crowd. The blindness of the self-deceived is, on one side, visited upon them.

Yet those who do not understand and produce fruit are responsible for their failure. In 13:18-22 these people have heard the word, but they have failed to persevere in the face of difficulties or they care for the world and delight in riches. The responsibility is on them. In view of what has happened in the midst of the cities of Galilee they should have seen the truth about God and themselves. Other people would have seen it (11:20-24). The refusal of the cities to see the significance of the mighty works virtually makes ironical the statement that it is God who has hidden something from them (11:25).

It is a part of the church's mission to make clear what has been obscure in the ministry of Jesus. Matthew 10:26 states the general principle that the hidden will be revealed. In 10:27a what Jesus says in the darkness to the disciples they are to speak in the light. In 10:27b what they hear with their ears they are to proclaim upon the rooftops. Matthew 10:27 suggests that in some way the church's proclamation will be clearer than Jesus'. This may accord with 12:31-32, where blasphemy against the Son of Man is forgivable but not blasphemy against the Holy Spirit which is in the church. There is less excuse in the latter case because the Spirit is more fully manifest in the church and its preaching than it was in the earthly Jesus.[8] It is possible that 10:27b makes the smaller and less theologically weighted point that what the disciples have heard privately (13:36, the parables' interpretations) they are to preach publicly. But given the theological significance of the parables' interpretations in chapter 13 and the stronger language of 10:27a, the point of 10:27a, and probably of the whole verse, is that the church's preaching is to be more revealing than Jesus' mission was.

Most of what I have said thus far about the hiddenness of the word pertains to the word in relation to nondisciples. In relation to disciples the word is definitely less obscure, but as our discussion of discipleship will show, it is still only relatively less obscure.

In any case, the word of the kingdom is made effective in the understanding of the disciples (13:11a, 16-17, 51). How is the disciples' knowledge of the mysteries of the kingdom related to the parables which exclude the crowd from the mysteries? Since the parables are a means to noncomprehension, there is an implication that parables would not be appropriate for disciples, to whom understanding is given. Nevertheless, Jesus does speak to the disciples in parables prior to 13:36 (13:18, 24), and after that by implication he continues to speak to the disciples in parables.[9] The disciples are given the mysteries of the kingdom, and there must be some connection between the mysteries of the kingdom and the parables of the kingdom (13:24, 31, 33, 44, 45, 47). In some way the parables communicate the mysteries. In 13:24 Jesus puts another parable before "them," and "them" at least has to include the disciples, since he has been speaking to them since 13:10.[10] Moreover, 13:24 defines a parable as a comparison of the kingdom to something. Thus, whenever we have the comparative introductory formula (with *homoioō* or *homoios*) we have what Matthew would regard as a parable. Therefore, the sayings in 13:44, 45, 47 are parables to disciples, as are those in 18:23; 20:1; 25:1.

So if Jesus does speak to the disciples in parables, why does he say, or strongly imply in 13:10-12, that he does not? The relationship of disciples to the crowd is adversative. Mysteries are given to the disciples so that they see (13:11a, 16), but parables = riddles are uttered to the crowd so that they do not see (13:11b, 14-15, 34-35). The disciples get revealed mysteries, not parables. Apparently the reason why Matthew, on the one side, denies that Jesus speaks to the disciples in parables is that there is a qualitative difference between parabolic revelation to disciples and to non-disciples. To say that the crowd gets parables is to say that they are *not* given to understand. To suggest that the disciples do not get parables, even though they do, is to say that they *are* given to understand. The parables are a problem even to the disciples. They have to ask for interpretations (13:36; 15:15), which are given (but not to the crowd). While the non-disciples are given parables = enigmas, the disciples are given parables-with-interpretations so that the parables are not enigmas for them. Parables-with-interpretations, then, are effective revelations of the mysteries of the kingdom.

A further move is made in 13:18, where the words addressed to the disciples—you (emphatic) hear the parable of the sower—really mean hear the interpretation of the sower, for it is the interpretation that immediately follows. Thus parable and interpretation have been fused; any difference between them has been erased. Parables-with-interpretations have become parables-as-interpretations. The parables spoken to the disciples are interpretations, explanations. That Jesus communicates the mysteries of the kingdom to the disciples in parables = explanations means that revelation is understood by Matthew as God's making the enigmatic effective (see 11:25-30). But why, from God's side, is the enigmatic not made effective for everyone? From the human side it is because people close their eyes (13:15c).

From God's side the only explanation suggested is that the contradiction between concealment and disclosure reflects the overlapping of the eschatological age and historical time. Since the kingdom has come, some see (13:16-17); and since it is future and so has not come, some do not see (13:11-15). The kingdom has not come with sufficient fullness to make all see. Matthew does not specifically connect the revelational dichotomy with his paradoxical eschatology: making the connection is the interpreter's construction. Nor does Matthew specifically acknowledge, as Mark does in 4:27, that the relationship between revelation and reception is a mystery that even the revealer does not understand.

There is a sense in which the crowd and the disciples hear the same word—the parables of the kingdom. That this word is stupefying for some and clarifying for others is a problem not resolved but rather left to the mystery of God's eschatological dealing in which Jesus makes the word clear for some but not for others (11:25-30). To speak of the parables alternatively as puzzles and explanations is to speak of their effects. But we have seen that the divine initiative is also a causal factor for both the positive and negative effects.

### The Interpretation of the Sower

We now need to look more systematically at this passage (13:18-23), which continues the interest in the word with a move from negative (13:19) to positive (13:23). The parable of the sower itself (13:3b-8) has three major images: sower, seed, and soil. The sower gets no direct attention in the interpretation. Matthew does not say as Mark does (4:14) that the sower sows the word. Matthew's version of the interpretation may seem to be most interested in the seed, but actually the soil turns out to be the most influential image.[11] Or do seed and soil balance each other?

There are four episodes of hearing the word in the interpretation. Each of these has a fourfold rhetorical structure which is identical in episodes two, three, and four but is modified in episode one. The content is essentially synonymous in episodes one, two, and three but changes in episode four. The basic structure I will illustrate with the third episode (13:22). (1) There is a reference back to the agricultural image of the parable: that sown among the thorns. (2) An allegorical interpretation is given of the sown seed: this (the seed) is the one hearing the word. (3) Then comes a comment on the nature of the hearing, which gives an allegorical interpretation of the developing fate of the seed-word: the cares of the world and the deceitfulness of wealth choke the word. (4) Finally there is a consequence of the negative fate of the word: it becomes unfruitful. The rhetorical structure is fused with a plot structure that is tragic in episodes two and three: the movement is downward to unfruitful failure.

Episode four has the same rhetorical structure, but the plot structure is comic: the movement is upward to fruitful success. In episode one the implicit plot movement is again downward; but the rhetorical structure has been rearranged in comparison with episodes two through four. (1) First comes the allegorical interpretation of the sown seed: when anyone hears the word of the kingdom (1a). (This was (2) in the other rhetorical structure.) (2) This is followed by the comment on the nature of the hearing, which gives an allegorical interpretation of the seed's fate: and does not understand it (19b). (This was (3) in the other scheme.) (3) Then comes the consequence of the failure of word and hearing: the evil one comes and steals away what was sown in his heart (19c). (This was (4) in the other scheme.) (4) Finally there is the reference back to the agricultural image: that sown along the way (19d). (This was (1) in the other scheme.) The second item from the other structure has become the first item in the first episode in order to state the theme of the whole interpretation: hearing the word of the kingdom.

Clearly Matthew's main interest in this passage is different kinds of hearing. Hearing appears in all four episodes as the referent of the agricultural image. The interpretation as a whole is framed by hearing and not understanding at the beginning (13:19) and hearing with understanding at the end (13:23b). Thus, for Matthew the broad meaning of the parable is the move from not understanding to understanding.

Natural logic, not to mention the recollection that Mark 4:14 identifies seed with word, leads us to expect that seed will mean word and soil will mean hearer. Hearing the word is Matthew's theme. But that expectation turns out not to be fulfilled—at first. That which is sown[12] is sown alongside (*para*), upon (*epi*), or into (*eis*) different kinds of soil so the sown is the seed sown upon soil. The seed then is said to be the hearer, not the word: this is the one hearing. This interpretation is reinforced by 13:37-38, where the good seed sown by the Son of Man is people. As sown seed, people are the object of the gracious action of the Son of Man—he sows them.

But what referent does the soil of the parable then have in the interpretation? Natural logic asserts itself. The hearer is also the referent of the soil and the word is the referent of the seed, for the hearer is the recipient of the word. In the relating of agricultural image to allegorical meaning the hearer of the interpretation is the seed of the parable. But within the allegorical interpretation itself, the hearer is also the soil that receives the seed-word. That the seed—what is sown—is not only the hearer but also the word is seen in the fact that in 13:19 it is explicitly both the word and the hearer that are sown. Two forms of the Greek word "to sow" (*speirō*) occur in the verse (see note 15). The word of the kingdom is sown because what is sown[13] in the heart in 13:19c has to be the word of 13:19a. In 13:19d that which is sown[14] might again be the word, for it is the word in 13:19a-c. But if that is so, it also has to mean the hearer, for that which is sown is the hearer in all three other episodes.[15] In relation to the hearer as soil or recipient of the seed-word, the word is represented as the means of grace. The Son of Man sows the hearer as seed into the world (13:37-38), and what the interpretation of the sower adds to that is the suggestion that he also sows the word as seed into the hearer-soil, the word being the means of affecting the hearer, producing understanding. Thus Matthew has a language-event theology. Grace occurs as the working of the word.

As soil (recipient of grace) and seed (placed in the world) the hearer is the instrument of grace, the means of affecting others. Being object of grace by means of the word, given understanding, the seed produces fruit (13:23), ethical action (7:16-20). And this leads others to glorify God (5:16).

In the parable of the sower there is one kind of seed and four kinds of soil. In the interpretation, since the hearers are the meaning of the seed, we have reason to expect one kind of hearer. But instead we have four kinds or two with three variations on the first. The reason for the diversification of hearers (seed) is, obviously, that the hearers are also the meaning of the soils, and there are four kinds of soil in the parable. The very fact of the fourfold diversity shows that the soil image exerts more force on the meaning of hearing than the seed image does. The fourfoldness of the soil in the parable turns the one seed of the parable into the four seed-hearers in the interpretation. At the same time the oneness of the seed in the parable maintains itself in the oneness of the word in the interpretation.

We have seen that in Matthew 13 the word is the event that gives understanding. This event character of revelation may be connected to Matthew's view of the redemptive power of Jesus' death. In 20:28 Jesus is the Son of Man who gives his life as a ransom for the many. Daniel Patte has observed that for Matthew Jesus' death is a ransom in that it enables people to receive his words and acts as divine revelation and to be saved by doing his teaching.[16] I think that this is on the right track, but I should like to push it a bit by pursuing the question of how Jesus' death enables saving obedience and to do this by connecting the ransom saying to its immediate context, the healing of the two blind men (20:29-34). For Matthew sight is an image for insight or understanding (13:14-17); therefore, the deliverance of people out of blindness and into sight, coming immediately after the ransom saying, interprets the death of Jesus as saving the many by conferring the understanding necessary for ethical fruitfulness (13:23). The death of Jesus and the word of the kingdom have the same effect. Matthew's view of the operation of the word interprets his understanding of Jesus' death. As in 20:28-34 the Son of Man gives his life as a ransom for the many by curing blindness and giving insight to follow him, so in 13:18-23, 37-38 the Son of Man sows people fruitfully into the world by sowing the word of the kingdom in them.

### From Word to Discipleship

To be a disciple one must both understand the word of the kingdom of heaven (13:11, 16, 19, 23)—what God is doing—and also see the truth about oneself (7:3, 5). The heart—the seat of understanding and will—is oriented to its treasure, what it values (6:21). Those who value the praise of others (6:2, 6, 16; 23:5) and the wide gate and easy way (7:13) will not be able to understand the real demand of the law, the radical will of God to which the law points. If you are looking at human praise and easy salvation, you will not be able either to look at—to see—the demand for mercy and justice (5:7; 9:13; 12:7; 23:23) or to enact these virtues (7:17b, 18b). Nor will you be able to see God as the only real source of well-being. The word has power to direct attention away from others to God as the source of approval and away from the easy way of external obedience to the inner self and the demand placed upon it. But obedience from the heart, of course, includes acts. The word both illuminates (13:11a, 16) and enables (13:23; 18:27, 33). It restores wholeness by bringing both to consciousness and to actuality what had been concealed.

I have been pointing to the power of the word in Matthew to disengage individuals from the crowd and turn them into a community of disciples. In Matthew revelation is more effective for disciples than it is in Mark, as will be developed below. Despite that, the situation of the disciples in Matthew is not unambiguous. The disclosed secrets are not immediately perceived (16:9), for the disciples like all others are in the position of having to see through the veil of Jesus' everyday ordinariness (13:53-58) in order to see him as the Son of God (14:33). So their faith is never complete, and they are often guilty of having little faith. Although Matthew understands the church as identified with (10:40) and empowered by (18:18-20) the exalted Son (28:16-20), this community of disciples will experience difficulty in the history of its mission (10:13-23, 34-39; 13:18-22; 24:4-14, 23-24) and must finally face judgment itself (13:36-43; 22:11-14; 25:1-12). Even at the moment of the climactic resurrection appearance, the disciples—or some of them—doubted or hesitated (28:17) as they worshiped. While the messianic secret in its aspect of discipleship failure is much attenuated in Matthew in comparison with Mark, it is nonetheless present.

### DISCIPLESHIP: UNDERSTANDING AND FAITH

Matthew has a special interest in the term "disciple," and, second only to John, he uses it more than any other Synoptic evangelist.[17] Let me suggest in summary fashion that as Matthew's narrative unfolds, several different discipleship roles emerge as correlatives of different christological roles. Jesus is conceived by the Holy Spirit (1:18, 20) and is from the beginning in principle God with us (1:23) and Son of God (2:15). But Jesus in Matthew is not who he is solely on the basis of principle. His identity is formed not only by his relationship to God but also by his varying relationships with human beings. And the disciples are who they are in relation to Jesus. Jesus as Son of God and Son of Man is manifested as teacher-judge, archetypal human being, revealer of knowledge of God, healer, miracle worker, and covenant sacrifice. The community of disciples, correlatively, enters fully into the precariousness of the human situation, merits salvation by its righteousness, but nevertheless is the graced recipient of healing, faith, understanding, and knowledge of God.[18]

Whatever conceptual tensions there may be among these discipleship roles, the disciple-reader as she is grasped by the story moves through all the roles or modes of existence. She experiences herself as under the command to forgive and to perform works of radical obedience in order not to be condemned in the judgment. But she also experiences herself as graced without regard for merit, one from whom faith and righteousness are evoked by a prior grace. In the unfolding of the story conceptual tension is transformed into personal or existential tension, which the disciple-reader experiences in the movement of the narrative through conflicting modes of existence; but the tension is nevertheless given a form by the very existence of the narrative.[19]

As we have observed, for Matthew the two fundamental requirements of discipleship are: (1) to do the kind of righteousness that the will of God requires (5:20; 7:21; 12:50) and (2) to understand the mysteries of the kingdom of heaven (13:11, 15-17, 23, 51-52). I will argue that the latter also includes faith. Since righteousness was treated in chapter 4, I shall here discuss—or continue to discuss—primarily understanding and faith.

### Understanding

The disciples are portrayed in Matthew as those who understand (13:52; 14:33; 16:12; 17:10-13). This is striking in comparison with Mark's picture of the disciples' lack of understanding during the course of the story. There are two scenes that present the difference between Mark and Matthew in a particularly dramatic way. At the end of the feeding of the five thousand and the walking on the water, in Mark it is said that the disciples were astounded, for they did not understand about the loaves but rather had hard hearts (6:52). Matthew has added Peter's walking on the water to this scene, and at the end of it in place of the hard-heartedness we find in Mark, Matthew places the disciples' confession: truly you are the Son of God (Matt. 14:33). In Mark when the disciples are perplexed about the meaning of the leaven of the Pharisees, they are harshly criticized by Jesus as hard-hearted and are put in the category of outsiders (8:17-18; cf. 4:11-12). The story ends on the question, Do you not yet understand? (8:21). But in Matthew the criticism of the disciples is much milder (16:8), and the pericope concludes with the affirmation "then they understood" (16:12).

What is the meaning of this difference between Mark and Matthew? According to Georg Strecker, this is an idealization of the disciples in Matthew which served Matthew's intention to historicize the tradition. That is, the ideal comprehension exercised by the disciples helps to give to the time of Jesus its own particular character, which is distinguished from the time of the church and the history of Israel.[20] I am more inclined to think that the motif is rather for Matthew one of the features that characterizes disciples at any time: A disciple in principle is one who understands.[21]

Matthew acknowledges that it is possible to have correct conceptual understanding of something but not to understand it existentially. This is the case with the priests and Pharisees, who understand the intellectual content of the parables of the two sons and the wicked tenants and even perceive (*ginōskō*) that they apply to them (21:45-46). But their perception does not shape their existence or conduct. They want to arrest Jesus. And in the end the leaders persuade the whole people to call for Jesus' death (27:15-26). The kind of understanding that constitutes discipleship, as we shall see, is a particular understanding that also reforms the heart. Matthew must presuppose that understanding and language are two sides of the same phenomenon, for he can say that salvation depends on having the appropriate understanding (13:11, 15-16) and that it depends on having the right words, words that put one in the right (12:37). In order for words to justify, they must correspond to one's heart, the inner core of one's will and thought (12:33-37). And they must also correspond to the reality that confronts one, specifically to the reality of who Jesus is. One must be able to say correctly the truth about Jesus. It is not enough to think that he is a prophet if he is the Son of God (16:13-20). Those who thought he was a prophet as late as the last week in Jerusalem (21:11) shortly thereafter cried out, "Let him be crucified!" (27:22). Words that express one's true inner core either justify or condemn because they govern how one lives.

### Faith

Faith is also for Matthew an important constituent of discipleship. Here I will treat faith primarily in theological terms, in terms of its object. Later, when I take up the relationship of understanding to faith, we will see something of how faith functions or works.

It has been widely recognized that in Matthew faith is very closely connected to miracle. Faith responds to Jesus' miracle-working authority (8:8-10) and includes both trust and will (15:28).[22] We might say in summary that faith is response to the circulating report about Jesus (9:26, 31) which takes the form of an expectant request to him (8:5-6; 9:21-22; 15:21-22) and as such is the means of access to his power (8:13; 9:29-30; 15:28). But faith is more inclusive than simply a volitional trust in the possibility of miracle. It is trust in God's general providential care for creation (6:30)[23] as well as response to God's eschatological dealing which determines whether one belongs to the true people of God (8:10-12; 21:32).[24]

When Heinz J. Held states that faith in the Synoptic tradition—including Matthew's Gospel—is most at home in miracle stories and does not involve recognition of the messianic status of Jesus or the acceptance of the Christian proclamation,[25] we are inclined to think that Held means Matthew's tradition before the Evangelist reinterpreted it, for Held himself has shown that Matthew interprets the miracle tradition in a highly kerygmatic and christological way. In Matthew's miracle stories Jesus is the one who (1) fulfills the Old Testament hope globally, (2) is the Servant of God, and (3) is the risen Lord, (4) who includes the church in his mission and authority.[26] But Held surprises us by saying that the theme of faith does not belong directly to Christology in Matthew itself.[27] My own view is that since faith is prominent in the miracle stories and since the latter are interpreted in a strongly christological way, it is atomistic and artificial to separate faith from Christology in Matthew's Gospel. For the reader of the Gospel, to believe in the Jesus of the miracle stories is to believe in the Christ of the Christian kerygma.[28]

### Understanding and Faith

How are these related in Matthew? Gerhard Barth, while acknowledging that understanding includes some of the functions of faith and is the opening of the heart to revelation,[29] nevertheless stresses the difference between faith and understanding. In understanding, the intellectual element is important; it is truly seeing and hearing.[30] As such it is the presupposition for faith, and faith is trust and volition from which the intellectual element has been excluded and transferred to understanding. Thus Matthew is different from Paul, Mark, and John, for whom faith does contain the intellectual component. Disciples in Matthew may have understanding but not faith (Matt. 14:31-33).[31] Essentially the same position is taken by Ulrich Luz, who also claims that the disciples may have little faith but still understand. Faith is directed to the person of Jesus, while understanding grasps his teaching.[32]

I want to argue, against the position of Barth and Luz, that in Matthew understanding and faith are not two separable stages or distinct levels in the life of discipleship. The very fact that there are two terms—understanding (*syniēmi* and related terms) and faith (*pistis* and related terms)—suggests different emphases: intellect and trust/will. But faith has its intellectual component: The conviction that Jesus can work miracles is a cognitive element.[33] And understanding is rooted in the heart, the core of human being. Faith and understanding significantly overlap and interpenetrate each other, and Matthew does not make a programmatic distinction between them.

If the confession of the disciples in Matt. 14:33—you are the Son of God—states the content of Christian understanding, as Barth suggests,[34] it must be very nearly the equivalent of faith because it is essentially identical to the confession of Peter (16:16) which Matthew attributes to direct revelation (16:17) and on which he regards the church as being built (16:18). On the basis of this confession the church will be able to withstand Hades, and Peter will have the power to bind and loose, a power sanctioned by heaven (16:18-19). This is power comparable to the power of faith for which nothing is impossible (17:20). The understanding, then, manifested in the confession in 14:33 cannot be merely the presupposition of faith.

The position that seems to be normative for Matthew is that understanding is the initial response to the word of the kingdom, which should take root in the heart (13:19, 23), for the heart is the seat of understanding (13:15). When it does take root, it produces ethical fruit (13:23), which means that it is understanding which has constituted the very being of the disciple—the tree that produces good fruit (7:17-18). That is to say, since proper understanding produces ethical fruit and the good person (tree or heart) produces ethical fruit, understanding virtually is, or at least constitutes, the person. Thus understanding embraces the life of discipleship from beginning to end and cannot be called the intellectual presupposition of faith.

Matthew 13:54-58 tells the story of Jesus' return to his own country and ends by informing us that Jesus did not do many miracles there because of the peoples' unbelief. Unfaith—*apistia*—sums up the response of these people to Jesus. Of what is it composed? Unfaith is characterized by resentful amazement at Jesus (*ekplēssō*, 13:54) and taking offense at him (*skandalizomai*, 13:57). This is a negative reaction to his teaching, for he taught them (*didaskō*, 13:54a), and they noted—sarcastically—his wisdom (*sophia*, 13:54b). The response is also a skeptical questioning of his miracles (*dynamis*, 13:54b) and his identity (13:55-56). Is this not the carpenter's son and do we not know his family? All of this is contained in unfaith, and it is very comprehensive. Its opposite—faith—would be equally comprehensive. Faith cannot be said to attach itself only to the person of Jesus and to lack intellectual content. Faith and understanding overlap extensively.

At the same time proper understanding requires nonliteral comprehension. In order to arrive at the appropriate theology one must be able to understand symbols and images whose meaning is not literal (16:5-12). One must be able to imagine. It is not without interpretive significance that the text on the right christological confession (16:13-20) follows immediately upon the story that stresses the need for nonliteral understanding (16:5-12). In order to get into this topic we will consider Jesus' discussion with the disciples about bread and the leaven of the Pharisees and Sadducees, which is an example of the call for imagination. To approach this and other texts in an appropriate way we should first look at the question of how the imagination works.

### The Nature of Imagination

What is the imagination and how does it work? The answer to this question is governed by the answer to the question about what is the locus of literary meaning. Imagination comes to expression where literary meaning is manifested. We may say that in a broad sense the imagination comprises the realm of the fictitious or the not literally true.[35] Matthew takes one position within the spectrum of possibilities regarding where the imagination is manifest. A further penetration of the matter requires us to pursue the question of what exactly is the locus of the imagination.

For our finer analysis of how nonliteral understanding occurs, we may turn to Samuel Taylor Coleridge for a suggestive thrust without comprehensively buying into his romanticism. The primary imagination is the living power of perception and is exercised by every human being insofar as he or she perceives anything. The secondary imagination is an echo of the former and is the power by which the poet reworks the perceptions of the primary imagination into concrete symbols. It dissolves, diffuses, and dissipates in order to re-create. Coleridge can refer to the imagination as "that synthetic and magical power" which balances and reconciles discordant qualities: sameness with difference, general with concrete, idea with image, novelty with the old and familiar.[36] Whatever the limitations of his poetics, Coleridge's basic conception of the imagination as the power to dissolve and re-create, to combine old and new, has stood the test of time.

In addressing the question about where the imagination is manifested, I propose a simplified communication model of author-text-reader. Given this model, where does the meaning lie? There seem to be two basic answers. (1) Meaning is a function of the relationship of the text to the author or (2) a function of the relationship of the text to the reader.

The first answer suggests two possibilities regarding where imagination is manifested. (1) It is in the mind of the author; the text is a means for reaching the author's intention, thought, and imagination. This position goes back to Friedrich Schleiermacher in modern hermeneutics, and while it is a minority opinion, it can be seen in the recent works of E. D. Hirsch,[37] P. D. Juhl,[38] and Helen Gardner.[39] (2) On the other hand, the author's intention can be bracketed out as not useful or as unobtainable. She is in some sense the exerciser of the imagination, but we have access only to the text that she produced, which has taken on a (semi-)autonomy of its own[40] as the manifestation of the imagination.

The text-and-reader relationship generates three possibilities, assuming that the text is or may be at least semi-autonomous. (1) There is imaginative activity on the part of the reader, and the text's meaning is actualized in her or him, but the meaning resides in the text, which strictly controls the reader's responses.[41] (2) The text has a verbal structure that guides the reader, but this structure is a potential for meaning rather than a formulated meaning. Following the clues in the text the reader turns the text into a work, constitutes its meaning, by exercising his or her personal disposition or imagination.[42] Meaning is a synthesis of the text and the reader's creative imagination. (3) There is no meaning embedded in the text. The formal features of the text are in fact the product, the creation, of the reader's interpretive acts.[43]

I want to argue that Matthew makes its own contribution to the view that imaginative meaning is a synthesis of the text and the reader's creative input, with the weight probably going on the text. Matthew in two ways suggests how readers receive a text by giving it concrete meaning in terms of their own horizons, their own predispositions. (1) In stories about the disciples' responses to Jesus or in instructions to the disciples about how to respond, the narrator indicates more or less directly how one is to receive the gospel and shows what the principles are for receiving the gospel with understanding. (2) Since we can assume that Matthew understood himself as a disciple, his own interpretive procedures demonstrate concretely how the imaginative reception of the gospel actually occurs.

### Understanding and Faith as the Exercise of the Imagination

Jesus' dialogue with the disciples about the meaning of the leaven of the Pharisees and Sadducees (Matt. 16:5-12) occurs in a story that calls on the disciples to exercise their imagination in the broad sense of nonliteral understanding. The interaction between Jesus and his disciples is grounded and contextualized by the initial state the narrator describes: the disciples had forgotten to bring any bread. This is a moment of potentiality, for lack—here absence of bread—is always the possibility for filling. The possibility becomes an actualized process moving toward filling when Jesus exhorts them to beware of the leaven of the Pharisees and Sadducees, which warning generates a discussion among the disciples and between them and Jesus about what the leaven means. They think that it has something to do with bread, but he corrects them. The process reaches its goal in the disciples' arrival at understanding. They perceive that he meant the teaching of the Pharisees and not literal leaven. A part of the story's artistry is the shift in the level of meaning of the central image: bread-leaven. At the beginning what they lack is real bread, but what they are filled with in the end is understanding. Although they lack bread, the lack that is liquidated is incomprehension.

Certainly a part of the story's meaning is to issue a warning against the teaching of the Pharisees and Sadducees. But it probably has more to say about the way in which one should understand than about the content of Jesus' exhortation. This brief paragraph (16:5-12) contains seven different Greek words for mental activity: forget (*epilanthanomai*), see (*horaō*), pay attention (*prosechō*), discuss or reason (*dialogizomai*), perceive (*noeō*), remember (*mnēmoneuō*) and understand (*syniēmi*). The most focused of the terms are those for perceiving and understanding. "Understand" sounds the climactic note on which the story ends: "Then they understood." "Perceive" occurs twice, as does "discuss," and only Matthew among the Synoptic Gospels has Jesus ask the pointed question, "How is it that you fail to perceive that I did not speak about bread?" (16:11a).

Notice also that the disciples are said to have little faith (16:8). Their little faith is a lack of proper perception; therefore, we see again that Matthew does not separate faith from knowledge or understanding as two different stages in the life of discipleship. And the faulty perception is that they take the leaven to have a literal meaning. Faith as proper perception is nonliteral understanding; thus faith is the exercise of the imagination.

In order to see more precisely how faith-as-imagination works, let us turn to the end (13:51-52) of Matthew's discourse on the parabolic word. Again the narrator stresses the disciples' understanding. After finishing the parables and interpretations, Jesus asks the disciples if they have understood all of this, and they unequivocally reply yes. The one who understands is then described as a scholar who has been made a disciple of the kingdom of heaven,[44] who is then compared to the master of the house who brings out of his treasure the new and the old. Understanding, then, is the imaginative combining of the new and the old.[45]

What is the treasure from which the new and old are to come? Matthew 12:34-35 identifies the treasure metaphorically with the heart and sees the heart as the source of language. The new thing to be brought forth from the heart is language adequate to the revelation that Jesus has brought. Jesus reveals what had been hidden (11:25) so that the disciples see and hear what others had longed to experience but did not (13:16-17). They are given a new understanding by the word of the kingdom which creates a new heart, since the heart is the seat of understanding (13:15, 18, 23). They then are to respond with appropriate answering words. The new that the disciple-reader is to bring forth is the understanding-in-language (12:35-37) that the word has put in the heart. The new embraces both Jesus' initiative and the elicited response.

What then is the old? Let us consider two contexts. In the context of the disciples' call (4:18-22; 9:9-13), the old is their natural condition, which Matthew assumes to be evil (7:11) and from which they should turn (4:17). The new is the call itself. This is to reshape the old, but in the light of 13:51-52 the old is not totally discarded. And it is not totally discarded because the natural person, though being evil, can still make valid judgments about what is good (7:11).[46]

In the context of 13:10-12 the secrets of the kingdom are given to the disciples because knowledge is given to those who already have. Thus the disciples are portrayed here as those who have. They have the call, ethical instruction (chaps. 5–7), and authority to preach, heal, and exorcise (10:1-8). The old is all of this, and the new is the further revelation of the mysteries of the kingdom. The old as revelation (call, teaching, authority) then makes possible more (new) revelation. Since in Matthew 13 revelation occurs in parable-and/as-interpretation, revelation is a kind of prior or prevenient imagination. It occurs by means of continuing interpretations that set the heart right and enable the receptive imagination of the disciple-reader to produce more interpretations. In some ways Matthew stresses the dominance of God's role in revelation even more than Mark does and attributes less to the human subject. For example, Mark's parable about the earth's producing *of itself* when seed is planted (4:28) attributes considerable initiative to the human subject as human, as does his statement that the measure of understanding that one contributes to hearing governs how much one gets (4:24). Matthew omits both of these Markan elements. Moreover, the principle that the one who has understanding will get more understanding Mark addresses to the crowd generally (4:25),[47] but Matthew shifts it to a context where it can apply only to the disciples (13:12), only to those who have already received, so that what they contribute is what they have been given by revelation.[48] Nevertheless, some contribution is made from the humanity of the interpreter—the old. What the nature of it is we must still consider. But let me draw out a tentative summary at this point. The natural imagination makes a slight contribution to the reception of revelation, and revelation once received creates an actively receptive imagination, of which the Gospel of Matthew itself is a manifestation.

But what indication does Matthew give that the imaginative re-thinking that occurs in interpretation is done in part by the interpreter and is not just done in her by the word of the kingdom? The very fact that Matthew identifies the new with what comes from God in itself implies that the old, which the disciple-scholar is to bring forth, comes from human beings. Furthermore, the use of the imperative—placing someone under responsibility—implies freedom and capacity to act. The description of the disciple-scholar as one who brings forth old and new from his treasure is not syntactically an imperative, but it is imperative in tone. The same point of view occurs in the passage that speaks of the heart as the source of one's words (12:33-37) except that here there is the specific demand to make one's words, as fruit, correspond to one's heart, as tree. And then there is the verb that Matthew uses for the action of "bringing out" the right language from one's treasure-heart in both 12:35 and 13:52. It is a strong verb, a verb of force, often used for the act of casting out demons.[49] In 24:32 there is a grammatical imperative addressed to the disciples to learn the parable of the fig tree, and, as we have seen, to learn or understand a parable is to give an interpretation of it. To give an interpretation is the disciple's responsibility.

Matthew does not tell us exactly how the divine and human initiatives meet and interact. He may not have thought about it systematically, and it is probably a mystery that has no conceptual solution. The unfathomableness of it is seen in the tension between two of his statements. People being evil are not able to speak the good (12:34). People being evil are able to do the good (7:11). What is said about acting can in principle be said about speaking because for Matthew both are the fruit of the heart (7:15-20; 12:33-37). So people, being evil, both are able and are not able to speak the good.

The parable of the talents (25:14-30) also has a bearing on the present issue. It is connected with the question of understanding the parables by means of the principle: to him who has will more be given, and from him who has not even what he has will be taken away. As we have noted, this is used to explain why the disciples are given more revelation (13:12). It is also used to explain why the one talent is taken from the one-talent man and given to the man who has ten (25:29). The presence of the principle "to him who has will more be given"both in 13:11-23 and in the parable of the talents invites us to interpret the parable in light of the topic in 13:11-23, the problem of understanding and interpretation.

So what does the parable of the talents tell us about the exercise of the imagination? The story moves for the one-talent man from the giving of opportunity—to use the talent—through the misuse of the opportunity and his being questioned about this to the loss of opportunity. The reason why the one-talent man lost everything is that he was too anxiety laden to take the risk of discovering what he could do. He would not take a chance with what he had. The kind of having that gains more having is that which risks its possession in the realm of the unknown. This means with regard to the exercise of the imagination in understanding that only the person who risks reaching into his or her unknown resources to find a horizon to be combined with the word of revelation, the person who will let the hitherto unknown in herself or himself be drawn out by the word of the kingdom, only such a one will become a part of the continuing process of revelation that occurs through interpretation. To have a true understanding of the kingdom one must risk the understanding one has. Having is risking a new interpretation to which God adds more revelation. Not having is not risking an interpretation of one's own and thus nothing new is given. The one-talent man is the interpreter who risks no new interpretations, has no new questions to pose to the text, but simply passes on the tradition more or less unchanged. If in the discussion of the disciples' receiving the mysteries of the kingdom in 13:10-17 revelation is dominant and the text is in control, when this text is juxtaposed with the parable of the talents, the creative power of the reader-interpreter is implicitly brought more into play. And since Jesus is the one who turns texts into meaning by giving interpretations (13:3-9, 18-23, 24-30, 36-43, 47-50), and since the disciples are to follow Jesus into the risky unknown (8:18-27), the interpretations a disciple is obligated to give—combining old with new (13:52)—should be adventurous interpretations. But imaginative interpretation is still receptive and responsive: The merchant gives the men the opportunity to take a chance.

What the disciple brings to the ongoing process of interpretation is natural human capacity renewed. Human understanding, which is evil but not incapable of good (7:11), is renewed by the disciple's being given a call, instruction in the kingdom, and authority to act; and this is what one has and brings to the task of understanding the mysteries of the kingdom (13:12). Old and new are not stable terms in the context of Matthew's view of the imagination. What comes from oneself is old in the sense that it was there prior to the encounter with the word of the kingdom, the parabolic text, the new. But the old is new in that it is the hitherto unactualized human understanding now elicited by the word of the kingdom and shaped by it into something not previously expressed. This means that the new given by the revelatory word of the kingdom is old in relation to the new interpretive horizon that the word of the kingdom evokes but that the reader-disciple also is to achieve and to risk from his or her own resources. Therefore, Matthew calls not only for the combining of new with old but also for the continuous reforming of the old into the new. New wine can be contained only in new wineskins (9:17). The form of the interpretation in which the word of the kingdom comes to expression is the old continually being transformed. In light of the ontological/ontic distinction I have used in interpreting Matthew, the old in human being that can be made new is the sense of the ontological wholeness of heart and act that has been rendered inaccessible by sin—destiny and choice—but not obliterated.

That the old must be turned into the new corresponds with the striking way in which Matthew introduced his allegorical interpretation of the parable of the sower (13:18). As we have observed, Jesus says to the disciples immediately before giving the interpretation, Hear then the parable of the sower. Is there a subtle difference between Mark and Matthew on this point? Mark creates more distance between parable and interpretation: The interpretation is a way of *knowing* the parable (Mark 4:13). But in Matthew to hear the interpretation is to hear the parable itself. The parable occurs *as* its interpretation. Matthew would probably not agree with the proposition that there are no texts, only interpretations. But it is his position that the texts of the gospel effectively occur as meaningful only in interpretations. And his interpretation of the sower shows that the interpretation grasps the text within a horizon quite different from that of the text. Unless the parable—the old—occurs in new forms, it does not occur as the effective word of the kingdom. The interpretation is the new wineskin for the new wine of the gospel. In Matthew's story Jesus gives his own interpretation, but the disciple is also summoned to give hers or his.

In the preceding discussion of the imagination the stress has been primarily on Jesus' instruction to the disciples about how to respond to the kingdom, which instruction contains Matthew's implicit reflection on faith as imagination. Relatively little was said about the narrator's own exercise of the imagination. The latter was somewhat in view in the discussion of Matthew's connecting the issue of understanding with the parable of the talents by means of the principle that to him who has more will be given. For other examples I call attention to Matthew's tacit critique of the law in his narration of the Joseph story and the tensiveness of the language when the parable of the sower and its interpretation are connected. The seed of the parable is both the word and the hearer in the interpretation. The hearer in the interpretation is both the seed and the soil of the parable.

In sum, the way faith and understanding come to expression in Matthew is by the exercise of the imagination, the breaking up of old connections and the making of new combinations. This puts one's outward expression—one's words—in touch with one's inner reality and with the reality that confronts one in the gospel of the kingdom.

### The Content of Faith as Lived

Throughout the Gospel narrative, until the trial of Jesus, the crowds are potential disciples. As late as the beginning of Passion week they still think that Jesus is a prophet (21:11), but they call for his death shortly thereafter (27:15-26). The course of the story may suggest, therefore, that given the kind of ultimate claim which Jesus makes—follow me, renouncing security and leaving the dead to bury the dead (8:18-22)—if one does not recognize who Jesus really is and that he has the right to make these claims, one will finally see him as a blasphemer (9:3; 26:62-66) and call for his death (12:14; 26:66; 27:23-26).

There are two complementary aspects of faith. (1) One is confessional: acknowledging in conceptually adequate terms—as the reception of revelation—who Jesus is. He is the Christ, the Son of God (14:33; 16:16). This is to recognize that what he brings into the world is from beyond. (2) The other aspect is existential: appropriating as the shape of one's own existence the story of Jesus' death and resurrection. He is also the suffering, dying, and rising Son of Man (16:21-23; 17:22-23; 20:17-19).

The existential aspect can be stated in conceptual terms, in Jesus' discourse with the disciples. They resist the idea that he is the Christ as the suffering one (16:21-23) and need to be told that they also must take up their crosses and find life by losing it (16:24-25). Only the renunciation of security offers true life. To deny oneself and lose one's life is to renounce the broad gate and easy way (7:13) of human approval (6:1-2, 5, 16; 23:5) and to acknowledge in love (22:37) the God who sees and rewards in secret (6:4, 6, 18) and to love the neighbor and enemy (5:44; 22:39) with deeds (25:31-46) grounded in a pure and merciful heart (5:7, 8, 28; 18:35). The ethical dimension is inseparable from the strictly faith dimension, but it is not identical with it. Fruit is organically connected to the tree but is not the same thing. The life that is found by the risking or renouncing of life is the wholeness of the self. In the lived posture of renouncing the easy way of external obedience and human approval, the concealed rebellion of the heart is brought to light, to consciousness, and the heart is given a new direction by the gracious enabling action of God which had also been concealed.

Faith as existential appropriation can also be presented dramatically. The blind men who have been given sight follow Jesus (20:34), and he is on the way to suffering and death in Jerusalem (20:17-19). This following into risk is as much given by the revealing word as is the capacity to confess who Jesus is (16:17). As we have observed, the giving of (in)sight is the way Jesus' death is a ransom for the many. Clearly, one of the main things from which people need to be released in Matthew is blindness. The addressees are blind to what they are: internally flawed and corrupt (7:3; 23:25-29). They are blind to what they might be—whole persons (7:16-20; 12:35). And they are blind to how God is dealing with the situation (11:20-25; 13:11-15). People are released from this blindness by the insight that draws them into the story—following Jesus to Jerusalem. Because the word of and about Jesus has power, the whole story of Jesus as word, especially its pointing to and culminating in his death and resurrection, has power to ransom. In terms of theological principle the word has power because it is the instrument of the Spirit. This is suggested very allusively by Matthew in that he attributes Jesus' power to cast out demons both to the word (8:16) and to the Spirit (12:28). The word has this power materially and specifically because it is able to effect in the disciple the losing of life that is necessary for the gaining of life by making the disciple, the follower, a participant in Jesus' death and resurrection. The story is the saving light. If it is the word that saves by giving the new understanding that transforms the heart (13:14-16, 19, 23), and if Jesus' death ransoms by giving insight (20:28-34), it is plausible to conclude that Jesus' death ransoms as the word—story—about his death and resurrection, which makes this event a reality in people's lives.

To give up old interpretations and to renounce the public proof of one's righteousness that comes from human approval is the other side of recognizing the Son of God in the ordinary man from Galilee. This is to be ransomed from unfaith, *apistia* (13:58).

We have seen that understanding and faith overlap and interpenetrate extensively. Faith-understanding as a function of the heart, the inner core (13:15-17, 19, 23), is a posture that is given by revelation and also grasps revelation, and it is the source of ethical fruit (13:19, 23). A change of understanding by changing the heart reconstitutes the self. In Matthew heart, tree, and treasure are analogous images of the inner self which should be in harmony with its acts or expressions (12:33-35).

### The Beatitudes

I want to deal with the Beatitudes (Matt. 5:3-10) so far as they bear on the relationship between discipleship and the recovery from self-deception and also to present them as a prime example of Matthew's poetic imagination. Some attention will be given to the virtues or qualities of character attributed to those pronounced blessed, especially to the poor in spirit. But my stress will be on the pertinence of form or structure for meaning.[50] I take my cue from the classical statement of Roman Jacobson that language functions poetically when items from the potential reservoir of equivalent terms constitute the sequence of the text. Or arrangement by equivalence is projected into the arrangement which combines the words in the sequence. For Jacobson "equivalence" includes comparisons both of similarity and dissimilarity.[51] And the equivalences I will point to in the Beatitudes involve phonetic, syntactic, and semantic or conceptual equivalences. The person pronounced blessed is one to whom there is attributed an ongoing, joyful fullness of life related in some way—in what way we shall have to see—to eschatological salvation.[52]

Each Beatitude is composed by two clauses: (1) a declaration of blessedness; (2) a grounding of the blessedness that takes the form either of an affirmation about the present or a promise for the future. The eight

Beatitudes in 5:3-10 form a whole with a tight internal structure of equivalences. At the same time each group of four has its own distinguishing internal structure. As is well known, Matthew's Beatitudes are composed of both Q and special Matthew source material. But the meaning that emerges from the poetic structure of the finished product overrides such source distinctions. I will offer a schematic presentation of the Beatitudes, setting forth enough of the terminology to make my discussion intelligible.

1.a. Blessed, poor in spirit (empty), b. because theirs is (present) kingdom (general).
2.a. Blessed, mourners (empty), b. because they will be (future) comforted (specific).
3.a. Blessed, meek (empty), b. because they will (future) inherit the earth (specific).
4.a. Blessed, those hungering for righteousness (empty), b. because they will be (future) filled (specific).
5.a. Blessed, merciful (full), b. because they will be (future) treated mercifully (specific).
6.a. Blessed, pure in heart (full), b. because they will see (future) God (specific).
7.a. Blessed, peacemakers (full), b. because they will be (future) called God's children (specific).
8.a. Blessed, persecuted for righteousness (full), b. because theirs is (present) kingdom (general).

I begin with a discussion of the poor in spirit because it is an important clue to the structural meaning of the Beatitudes as a whole, and the structural meaning of the whole supports the initial suggestion about the meaning of the poor in spirit. It is well known that Luke has "blessed are you poor" (6:20) while Matthew has "poor in spirit." There has been a strong tendency to interpret being poor in spirit against its Jewish background as a religious posture as well as an economic condition. These people are driven by their economic need into a dependent relationship with God.[53] This posture is generally interpreted in a religiously positive way. The poor in spirit are to be understood as humble in contrast with the high self-estimation of the Pharisees and scribes; they stand before God without pretense, stripped of all self-righteousness.[54]

The interpretation I want to argue for is that the context of Matthew's Gospel confers on poor in spirit a negative connotation[55] that is as much moral as religious, if not more so. Or, perhaps more precisely, poor in spirit in itself is a thoroughly negative category, but in the context of the Beatitudes and the whole of the Gospel it is potentially positive.

One of the best clues to the meaning of poor in spirit is the one other passage in Matthew that refers to the human spirit in a substantive way. In the Garden of Gethsemane scene Jesus tells the sleeping disciples that the spirit is willing but the flesh is weak (26:41). Here the human spirit is the seat of willingness to be faithful and loyal and is positively evaluated over against the flesh, which is weak. Thus poverty of spirit is not the positive virtue of humility or lack of pride but is, negatively, a lack of spiritual or ethical substance, a lack of will to faithfulness.

The other main clue to the meaning of poor in spirit is the structure of the Beatitudes as a whole, my discussion of which begins with the equivalences in the first clauses.

1. The term "blessed" occurs in all of the eight clauses, joining them together.

2. The first four are similar in that all of them express lack or emptiness. The lack of spiritual substance in the first is followed by the mourners, who lack joy, the meek, who lack power, and those who hunger and thirst for righteousness and therefore obviously do not have it.

3. The first four are also similar in that they paradoxically combine lack with blessedness. Fullness of life is not there for those who are full of positive qualities but for those who are lacking in various ways. Full of life are the empty.

4. The second four Beatitudes are similar because all of them express fullness. The merciful, the pure in heart, the peacemakers, and those who accept suffering for their righteousness are all morally or spiritually filled.

5. The second four are also equivalent in that in a conventional way they combine blessedness and achievement. Full of life are the morally and spiritually filled.

6. The two groups of four are held together by the appearance of the word "righteousness" in the last members of each group.

7. The two groups of four are paradoxically equivalent to each other: emptiness equals fullness because both are equal to blessedness. This paradoxical connection between the two groups reiterates the paradox within the first group—the joining of blessedness and lack.

There are five instances of equivalence in the second clauses.

1. All eight are held together by the "because" (*hoti*) which introduces each of them.

2. The first and last of the second clauses are equivalent in that both have the present tense—theirs *is* the kingdom. The two framing members express realized eschatology.

3. The framing members also speak of the kingdom of heaven in a general or abstract way. They refer to God's sovereignty in principle rather than to concrete manifestations of it.[56]

4. Items 2-7, the framed members, are equivalent because all of them mention a concrete manifestation of the kingdom: They will be comforted, they will be filled, they will be treated mercifully, and so forth.

5. The framed members are also equivalent in that the grounding for blessedness is in each case a promise expressed in the future tense.[57]

What is the relationship of the first clauses to the second? The binding together of lack and fullness in the first clauses suggests that emptiness is the potentiality for fullness. Emptiness can be filled. Together lack and fullness form a process of becoming. This is related to the second clauses because the kingdom as both present and future also suggests a process. The kingdom though eschatologically present is yet not eschatologically present and so moves toward its future realization. The actualization of possibility hinted at in the first clauses by calling the empty blessed and by equating the empty and the full is affirmed in the second clauses. That the kingdom is present means that emptiness has been filled, that possibility has become actuality. But since the kingdom is also future, the present as actuality is turned into potentiality for further actualization in the future. We might diagram the relationship between the first and second clauses in the following way.

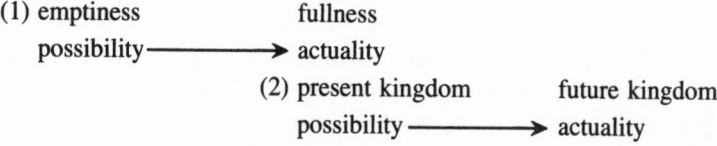

This interpretation raises the question whether emptiness is necessarily a dynamic potentiality that always leads to the fullness of actualization, but that question is answered only in the remainder of the narrative. It might seem that since both the empty and the full are pronounced blessed—full of life—there is no one who is not blessed. But we have seen that for Matthew there are the self-deceived who are empty and in fact corrupt within but do not know it. They are blind to their true condition (7:3; 23:24-28), and they are not blessed but are rather under woe (Matthew 23). Thus the positive potentiality of emptiness is contingent upon recognizing oneself as empty. Since the empty who do not see what they really are are under woe, the empty who are blessed (5:3-6) must have seen their lack of spiritual substance. That they do know this truth about themselves is confirmed by the fact that they hunger and thirst for righteousness (5:6). Matthew then envisions two fundamental human situations: (1) the empty who are blind to it; (2) the empty who have had their eyes opened and thus are simultaneously empty and in the process of being filled. These are the disciples, those who have been given to see (13:11, 16-17).

Since Matthew represents the blessed ones in 5:3-10 as having had their eyes opened to sight, they have received the word that illumines. Therefore, the Beatitudes are not entrance requirements stating the conditions that must be met in order to enter the kingdom,[58] but rather they are descriptions of people who have entered it, descriptive words that help to bring about life.[59] We do not have imperatives in the Beatitudes but affirmations about people with a certain kind of character and promises that they will persist into the future. There is a strong presence of the divine passive in the assuring promises. God will comfort, fill with righteousness, and give mercy. These disciples have the character that God wills and the fullness of life that goes with it, and God will carry them into the future.

That the Beatitudes describe the effects of grace as enabling power rather than the conditions for receiving salvation is suggested by certain other features in Matthew, such as the parables in Matthew that accent the initiating activity of God: the unforgiving servant (18:27); the workers in the vineyard (20:1-2, 9, 15); the wedding feast (22:1-2, 9-10). Another supporting theme is the various ways in which Matthew represents humankind as dependent on the revealing word for insight about oneself and reality.

So for Matthew God gives the character that integrally contains the blessedness of life that continues into the future. But we have seen that the character described in 5:3-10 is an existential stance defined by possibility becoming actuality, emptiness becoming fullness. What God gives is not a fixed possession but a dialectical movement. Thus it can slip away just when one thinks one has it. One must do himself what God has done in him. God has made you a merciful person (5:7; 18:27, 32-33), but if you do not show mercy, God will put you in jail forever (18:33-35). This last issue needs further consideration.

### Grace as Power and the Ethical Imperative

We have seen that ethical action is given with the revelation that re-creates the heart. It is a part of the redemptive event, God's action in human beings. Revelation produces new understanding (13:11, 16-17), a new disposition that constitutes a new tree (7:17a, 18a) or treasure (12:35a) from which come good acts (7:17a) or words (12:35). For Matthew an act cannot be good unless it manifests a heart, tree, or treasure which is also good (7:17-18; 12:33-35). Both character and action are given by God's grace as power to transform.[60]

Yet both character or ethical disposition and action or fruit are placed under the imperative. Both of them are a moral obligation to be achieved by human beings, as well as a gift of grace, although carrying out the demand is enabled by grace. Let me begin with the character or disposition side of the imperative. Matthew puts the reader under the command to cleanse the inside of the cup in order that (*hina*) the outside might be clean (23:26). That really entails bringing the inner self again to consciousness since it has been lost sight of through self-deception. The hypocrite or self-deceived one whom Matthew repeatedly addresses is not a member of a small, especially vicious part of humanity. This is rather Matthew's term for human beings apart from grace, the blind who have not been given to see. Matthew can also apply it to disciples (7:5, as a part of the Sermon on the Mount, is addressed to disciples) inasmuch as they are sometimes guilty of little faith (6:30; 8:26; 14:31; 16:8) and they doubt while they worship (28:17). Hypocrite is not just a term for those who believe that tithing and keeping the Sabbath earn the divine reward. It also includes those who do not kill or commit adultery, who tell the truth under oath and love their neighbors, who care for the sick and hungry. Outwardly they appear to be righteous but inwardly they are full of rebellion (23:27-28). That is to say, Matthew holds open the possibility that people may and in fact do perform acts that are in accord with a very high level of moral expectation while they are still corrupt on the inside. These people, whom he describes as hypocrites or self-deceived, are blind to the inner reality so that it must be restored to consciousness.

But how do you become aware of your inner being, your heart, and the ethical demands placed upon it, and the necessity of bringing it into accord with outer action? How do you come to see what you do not and cannot see because you do not know that it is there? You do not know that it is there because you have intentionally concealed it (7:13-14; 11:20-24; 13:15c), and the concealment has become a fate (11:25; 13:13-15b).

How can the ethical address to the inside be heard when the inside does not know that it exists? How do you deal with an inside that you do not know you have?

As we have seen, for Matthew the heart is restored to understanding (13:11a) and insight (13:16-17) from beyond itself, by the word of the kingdom and cross (4:17; 13:19; 16:21; 20:28-34). You must be shown what you cannot see, your own lost dimension of depth. This brings the concealed inner dimension back to consciousness (13:16-17, 23); wholeness is restored. Thus the person can grasp his or her inside, can cleanse it (23:26) by installing in it the disposition to the weightier matters of the law—justice, mercy, and faith (23:23). This disposition or inside will generate action or an outside that will be clean or righteous because it will correspond to the inside (23:26). The inside qualifies the outside.

But Matthew can also begin at the other end of the dialectic, with action and the imperative to act. He is saying in effect: cleanse the outside in order that the inside might be clean. A new kind of action will reshape the heart, so start with action. Take the log out of your eye, hypocrite, and then you will see (7:5). Do the thing that the will of God requires, and the heart and understanding (seeing) will be redirected.

Grace as power and ethical action are thus united in an insoluble paradox: (1) The word of the kingdom gives new understanding that generates new character and action as part of the saving event; ethical fruit is in fact given by God, achieved by God in human beings (13:11, 16, 23; 7:16-18). (2) This actuality given as part of the re-creation of wholeness is lost if it is not achieved by the person through his or her own effort (5:20; 6:14-15; 7:21-27; 16:27; 18:35; 22:1-15). God's act enables the response, but the response must also be one's own. Grace as enabling power and theological legalism go hand in glove. God enables people to do what they must do to enter the kingdom (5:20; 7:17-18; 16:27; 19:25-26).

## THE REPRESENTATION OF WHOLENESS IN THE FAILURE TO ACHIEVE IT

The parable of the unforgiving servant (Matt. 18:23-35) expresses in concentrated narrative form the Gospel's broader theological and ethical point of view: Well-being resides in the wholeness of the self, in the correspondence between inner and outer, between possibility and actuality.

The story has a three-part plot with beginning, middle, and end. The beginning (18:23-27) is in its turn a miniature three-part plot composed of a crisis, a response, and a consequence. The middle (18:28-30), which is a response to the resolved crisis of the beginning, is also composed of crisis, response, and consequence. The end (18:31-35), which is a consequence of the middle, is composed of a report and a response.

In the beginning the crisis for this servant of the king, probably a high-level tax farmer, is that he owes the king an improbably, if not impossibly, large debt. He owes ten thousand talents while the annual revenue of Herod the Great was only nine hundred. The servant responds to his crisis by asking for more time to pay—a hopeless request given the size of the debt, but understandable in the circumstances. The consequence is that the king gratuitously cancels the debt. The servant has asked for an extension of his chronological time, more time, but the king has given him a new kind of time. He has turned a time of heavy obligation with a closed future into a time of freedom with an open future. The extravagance of the forgiven debt alerts us to the fact that we are dealing with a metaphor of the kingdom of heaven and not simply with a realistic story. In the middle this official of the king responds to his unexpected and undeserved blessing by precipitating a crisis for a fellow servant. He seizes him by the throat and demands payment of a relatively small debt. The fellow servant responds using the same words with which the first servant had so recently pled before the king: Have patience with me, and I will repay you. The debt is small enough to be repaid, given time, but the reaction of the servant whose huge debt has been cancelled is to throw his fellow servant into jail. Not only did he not give him a new kind of time, as he had been given, he would not even give him a little more time.

The consequence of the whole story is that the king, in response to a report from his servants, turned the first official over to the jailers in whose prison he would languish until he paid back the debt—forever. There is also an element of the extraordinary here. The king's final withdrawal of his initial forgiveness would be for that Middle Eastern audience the introduction of chaos. The order of the world has been destroyed, for a king does not retract forgiveness once given.[61] If the word of the king cannot be counted on, what can be? In talking with the first servant, the king told him that it was *necessary* for him to have been merciful as mercy had been shown to him. Two questions present themselves to us. (1) What was the nature or ground of the necessity imposed on the servant? (2) What is the theological import of the chaos introduced into the ending of the story—the withdrawal of forgiveness?

Why was it necessary for the servant to be merciful? David Little in his study of Matthew's ethics suggests that for Matthew it was necessary because in the Evangelist's view the law of reciprocity was an intrinsic validating principle: Insofar as possible there should be an equivalence between others' treatment of one and one's treatment of others.[62] But we could respond that in the context of the parable the king's statement could mean that it was necessary to be merciful in order to stay out of jail. There is in the parable a failure of reciprocity, but in Matthew reciprocity as a justifying principle for ethical norms rests on a deeper justification. And the movement toward prison with its final cutting off of freedom and the future simply externalizes the inner existential transaction in the plot of the parable. The king's act of forgiveness as power for a new kind of action was not actualized by the servant. It should have been. The necessity for the servant's mercy was based on the implications of the story's development, as we shall see in the next paragraph.

The overall movement of the story does not put the emphasis on the *demand* for merciful behavior but on the *enablement* of it by the king's forgiveness as power for a new kind of life. The cancellation of the debt is, in theological terms, both grace as forgiveness and grace as power or enablement. Forgiveness gives power or possibility. The necessity for mercy is grounded on the parabolic narrative structure of human existence in which everyday reality is intersected by the unexpected, by the kingdom of heaven. The superabundance of grace—the cancellation of an impossible debt—opens up a possibility of such power that it must be actualized. Mercy is necessary because the new possibility propels itself with such force. Yet the ending of the story shows that mercy is also demanded. It is also a human responsibility, and the ironic tragedy of human existence is that it can thwart the necessary thrust of God's grace as power. And it should be pointed out that while the parable itself puts the emphasis on grace, Matthew's interpretive conclusion (18:35) shifts the stress to demand. Matthew makes it a matter of strict reciprocity, equal retaliation: If you do not forgive your brother from your heart, God will put you in jail forever. The necessity for the merciful behavior, then, is grounded in the powerful effect of salvation history, and is intentioned by the need to escape punishment.

But if we view the parable in the context of Matt. 7:16-20—the text on tree and fruit—the necessity for merciful behavior resides also in the structure of human existence as created. Grapes are not gathered from thorn bushes. A sound tree produces good fruit; in fact, it is not possible for it to produce bad fruit. There is then in human existence as such an impulse toward wholeness, toward the correspondence between interior heart and external act. The flaw in the human condition is that this wholeness has been lost, and we exist in contradiction between inside and outside, the wolf in sheep's clothing. The word of the gospel is the event that restores the heart (13:16-17, 23; 20:28-34) which can produce corresponding good acts (13:23; 23:26). Thus what was latently and in principle the case with human beings as created is now actually the case for the believing disciple. Salvation realizes what God had always intended for human beings as created. There is then actually in the renewed human being the same impetus toward wholeness which is latently present in human being as such. In our parable the king's cancellation of the debt is the equivalent of creating a new heart, a new possibility, in the servant. The necessity for the servant's acting mercifully is then grounded in the pressure that comes from the thrust of human existence as such—now re-created—toward wholeness.

And what of the social chaos introduced by the king's withdrawal of forgiveness in the story? Its theological import is that God's forgiveness is not effective unless internalized as a disposition toward other human beings. In the beginning the possibility of freedom for the future is given, and in the end it is taken away. In between it was not actualized by the servant. Therefore, the possibility offered by God remains an unfulfilled possibility unless it is enacted by the person. The narrative understanding of existence in faith here presented does not permit us to think of any moment or situation as existing as it is in itself, defined and self-contained, disengaged from the story process. Each moment—like the cancellation of the servant's debt—can become one thing or another. Such a moment can become an occasion to extend the freedom of another or it can become the loss of freedom. But it cannot merely remain what it is; it cannot simply remain *my* forgiveness. If one tries to freeze the moment rather than letting it open out into something new, it becomes a prison, as the unforgiving servant discovered.

# 6

## CONCLUSION AND IMPLICATIONS

Both Paul and Matthew see human beings as enmeshed in a self-deception that promotes a cover story of righteousness in order to conceal a real story of unrighteousness (Gal. 6:3; Phil 3:6-10; Rom. 9:30—10:3; Matt. 23:25-28). Both writers view the righteousness claimed by human beings as flawed, but they understand it as flawed in different ways. Also both of them consider the condition of self-deception to be a result of both choice and victimization. Let us now briefly consider how the two writers differ in their understanding of the flaw in the righteousness of the self-deceived.

For Paul the claim of a righteousness of my own based on obedience to the law is wrong-headed and misdirected. In witnessing to my own attainments as a means of establishing a right relationship with God, I refuse to submit to God's sovereign will to establish that relationship without regard to human obedience or merit. In so doing I reject the posture of faith, which is the acceptance of God's dealing (Rom. 4:14-16; 9:10-18; 9:30—10:3). Overcoming self-deception shows that faith is what is required for salvation. And the light of the gospel reveals that ethical conduct is the fruit of the Spirit, the outflowing of the gift of salvation, and not a means of achieving salvation. Wholeness is the actualization of a consciously understood connection between my flawed finite concreteness and God's sovereign and gracious freedom. In justifying me, putting me in a proper relationship with God, despite my sin, God exercises sovereign freedom and power over my evil, and this enables me to be engaged responsibly in the world while also moving with freedom into a future governed by God. The word of the cross is a light that brings the hidden secrets of the heart to consciousness. And this initial restoration of wholeness generates a process in which the poles of several polar relationships are brought into accord: life (or faith) and obedient action, sacramental life and moral life, body and spirit.

For Matthew, by contrast, the claim to have righteousness is not misdirected, is not an affront to God's way of establishing salvation, but rather the righteousness of the self-deceived is not enough. It does not comprehend the whole self. God does require works of righteousness as a condition for salvation (5:20; 6:14-15; 7:24-27; 16:27; 18:35; 25:31-46). But even avoiding murder and adultery, telling the truth under oath, pursuing justice, loving the neighbor, caring for the poor, and so forth, are not enough if they do not issue from a good tree, a heart disposed to love (7:16-20; 9:13; 12:7; 12:34-35; 18:35; 22:34-40). Thus it turns out that for Matthew what God requires and enables as the condition for salvation is acts of obedience that proceed from a heart renewed by understanding. This is what the overcoming of self-deception discloses. And wholeness is correspondence between inside and outside, heart and act.

It is not the case that Matthew does not relate ethics directly and explicitly to grace,[1] nor is it exactly true that Matthew assumes without question the Jewish view (Eccles. 15:14-15) that human beings can perform what God commands.[2] In the most direct way Matthew makes ethics depend on the gospel's transformation of the heart. Grace as power enables both inner being and ethical acts (13:14-17, 23; 19:25-26; 20:28-34). Thus it is not human beings as such but human beings transformed by grace who are assumed to be able to fulfill the demand of God for obedience from the heart. But the presence of grace in Matthew's theology does not remove the legalistic strain. Matthew does not have a legalistic ethic in the last analysis. He does not think that the believer's moral responsibility can be formulated finally in rules. But he does have a legalistic theology. Works of radical obedience do count for salvation. Grace as power and legalism can go hand in hand. Grace, the power of the gospel, enables the acts that are required, but the acts must be performed in order for salvation to take place. With Matthew it is not a matter of showing that acts of obedience do not count for salvation (as with Paul) but rather of showing that it is only the total obedience of the whole self that counts. For Paul the gospel is that God accepts us without regard for the acceptability of our works. For Matthew the good news is that God makes our works acceptable.

In drawing this sharp contrast between Paul and Matthew I have oversimplified both of them. Paul like Matthew regards wholeness as correspondence between inside and outside, between faith or intention and act (2 Cor. 8:1-15; Gal. 5:6, 25), and calls for the obedience of heart and act (Rom. 2:25-29; 6:17). And while I judge the emphasis in Paul to be justification by grace through faith, the apostle also proclaims judgment by works (1 Cor. 6:9-11; 2 Cor. 5:10; Rom. 14:10-12). Matthew, however, stresses that the obedience of the whole self is the necessary condition for salvation, but he also grounds salvation on the forgiveness of sins (1:12; 20:28; 26:28).[3] There is within each of our figures the same tension that I have posited between them. It would move beyond my present purpose to pursue the internal tension in each of these great theologians, but I should like to develop and nuance Matthew's position slightly.

It appears to me that Matthew has two schemes for relating grace, ethical performance, and eschatological salvation. According to the first one—the one that has received the most attention in this work—grace is the power (13:20, 23, 37-38) that enables the inner disposition and action (7:16-20; 12:33-37; 13:23) necessary for salvation (7:24-25; 16:27). Salvation is achieved in human beings by God. The paradox in this scheme is that human beings must achieve that same salvation by their own effort (5:20; 6:14-15, 27; 18:35). What they must do seems to be calculable: They stand or fall on the basis of their actions (7:24-25; 16:27). And yet this calculability in Matthew's theological legalism is challenged by his nonlegalistic ethic. What one must do cannot be stated in laws or rules that constitute a formal authority and definitively specify what one must do.

The second scheme is based on grace as forgiveness, and this has a paradoxical relation to the first scheme. Action grounded in a renewed heart and produced both by God and by human beings is necessary for salvation, but if that necessary righteousness fails, God still saves by forgiving, cancelling the debt (1:21; 9:1-8; 18:27; 20:9-15; 20:28; 26:28). We have seen that Jesus' death ransoms (20:28) by giving the insight that enables following (20:29-34). But the ransom saying is also connected to the eucharistic saying in 26:28 because both interpret Jesus' death redemptively. Given this connection and seeing that 26:28 understands Jesus' death as conferring forgiveness, the ransom must be understood as forgiveness as well as enablement.

Obviously forgiveness undermines the calculable continuity in the scheme demand-performance-reward. And in Matthew the theme of incalculability comes most forcefully to expression in the parable of the workers in the vineyard (20:1-16), which I now want to consider in its immediate context.

The parable is framed by the repetition of the motif that the first will be last and the last will be first (19:30; 20:16). This reversal will take place because (*gar*) (20:1) God's kingdom happens like the events in the parable. God acts contrary to the expectation of popular morality.[4] God's relationship to human beings is like the situation described in the parable. The reversal is reiterated at the end of the parable. The kingdom reverses expectations, thus (*houtōs*) the last will be first.

Prior to 19:30 Peter has reminded Jesus that the disciples have left everything to follow him, and he has asked Jesus what they can expect to get for this sacrifice (19:27). Jesus replies that in the rebirth of the world those who have followed him will share the Son of Man's role as judge (19:28) and that all who have left house and family for his sake will inherit eternal life. The assertion then that the first will be last and the last first could simply reinforce this promise. The disciples have made themselves last by giving up family and property to follow Jesus. Thus Jesus has made them first—judges and inheritors of eternal life. On the other hand, the first to last and last to first theme could be a warning to these same disciples. Having been moved from last to first, if they become presumptuous, if they forget God's proclivity to reverse expectations (20:1-15), if they fail to manifest the servanthood appropriate to discipleship (20:26-27), they will be made last again. So our theme could be promise or warning, or both.

In this parable the plot is shaped by the fate of the full-day workers, although there are also subdominant elements. The plot moves downward (tragically) from the workers' being given the opportunity to work productively, through their complaint about the owner's method of payment, to their exclusion from the presence of a good man. The theme is comic or redemptive. The owner does not deal with the workers, or at least not with some of them, on the basis of merit or performance but out of a surprising—offensive—generosity. But the plot is tragic because of the full-day worker's response to this: Those who work more should get more. To speak theologically, the theme of grace as forgiveness—performance does not count with God[5]—is present in this parable but is not the focus. The focus is the attitude that rejects this graciousness and generates the plot. Grace is there not so much for its own sake as to disclose what kind of self-understanding rejects grace as forgiveness.

The fact that the full-day workers complain because the owner breaks with the performance or merit principle—he pays all the same regardless of how long they have worked—shows that they believe that they can secure their existence by their performance. But if someone is seen to be sustained not by his own achievement but by the generosity of another, there is an incalculable element in human existence and one's faith that she can secure herself is challenged. The desire of the full-day workers to be able to manipulate reality themselves causes them to see the incalculable as injustice rather than as grace. The tragic fault in the full-day workers is not their failure to perform in a certain way but their failure to change their self-understanding so as to be able to grasp the comic-redemptive possibilities of life. From God's side human life is comic, for God works incalculably for the good of humankind, but people in their desire to have life calculable and on their own terms work against their own good.

Grace as enablement and grace as forgiveness stand over against each other in a very tensive relationship in Matthew. Everything depends on disciples' doing what God has done in them. Everything depends on God's generous but incalculable dealings, which ignore human performance. Those who want to rest on performance are alienated from the source of life.

Or have grace as power and grace as forgiveness been synthesized into the same thing? That seems to be the case in the unforgiving servant. It is forgiveness, cancelling the debt, that is the power that made it necessary (18:33) for the forgiven servant to forgive his fellow servant. But the power that made it necessary did not make it happen. Therefore, if forgiveness does not distinguish itself from enabling power and simply is nothing other than the power that enables people to do what must be done, and yet the power does not empower what is necessary, then where does one look for hope, if not to forgiveness?

I conclude with some statements of implication and commentary.

First, differences between Paul and Matthew alert us to the fact that there is more than one way of being self-deceived. The differences are in fact more far-reaching. The tensions between Paul and Matthew and within each of these writers require a decision between two alternatives from anyone who would take the Bible seriously. In this instance I will let these two central figures represent the text of the New Testament as a whole. Either the text of the New Testament is seriously deconstructed and one cannot decide what it means or, despite the tensions, it has something profound and constructive to say about living in the world before God even if the content cannot be systematically resolved. Living in this particular tension is a redemptive shaping of life.

Second, the concept of self-deception presents a thread of continuity in Western reflections on human nature from antiquity to the present.

A third implication is that since those inside and outside the biblical tradition understand self-deception in similar ways (though also with differences), the gospel, as the answer to this human problem as seen by Paul and Matthew, is also a plausible answer to the problem as seen from outside the biblical tradition.

Fourth, the New Testament deepens our understanding of self-deception by seeing it not just as the way the human mind works nor as an inevitability of human existence but as a cause of sin (an initiating act) and as a result of demonic evil (a fate). Our understanding of self-deception is also deepened in that the condition is seen not just as against oneself and others but also as against God.

Finally, I have sought to use psychological categories, especially the conscious/unconscious opposition or levels of consciousness so as to help us organize Pauline and Matthean themes related to self-deception in a way that is psychologically credible and illuminating. But I have endeavored to use an approach that does not reduce or diminish the theological and ethical dimensions of these themes. I hope I have placed the New Testament material in a structure that brings out its psychological import and significance but without diminishing its theological and ethical substance.

# Notes

### Preface

1. See Brian P. McLaughlin and Amélie Oksenberg Rorty, "Introduction," in *Perspectives on Self-Deception*, ed. B. P. McLaughlin and A. O. Rorty (Berkeley: University of California Press, 1988), 1. This book, which contains many useful articles on self-deception, will be cited hereafter as *Perspectives*.

2. See Robert Audi, "Self-Deception, Rationalization, and Reasons for Acting," ibid., 108; Brian P. McLaughlin, "Exploring the Possibility of Self-Deception in Belief," ibid., 29; Sissela Bok, *Secrets* (New York: Pantheon Books, 1982), 60.

3. Good bibliographies on self-deception may be found in Alfred Mele, "Recent Work on Self-Deception," *American Philosophical Quarterly* 24 (January 1987); McLaughlin and Rorty, eds., *Perspectives*, 553–58.

### 1. THE NATURE OF SELF-DECEPTION

1. See Sissela Bok, *Lying* (New York: Random House, Vintage Books, 1979), 6, 14, 17.

2. See Sissela Bok, *Secrets* (New York: Pantheon Books, 1982), xv, 5–7.

3. See Robert Audi, "Self-Deception, Rationalization, and Reasons for Acting," in *Perspectives*, 96, 109.

4. See Stephen L. White, "Self-Deception and Responsibility for the Self," *Perspectives*, 451.

5. Bok, *Secrets*, 64.

6. J. V. Langmead Casserley, *The Christian in Philosophy* (New York: Charles Scribner's Sons, 1951), 179–82.

7. Flannery O'Connor, "Good Country People," in *Three by Flannery O'Connor* (New York: New American Library, Signet Books, n.d.).

8. Flannery O'Connor, "Everything That Rises Must Converge," in *Everything That Rises Must Converge* (New York: The Noonday Press, 1966).

9. Fyodor Dostoevsky, "Notes from the Underground," in *The Best Short Stories of Dostoevsky*, trans. D. Magarshack (New York: The Modern Library, n.d.), 232.

10. Reinhold Niebuhr, *The Nature and Destiny of Man*, vol. 1 (London: Nisbet and Co., 1949), 198.

11. Ibid., 190, 198.

12. Ibid., 213.

13. Ibid., 198–216.

14. Ibid., 216, 218.

15. Ibid., 217.

16. Ibid., 191.

17. Jean-Paul Sartre, "Existentialism Is a Humanism," in *Existentialism from Dostoevsky to Sartre*, ed. W. Kaufmann (New York: Meridian Books, 1957), 290–91.

18. Jean-Paul Sartre, *Being and Nothingness*, trans. H. E. Barnes (New York: Philosophical Library, 1956), 49, 56.

19. Ibid., 56, 58, 60, 62, 67, 70, 77, 631, 635.

20. Ibid., 58–60.

21. Ibid., 56–57, 66–67.

22. Ibid., 56, 64.

23. Ibid., 439–40.

24. Ibid., 60, 439–40, 632. See also on this Bok, *Secrets*, 62.

25. For a brief discussion of Freud and the issue of the unconscious, see chapter 2.

26. See Allen W. Wood, "Self-Deception and Bad Faith," in *Perspectives*, 211.

27. Ibid., 215, 222–25.

28. *Being and Nothingness*, 49.

29. Herbert Fingarette, *Self-Deception* (London and Henley: Routledge and Kegan Paul, 1977), 5.

30. Ibid., 1, 70–71, 130.

31. Ibid., 140, 141, 143, 146.

32. Ibid., 5–6, 64. It has been argued that Fingarette has regenerated the paradoxes he wished to avoid. The self-deceived person is both conscious (in some way) and not conscious (in some way) of the engagements he disavows. See Alfred Mele, "Recent Work on Self-Deception," *American Philosophical Quarterly* 24 (January 1987): 13.

33. Fingarette, *Self-Deception*, 34–35, 38–39, 41–43.

34. Ibid., 42–43, 47, 53, 66–67, 70–71, 99.

35. Ibid., 27–29, 49, 134.

36. Ibid., 27–29.

37. Ibid., 70–71, 134.

38. See Mele, "Recent Work," 12.

39. Fingarette, *Self-Deception*, 64–65, 87.

40. Sigmund Freud, *The Ego and the Id*, trans. J. Riviere, ed. J. Strachey (New York: Norton Library, 1962), 5, 7, 8.

41. Sigmund Freud, "Repression," in *The Standard Edition of the Complete Psychological Works of Sigmund Freud*, vol. 14, trans. and ed. J. Strachey (London: Hogarth Press, 1957), 147, 150, 153–54, 156.

42. Fingarette, *Self-Deception*, 119–24.

43. Blaise Pascal, *Pensées*, trans. W. Trotter (New York: The Modern Library, 1941), 38–40 (no. 100).

44. Augustine of Hippo, *Confessions*, trans. R. Pine-Coffin (New York: Penguin Books, 1982), 64, 169, 245–47 (III:7; VIII:7; X:37).

45. See Allen W. Wood, "Ideology, False Consciousness, and Social Allusion," *Perspectives*, 358; Stephen L. Darwall, "Self-Deception, Autonomy, and Moral Constitution," *Perspectives*, 411.

46. Stephen Crites, "The Aesthetics of Self-Deception," *Soundings* 62 (1979): 114–18.

47. Ibid., 118, 120, 123.

48. See Fingarette, *Self-Deception*, 50. Georges Rey ("Toward a Computational Account of Akrasia and Self-Deception," *Perspectives*, 277–78, 281) makes a similar distinction between avowed attitudes (cover stories) and central beliefs (real stories).

49. Crites, "The Aesthetics of Self-Deception," 126–27.

50. The illustration is from Rey, "Self-Deception," *Perspectives*, 281.

51. Crites, "The Aesthetics of Self-Deception," 126–27.

52. Bok, *Secrets*, 61–62; Mark Johnston, "Self-Deception and the Nature of Mind," *Perspectives*, 63; Darwall, "Self-Deception," 415; Mele, "Recent Work," 1.

53. Bok, *Secrets*, 61–62; Johnston, "Self-Deception," 63, 65.

54. Johnston, ibid.

55. Bruce Wilshire, "Mimetic Engulfment and Self-Deception," *Perspectives*, 391; White, "Self-Deception," 451.

56. Johnston, "Self-Deception," 65, 66, 76, 86. Fingarette (*Self-Deception*, 28–29) seems to use the terms "purposive" and "intentional" interchangeably.

57. Rationalization is giving reasons for an action that provide prima facie rationality for the act but that do not really explain the action. See Audi, "Self-Deception," 98.

58. Brian P. McLaughlin, "Exploring the Possibility of Self-Deception in Belief," *Perspectives*, 53–54.

59. Mele, "Recent Work," 1.

60. See Amélie Oksenberg Rorty, "The Deceptive Self: Liars, Layers, and Lairs," *Perspectives*, 12, 13.

61. Rom Harré, "The Social Context of Self-Deception," *Perspectives*, 376, 378. See also William Ruddick, "Social Self-Deception," *Perspectives*, 380, 388.

62. "Recent Work," 8.

63. I have substituted the terms "real story" and "cover story" for the philosopher's "p" and "not-p" here and in some other places.

64. "Self-Deception," 65–66.

65. White, "Self-Deception," 450–53; Darwall, "Self-Deception," 415.

66. White, ibid., 453.

67. Donald Davidson, "Deception and Division," in *Actions and Events*, ed. E. LePore and B. McLaughlin (Oxford: Basil Blackwell, 1985), 139, 142, 144, 146.

68. Ibid., 144, 146.

69. Ibid., 145, 146.

70. Ibid., 138, 139, 147, 148.

71. McLaughlin, "Self-Deception," 47, 49, 50, 51, 61.

72. Ibid., 51, 52.

73. This is Robert Audi's formulation ("Self-Deception," 94) although he actually uses the term "unconscious" in a nontechnical sense.

74. See Wilshire, "Self-Deception," 392–93.

75. Michael Polanyi, *The Study of Man* (Chicago: University of Chicago Press, 1963), 26–30, 32, 44; *Personal Knowledge* (New York: Harper and Row Torchbooks, 1964), 57; *Knowing and Being* (Chicago: University of Chicago Press, 1969), 128, 133–34, 140–41.

76. On this see Rorty, "Deceptive Self," 12, 13, 17, 21–25.

## 2. SELF-DECEPTION IN PAUL

1. Stephen Crites, "The Aesthetics of Self-Deception," 109.

2. Paul's word "to boast" means to put one's trust in. One can boast of what is of human origin, as above, or one can boast of God (1 Cor. 1:31; 2 Cor. 10:17; Gal. 6:14; Jer. 9:23-24). See Rudolf Bultmann, *Theology of the New Testament*, trans. K. Grobel (New York: Charles Scribner's Sons, 1951), 1:242-43; Ernst Käsemann, *Commentary on Romans*, trans. G. Bromiley (Grand Rapids: Wm. B. Eerdmans, 1980), 69–70.

I am here discussing Paul's understanding of human wisdom, or knowledge, in terms of its formal function and not in terms of its particular historical content. With regard to the latter Schmithals holds that the Corinthian wisdom Paul opposes is full-fledged gnostic wisdom or gnosis which has replaced faith, hope, and love and displaced the word of the cross. This gnosis is an explanation of who God is, who we are, and where we are going, the apprehension of which realizes the divinity we have by nature. See Walter Schmithals, *Gnosticism in Corinth*, trans. J. Steely (Nashville: Abingdon, 1971), 143, 147–51. I think that Conzelmann (among others) is more likely to be right in maintaining that Paul's Corinthian opponents were probably proto-gnostic enthusiasts for whom knowledge has turned faith into a speculative principle that ignores the cross and focuses solely on the exalted Lord. Faith then becomes the movement of the believer along with the ascent of the Redeemer, a movement that detaches the believer from the world. See Hans Conzelmann, *1 Corinthians*, trans. J. Leitch (Philadelphia: Fortress, 1975), 14–16. It should also be pointed out that sometimes when Paul speaks about human wisdom or the wisdom of the world (as in 1 Cor. 1:17ff.; 2:5) he seems not to have in mind something as specific as gnostic, or even enthusiastic, wisdom but simply a broadly Hellenistic sense of wisdom.

When gnostic or enthusiastic wisdom becomes a functional cover story in self-deception, the self-deceived person believes (mistakenly) that he or she is divine or at least has been lifted above the struggles of natural and historical existence by his or her union with the exalted Christ.

Seneca observed that we often do not notice or pay attention to the facts before our eyes. See Abraham J. Malherbe, *Moral Exhortation, a Greco-Roman Sourcebook* (Philadelphia: Westminster, 1986), 127–28. Hans Dieter Betz notes the relationship generally of Paul's view of self-deception to the Greek gnomic tradition which goes back to the Delphic maxim "know yourself." But Betz does not analyze or penetrate the self-induced dimension of the self-deception that Paul attributed to humankind. See H. D. Betz, "Self-Deception and Boasting," in *Plutarch's Ethical Writings and Early Christian Literature*, ed. H. D. Betz (Leiden: E. J. Brill, 1978), 379–81.

3. Paul's connecting of self-deception with his appraisal of the human situation in Romans 1–2 shows that he regards self-deception as universal. Other interpreters regard it rather as a problem only of some people. See Amélie Oksenberg Rorty, "The Deceptive Self," *Perspectives*, 25.

4. On the ontological-ontic distinction see: Martin Heidegger, *Being and Time*, trans. J. Macquarrie and E. Robinson (New York: Harper and Row, 1962), 31–35; Rudolf Bultmann, *Theology* 1:198–99, 209–10, 212, 227–28; R. Bultmann, "The Historicity of Man and Faith," in *Existence and Faith*, trans. S. Ogden (New York: Living Age Books, 1960), 94–99, 108; Dan O. Via, *The Parables* (Philadelphia: Fortress, 1967), 41–42; Russell Pregeant, *Christology beyond Dogma: Matthew's Christ in Process Hermeneutic* (Philadelphia and Missoula: Fortress and Scholars, 1978), 147; Dan O. Via, "Structure, Christology, and Ethics in Matthew," in *Orientation by Disorientation*, ed. R. Spencer (Pittsburgh: Pickwick, 1980), 210–13.

5. Roland Barthes, "La Lutte avec l'ange: Analyse textuelle de Genèse, 32:23-33," in *Analyse Structural et Exégèse Biblique* (Neuchâtel: Delachaux et Niestlé, 1971), 37.

6. If 2 Thessalonians is not by Paul, and Paul, therefore, did not create this relationship, the relationship is still created by the canonization of both 2 Corinthians and 2 Thessalonians.

7. On metaphor as mini-myth see James Hillman, *Re-Visioning Psychology* (New York: Harper and Row, 1975), 156.

8. Ibid., 12, 16–17, 35. That personification—specifying a physical (nonpersonal) object as a person—is a type of metaphor (understanding one kind of thing in terms of another) is also held by George Lakoff and Mark Johnson, *Metaphors We Live By* (Chicago: University of Chicago Press, 1980), 5, 33–34.

9. See E. P. Sanders, *Paul, the Law, and the Jewish People* (Philadelphia: Fortress, 1983), 66, 75, 78–81, 143, 147; Heikki Räisänen, *Paul and the Law* (Tübingen: J. C. B. Mohr, 1983), 82–83, 229.

10. See Barnabas Lindars, *New Testament Apologetic* (London: SCM Press, 1961), 162–63. In light of my argument I take Räisänen to be wrong when he

holds (*Law,* 82) that for Paul the law is letter "by nature." That the law is letter (*gramma*) (Rom. 7:6; 2 Cor. 3:6)—demand for good works—is not the most fundamental thing about it.

11. This has been elaborately argued by Bo Reicke, "The Law and the World According to Paul," *Journal of Biblical Literature* 70 (1951): 259, 273–74.

12. Räisänen, *Law,* 145–46.

13. As claimed by E. P. Sanders, *Paul, the Law,* 20, 31–35, 155; *Paul and Palestinian Judaism* (Philadelphia: Fortress, 1977), 489–90, 496–97.

14. Again as claimed by Sanders, *Paul, the Law,* 27, 47, 155; *Paul and Palestinian Judaism,* 489–90, 496–97.

15. In Rom. 8:7 the law of God to which one should submit has to be understood as the law in the sense of its original intention to evoke faith.

16. See Räisänen, *Law,* 141–42, 251; Gerd Theissen, *Psychological Aspects of Pauline Theology,* trans. J. Galvin (Philadelphia: Fortress, 1987), 208.

17. Bultmann, *Theology* 1:246–49.

18. Theissen, *Psychological Aspects,* 209–10.

19. Theissen seems uncertain about whether the conflict in Rom. 7:14-25 was conscious or unconscious but evidently finally takes the position that it was unconscious (*Psychological Aspects,* 177, 188, 217, 221, 234).

20. For other reasons see Käsemann, *Romans,* 199–212.

21. Thus I disagree with Theissen's contention (*Psychological Aspects,* 248) that the conflict was completely unconscious and repressed.

22. Thus there is both a theological and psychological warrant for the structure of Romans (from sin to justification and liberation, or from the wrath of God to the righteousness of God) even if Paul also operated with theological logic that moved from the reality of salvation in Christ to human bondage in sin seen as the opposite of salvation (as claimed by Sanders, *Paul and Palestinian Judaism,* 484, 499, 500, 506, 507, 510). The nature of redemption helps to define the human plight, but the plight must be presupposed in order to see the relevance of salvation.

23. Johnston, "Self-Deception," 85.

24. The semantic (contextual) constraints require that Paul is suggesting that the law cannot make alive. That point would have been clearly undergirded if he had used a second-class condition, which assumes that the condition is untrue (if a law was given that could make alive, which was not the case). But Paul did not do that. He rather used a first-class condition to express a contrary-to-fact case. That is syntactically possible but rare for Paul. It is more natural for a first-class condition to assume that the conditional case is true. Thus the semantic context requires that the law cannot make alive and favors the ontic sense of the law. But the syntax elusively suggests that the law might make alive and thus alludes to the ontological sense. On conditional clauses see F. Blass, A. Debrunner, and R. Funk *A Greek Grammar of the New Testament,* trans. R. Funk (Chicago: University of Chicago Press, 1962), 182, 188–90; Robert W. Funk, *A Beginning-Intermediate Grammar of Hellenistic Greek* (Missoula, Mont.: Society of Biblical Literature, 1973), 2:680–83.

25. Räisänen, *Law*, 82–83. Is Räisänen presupposing that the text is a fixed and closed work rather than a set of possibilities to be turned into a work by the interpreter with his or her presuppositional categories?

26. See Jacques Derrida, "Structure, Sign, and Play in the Discourse of the Human Sciences," in *The Language of Criticism and the Sciences of Man*, ed. R. Macksey and E. Donato (Baltimore: Johns Hopkins University Press, 1970), 249; "Differance," in *Speech and Phenomena*, trans. D. Allison (Evanston: Northwestern University Press, 1973), 140–41; *Of Grammatology*, trans. G. C. Spivak (Baltimore: Johns Hopkins University Press, 1980), 7, 61–62, 73; Jonathan Culler, *On Deconstruction* (Ithaca: Cornell University Press, 1983), 85–86, 166, 198–99, 205.

27. This is consistent with the view of Robert Audi ("Self-Deception," 93, 96) that self-deception involves both an act and a state.

28. See Bultmann, *Theology* 1:226, 241–43.

29. Theissen, *Psychological Aspects*, 146.

30. Pauline usage requires that the verb *katargeō* be understood in the strong sense "abolish." See Victor Paul Furnish, *2 Corinthians*, Anchor Bible series (Garden City, N.Y.: Doubleday, 1984), 203.

31. The feminine participle of *katargeō* (abolish) agrees with the feminine noun *doxa* (splendor).

32. This is suggested by the fact that in these verses he has shifted to the neuter participle of *katargeō*.

33. Theissen, *Psychological Aspects*, 146.

34. See McLaughlin, "Self-Deception," 50–52.

35. Sartre, *Being and Nothingness*, 50, 64, 68.

36. Ibid., 64.

37. Ibid., 60, 439–40.

38. Ibid., 262–63.

39. Philip Wheelwright, *The Burning Fountain* (Bloomington: Indiana University Press, 1954), 25; *Metaphor and Reality* (Bloomington: Indiana University Press, 1962), 33–37.

40. Wheelwright, *Fountain*, 25–26; *Metaphor*, 42–44, 46–50, 53–55.

41. Wheelwright, *Metaphor*, 72–74, 78–80, 86.

42. Ibid., 70–71.

43. Ibid.

44. For example David S. Miall, "Metaphor as Thought-Process," *Journal of Aesthetics and Art Criticism* 38 (1979): 22.

45. Hillman, *Re-Visioning Psychology*, 156. This position is also taken by Sallie McFague, *Metaphorical Theology* (Philadelphia: Fortress, 1982), 38.

46. Wheelwright, *Fountain*, 25–26, 49–51; *Metaphor*, 43–44.

47. Frank Burch Brown, *Transfiguration* (Chapel Hill: University of North Carolina Press, 1983), 15–16, 42, 44–45.

48. Ibid., 28–29, 175.

49. Paul Ricoeur, *The Rule of Metaphor*, trans. R. Czerny (Toronto: University of Toronto Press, 1984), 14, 15, 20, 44.

50. Ibid., 44, 48, 98, 231, 299; Paul Ricoeur, *Interpretation Theory* (Fort Worth: Texas Christian University Press, 1976), 47, 49–50.

51. Mary Gerhart and Allan Russell, *Metaphoric Process* (Fort Worth: Texas Christian University Press, 1984), 161.

52. Janet Martin Soskice, *Metaphor and Religious Language* (Oxford: Clarendon Press, 1985), 19, 21–23.

53. Ricoeur, *Interpretation Theory*, 50.

54. Ibid.; *Rule*, 230, 290–91.

55. *Rule*, 229–30, 290–91. Soskice seems to oppose the view that a metaphor has multiple meanings when she contends that the literal sense of a metaphor should direct the metaphorical construal in order to prevent the "absurdity" of a number of different readings (*Metaphor*, 31).

56. *Interpretation Theory*, 37, 68; *Rule*, 229.

57. *Interpretation Theory*, 68; *Rule*, 249, 298–99. The "is" and "is not" tension is also important to McFague, *Metaphorical Theology*, 13–15.

Soskice (*Metaphor*, 88–89) is critical of Ricoeur's split reference and seems to want to affirm only one reference. In her view the alternative to the metaphorical reference is not the shattered literal reference but no reference. I think that what is at stake here is the necessity of maintaining both the literal meaning of the terms in the metaphorical utterance and the new twist. Apart from the tension at the literal level there would be no new twist. I think that Ricoeur underestimates that. And Soskice's single reference does not take account of it. But Ricoeur does recognize the importance of both dimensions of meaning when he says that it is not really a matter of two significations but of a single movement from one to the other (*Interpretation Theory*, 55). But the literal must not be dropped. The law could not function—metaphorically—as a person if it lost its standing in reality as a code.

Soskice (*Metaphor*, 89) is also (vaguely) critical of the is/is not tension and claims that it tends to turn metaphor into comparison. In response I should say that metaphor does inevitably involve some degree of comparison (recall Wheelwright and Brown). Nor is any understanding at all possible apart from seeing one thing *as like* another. Perhaps metaphors for God are the clearest evidence why both the "is" and "is not" must be maintained. The Bible both says that God is indescribable and describes God with many images. God must then be in some way like the images or we have no knowledge of God. But God must also not be like the images in order to avoid idolizing the images and in order to do justice to God's indescribability.

58. Ricoeur, *Interpretation Theory*, 51–53, 55, 57, 67–69, 81; "The Specificity of Religious Language," *Semeia* 4 (1975): 124–26; *De l'interprétation* (Paris: Editions du Seuil, 1965), 40.

59. For example, John Dominic Crossan, *In Parables* (New York: Harper and Row, 1973), 13.

60. As Räisänen does (*Law*, 150).

61. Miall, "Metaphor," 22, 23, 25–28.

62. As in Stephen Ullmann, *Semantics* (Oxford: Basil Blackwell, 1970), 195.

63. Miall, "Metaphor," 22, 23, 25–28.

64. See C. G. Jung, "The Psychology of the Child Archetype," trans. R. F. Hull in *Psyche and Symbol: A Selection from the Writings of C. G. Jung*, ed. V. S. de Laszlo (Garden City, N.Y.: Doubleday, Anchor Books, 1958), 115, 117. See further *Psyche and Symbol*, xvi, 19, 61, 118–19, 129; C. G. Jung, *The Archetypes and the Collective Unconscious*, trans. R. F. Hull (New York: Pantheon Books, 1959), 5, 38, 48, 57, 66, 70; *Two Essays on Analytical Psychology*, trans. R. Hull (New York: Meridian Books, 1959), 230.

65. Hillman, *Re-Visioning Psychology*, xiii, 44, 115–17, 120, 122–23, 127, 130, 132, 142, 145, 156. Lakoff and Johnson (*Metaphors*, 3–5) also understand experience and action as metaphorical.

66. Hillman, *Re-Visioning Psychology*, xiii, 12, 35, 142, 145, 169.

67. See Hans Dieter Betz, *Galatians* (Philadelphia: Fortress, 1979), 177.

68. See Walter Wink, *Naming the Powers* (Philadelphia: Fortress, 1984), 68; Wesley Carr, *Angels and Principalities* (Cambridge: Cambridge University Press, 1981), 72–73. Richard Hays has given an illuminating interpretation of the narrative structure of Gal. 3:1—4:11. His focus is on the Christology while mine is on the anthropology. See Richard B. Hays, *The Faith of Jesus Christ*, SBL Dissertation series, 56 (Chico, Calif.: Scholars Press, 1981), 104–10, 124–25, 193–96.

69. Betz, *Galatians*, 204–5. In basic agreement with Betz on this point are Käsemann, *Romans*, 251; Wayne A. Meeks, *The First Urban Christians* (New Haven: Yale University Press, 1983), 184; Sanders, *Paul, the Law*, 69; Gerhard Ebeling, *The Truth of the Gospel*, trans. D. Green (Philadelphia: Fortress, 1985), 216, 219; David J. Lull, "The Spirit and the Creative Transformation of Human Existence," *Journal of the American Academy of Religion* 67 (March 1979): 51.

70. Eduard Schweizer, "Slaves of the Elements and Worshippers of Angels: Gal. 4:3, 9 and Col. 2:8, 18, 20," *Journal of Biblical Literature* 107 (September 1988): 455–64. In basic agreement with him are Wink, *Naming the Powers*, 67; Carr, *Principalities*, 37.

71. Schweizer, "Slaves," 456, 466.

72. Carr, *Principalities*, 75; Wink, *Naming the Powers*, 70, 72.

73. Schweizer, "Slaves," 460, 467–68.

74. Lull, "Spirit," 51.

75. Carr, *Principalities*, 7; Wink, *Naming the Powers*, 16–17.

76. Carr, *Principalities*, 12, 15–18, 24, 30, 35, 42–43, 174–75.

77. Ibid., 52, 63, 90–92, 113. One of Carr's presuppositions throughout (as 72, 74) seems to be that Paul's thought was rigorously confined by the conventions of his readers. It is true that people cannot understand what is too foreign to be assimilated. But understandings can be extended; otherwise people could never grasp anything new. And innovative thinkers like Paul do not stay exclusively within current conventions. Paul could have wanted his readers to see something they had not seen.

78. Wink, *Naming the Powers*, 23–24.

79. Ibid., 5, 11–12, 47, 105–7.

80. See C. B. Caird, *Principalities and Powers* (Oxford: Clarendon Press, 1950), 2–5, 11–16.

81. Wink, *Naming the Powers*, 7, 9.

82. See on this also J. Christiaan Beker, *Paul the Apostle* (Philadelphia: Fortress, 1980), 189–92.

83. Recent interpreters of self-deception also recognize that it keeps people from acknowledging the full extent of their moral responsibilities. See Marcia Baron, "What Is Wrong with Self-Deception?" in *Perspectives on Self-Deception*, 437–40.

Räisänen (*Law*, 200–201, 264–65) says in effect that Paul was self-deceived in that he concealed the truth that he had abrogated the law with the false belief that he was the only one who really upheld it. I am sure that Paul would have acknowledged that he suffered from self-deception, if pushed, since he regarded it as universal. But I doubt that he was self-deceived on the particular issue that Räisänen raises here. When Paul uses explicitly negating language about the law, it is hard to imagine that he does not know that he is negating it. For example, in Rom. 10:5-13 in the clear light of day he draws a line between what he regards as valid and what he regards as invalid in the Hebrew Scriptures.

Räisänen deals with the problem of tensions in Paul's view of the law by attempting to reconstruct Paul's psychological history (*Law*, 257–62). There are probably times when I also sound as if that is what I am trying to do, but generally that is not my purpose and not the way I hope to be understood. I have rather at points employed psychological categories in the effort to interpret Paul's text and Paul as he comes to expression in his text, without assuming that we have immediate access to the psyche of the historical Paul.

## 3. THE RECOVERY OF WHOLENESS IN PAUL

1. See Dan O. Via, "Justification and Deliverance: Existential Dialectic," *Studies in Religion/Sciences Religieuses* 1 (1971): 203–6.

2. On the idea of the power of the *philosophical* word to transform people in Greco-Roman philosophy, see Abraham J. Malherbe, *Moral Exhortation*, 56–59.

3. Theissen, *Psychological Aspects*, 11, 123, 151–52.

4. Hans Dieter Betz, *Paul's Concept of Freedom in the Context of Hellenistic Discussions about the Possibilities of Human Freedom* (Berkeley: Center for Hermeneutical Studies, 1977), 9–10.

Other Greco-Roman thinkers were aware of the need for drastic action—the whip, an overlord, cutting, cautery, medication—in order to overcome self-deception. See Malherbe, *Moral Exhortation*, 47.

Seneca believed that people needed the constant reminder of moral exhortation to make them attend to the facts they know but do not notice. See Malherbe, *Moral Exhortation*, 127–28. We have seen that for Paul the power of the Spirit is necessary to make people see the unnoticed truth. But had Paul not believed that moral exhortation could also perform this function, he would hardly have made so much use of it.

5. Theissen observes that in 1 Cor. 4:5 we find the three basic presuppositions that are necessary for a concept of the unconscious: (1) God's knowledge of the heart; (2) limited human self-knowledge; (3) the significance of inner reality. See *Psychological Asepcts*, 62. I am not sure why the first one is necessary for an understanding of the unconscious per se.

6. Heinz Kohut, *The Restoration of the Self* (New York: International Universities Press, 1977), 53–54.

7. The human spirit is to be discussed later in this chapter.

8. Victor Paul Furnish, *Theology and Ethics in Paul* (Nashville: Abingdon, 1968), 224–26.

9. Ernst Käsemann, *Romans*, 174–75.

10. Bultmann, *Theology* 1:332.

11. Kohut, *Self*, 30–31, 63, 171.

12. See C. A. Pierce, *Conscience in the New Testament* (London: SCM Press, 1955), 16, 17, 40–41, 45–46, 50, 77; W. D. Davies, "Conscience," *The Interpreter's Dictionary of the Bible* (Nashville: Abingdon, 1981), 1:674; Bultmann, *Theology* 1:217, 218; W. David Stacey, *The Pauline View of Man* (London: Macmillan, 1956), 206–8; Richard A. Horsley, "Consciousness and Freedom among the Corinthians: 1 Corinthians 8–10," *Catholic Biblical Quarterly* 40 (October 1978): 582; Robert Jewett, *Paul's Anthropological Terms* (Leiden: E. J. Brill, 1971), 425.

13. See Jewett, *Anthropological Terms*, 426.

14. For a somewhat different view see ibid., 425.

15. John Knox, *The Epistle to the Romans, The Interpreter's Bible* (Nashville: Abingdon, 1984), 9:471.

16. See Peter Richardson, *Paul's Ethic of Freedom* (Philadelphia: Westminster, 1979), 13, 164; Betz, *Paul's Concept of Freedom*, 1.

17. On the background of freedom as political and as an internal dimension of the self in the Greco-Roman world, see Betz, *Paul's Concept of Freedom*, 2–5. Also in the same volume (19, 20, 24) see the well-taken criticisms of his respondents, Thomas Conley and M. Pohlenz. On internal freedom in Epictetus (from assenting to falsehood or from fear) and Seneca (from craving wickedness or excess) see Malherbe, *Moral Exhortation*, 36–37, 46, 158.

18. See Betz, *Paul's Concept of Freedom*, 6, 8, 9; Bultmann, *Theology* 1:330–52.

19. For the contrasting view in Epictetus that freedom is self-attained see Malherbe, *Moral Exhortation*, 159.

20. Betz (*Paul's Concept of Freedom*, 7) states that Paul rejects the Corinthians' "all is permitted" in the tone of a Roman disgusted with Greek individualism. But I am trying to show that Paul's reasons for qualifying "all is permitted" run deeper than a difference of political culture.

21. Note that the freedom the believer has in Christ can be lost because of specific decisions and actions just as the freedom of human beings in general as created is lost because of specific decisions and actions (Rom. 1:19-28). In both cases freedom for God and obedience is lost.

22. I do not see any reason to read 1 Cor. 9:16-23 as describing a linear movement from freedom to slavery. Paul is rather describing his stance toward his churches as he writes at that time, expressing the simultaneity of freedom and slavery. We have in 9:19 a plausible concessive participial phrase (although being free) followed by an affirmation (I made myself a slave of all). This interpretation is supported by the simultaneity of being free for the world and belonging to Christ in 1 Cor. 3:21-23. Contra Dale Basil Martin, "Slave of Christ, Slave of All: Paul's Metaphor of Slavery and 1 Corinthians 9" (dissertation, Yale University, 1988), 231–32.

23. See Vincent L. Wimbush, *Paul the Worldly Ascetic* (Macon, Ga.: Mercer University Press, 1987), 21–22, 83.

24. I follow Wimbush (*Paul,* 23–25) on this although I differ with some of his interpretations.

25. As Wimbush claims (*Paul,* 34, 42).

26. The tightly structured form of the passage with its eschatological inclusio obviates the claims of Wimbush that the text is not strongly eschatological (*Paul,* 34, 42, 47), that there is a lack of agreement between 29a and 31b (34, 42), and that the two terminal parts are freestanding (44). Wimbush sees a kinship between Paul's "as though not" and Stoic *apatheia* (*Paul,* 68).

27. The imperative here is not expressed by the more customary imperative form but by *hina* with the subjunctive. See Blass, Debrunner, and Funk, *A Greek Grammar of the New Testament,* 195–96.

28. As argued by Wimbush, *Paul,* 22, 50–52, 87.

29. That Paul has in mind here two kinds of anxiety is supported by Hans Conzelmann, *1 Corinthians,* 134. That Paul regards anxiety about both the Lord and the spouse as negative is argued by C. K. Barrett, *The First Epistle to the Corinthians* (New York: Harper and Row, 1968), 179.

That there is a kinship between Paul's view of marriage and certain strains of Stoic thought is argued by Wimbush (*Paul,* 87) and David L. Balch, "1 Cor. 7:32-35 and Stoic Debates about Marriage, Anxiety, and Distraction," *Journal of Biblical Literature* 102 (September 1983): 430, 434, 439.

30. Wimbush (*Paul,* 39) sees the passage as not quite at home in Paul.

31. On the dialectic between coherent center and contextual modification in Paul's theology, see Beker, *Paul the Apostle,* 23–36.

32. See F. W. Beare, *A Commentary on the Epistle to the Philippians* (London: Adam and Charles Black, 1959), 133–36.

33. The parallelism and antitheses of these verses are characteristic of the diatribe style. See Malherbe, *Moral Exhortation,* 130.

34. See Gerd Theissen, *The Social Setting of Pauline Christianity,* ed. and trans. J. Schütz (Philadelphia: Fortress, 1982), 42–49.

35. Thus the freedom Paul seeks is much more than economic independence, which seems to be suggested in Ronald F. Hock, *The Social Context of Paul's Ministry* (Philadelphia: Fortress, 1980), 61.

36. Dale B. Martin has done a very instructive study of the social phenomenon of slavery in the Greco-Roman world and of the pertinence of social-historical knowledge for understanding Paul. However, I believe that his tendency to stress

the possibilities for influence and upward mobility present in some levels of slavery is clearly discordant with the connotation of obedience present in the text. See Martin, "Slave of Christ," 9–11, 127–28.

37. Very briefly I assume that the moral or ethical as a human category has to do with prescribing attitudes and actions that are relational and social and are aimed at promoting the welfare of human beings. David Little and Sumner B. Twiss, *Comparative Religious Ethics* (New York: Harper and Row, 1978), 26–29.

38. Krister Stendahl's interpretation is one-sided and wrong because it recognizes only that Paul contrasts love with spiritual experience. Thus Stendahl concludes that love in Paul has nothing to do with "Western introspection" or with "feeling more deeply" but is simply reasonable concern for building up one's brothers and sisters in the church. See Krister Stendahl, "Love Rather Than Integrity," in *Paul among Jews and Gentiles* (Philadelphia: Fortress, 1976), 56–58.

Love for Paul is certainly more than feeling more deeply, but to deny that it includes an inner direction of oneself is, I believe, a distortion of Paul.

39. On the comprehensive inclusiveness of the moral demand in Paul, see Wolfgang Schrage, *The Ethics of the New Testament*, trans. D. Green (Philadelphia: Fortress, 1988), 186–87.

40. Stendahl, "Love," 60–61. Dale Martin points out that in the Greco-Roman world the accusation of accommodation was generally an insult hurled at demagogues who changed their speech and life-style in order to gain influence with the many. See "Slave of Christ," 172.

41. Martin, "Slave of Christ," 213–14; also see Hock, *The Social Context of Paul's Ministry*, 35–36, 60.

42. Stendahl, "Love," 60–61, 67.

43. Ibid., 61.

44. On active love in Paul see Luise Schottroff, "Non-Violence and Love of One's Enemies," in *Essays on the Love Commandment*, ed. R. Fuller (Philadelphia: Fortress, 1978), 22–24.

45. Peter Richardson (*Paul's Ethic of Freedom*, 90) states Paul's accommodation principle as a willingness to compromise on behavior but not on the essentials of the gospel (Gal. 1:6-9). In the light of 1 Cor. 10:27-29, especially 10:29b, Richardson says that Paul's position is: The conscience of the weak should be carefully considered but not deferred to if it is being oppressively used to control others (129).

46. Sanders, *Paul, the Law, and the Jewish People*, 96-98. I believe that Räisänen is wrong (*Paul and the Law*, 83) in holding that in 2 Cor. 3:6-7 Paul rejects the belief that the law is still in force as an expression of God's moral will. It is true that in this passage Paul includes the law within the category of letter—a power that kills. But it is specifically the law as letter—the demand for good works that save—and not the law as moral that Paul here negates. We should note, however, that since Paul can give the moral law as an example of letter, he is implying that even in the Christian *kairos*, law as moral authority always threatens to become and can become letter.

47. See Joseph Jensen, "Does *Porneia* Mean Fornication? A Critique of Bruce Malina," *Novum Testamentum* 20 (1978): 165–69.

48. On love as a basis for subsidiary rules and principles, see Gene H. Outka, "Character, Conduct, and the Love Commandment," in *Norm and Context in Christian Ethics*, ed. Gene H. Outka and Paul Ramsey (New York: Charles Scribner's Sons, 1968), 40–41.

49. For helpful discussions of the types of justification see Little and Twiss, *Comparative Religious Ethics*, 96–109; Thomas W. Ogletree, *The Use of the Bible in Christian Ethics* (Philadelphia: Fortress, 1983), 15–45.

50. See Schrage, *Ethics*, 200; Beare, *Philippians*, 148.

51. For examples of deontological, consequentialist, and self-realization warrants in Greco-Roman moral philosophy, see Malherbe, *Moral Exhortation*, 89, 91, 94, 156–57, 158.

52. See Bultmann, *Theology* 1:15.

53. See Richardson, *Paul's Ethic of Freedom*, 69; L. William Countryman, *Dirt, Greed, and Sex: Sexual Ethics in the New Testament and Their Implications for Today* (Philadelphia: Fortress, 1988), 206; Robin Scroggs, "Paul and the Eschatological Woman," *Journal of the American Academy of Religion* 40 (September 1972): 289–91. This last mentioned work is still important.

54. *Exousiazō* and *kyrieuō* were related terms. In Mark 10:42 *katexousiazō* and *katakyrieuō* are used more or less as synonyms.

55. See Countryman, *Dirt*, 206.

56. Samuel Terrien argues that "to burn" refers not to passion but to burning in judgment because of immorality. His reason is that the verb *puroō* is almost never used metaphorically and never has such a psychological sense in the Septuagint. See Samuel Terrien, *Till the Heart Sings* (Philadelphia: Fortress, 1985), 162–63. But whatever the customary usage, Paul's language in 1 Cor. 7:36-38 about strong passions, standing firm, not being under necessity, and having authority over one's own will or desire suggests that he is using *puroō* as a metaphor for the psychological condition of burning with passion. Moreover, in 2 Cor. 11:29 Paul uses *puroō* as a psychological metaphor.

57. See Hubert Martin, Jr., "Plutarch on Eros," in *Plutarch's Ethical Writing and Early Christian Literature*, ed. Hans Dieter Betz (Leiden: E. J. Brill, 1978), 472, 476, 513.

58. See in Malherbe, *Moral Exhortation*, 153.

59. See Stanley K. Stowers, "A 'Debate' over Freedom: 1 Corinthians 6:12-20," in *Christian Teaching*, ed. E. Ferguson (Abilene, Tex.: Abilene Christian University, 1981), 68–69. Stowers points to the diatribe style of this text.

60. Stowers (ibid., 62–67) believes that the libertine group is influenced by a Cynic view of unlimited freedom and that Paul imposes limits from a Stoic perspective.

61. Jensen, "*Porneia*," 163, 180; Countryman, *Dirt*, 104.

62. The unclean is that which confuses, confounds, disorders, fragments the order of reality. It is matter out of place, outside the system. Purity rules relate especially to the boundaries and orifices of the human body. See Countryman, *Dirt*, 11–13; Dan O. Via, *The Ethics of Mark's Gospel* (Philadelphia: Fortress, 1985), 88–96.

63. Countryman, *Dirt,* 104–9, 147, 164.

64. Bultmann, *Theology* 1:192–96, 201–3. Bultmann has been followed by many, including John A. T. Robinson, *The Body* (Chicago: Henry Regnery, 1952), 28–33; Countryman, *Dirt,* 203–4.

65. See Robert H. Gundry, *Soma in Biblical Theology* (Cambridge: Cambridge University Press, 1976), 59, 79–80.

66. Ibid., 6. Among others who argue that body in Paul has a physical and not holistic meaning are Jewett, *Anthropological Terms,* 211; Stowers " 'Debate,' " 60; Jerome Murphy-O'Connor, "Corinthian Slogans in 1 Cor. 6:12-20," *Catholic Biblical Quarterly* 40 (1978): 393.

67. Gundry, *Soma,* 68.

68. Jewett (*Anthropological Terms,* 260) evidently wants to see the body's union with Christ in 6:15-16 as simply physical.

69. While my emphasis is different, I think that I am not in total disagreement with Brendan Byrne, who argues that the two primary dimensions of the body are its physicality and its being the vehicle of communication and relationship. Byrne seems to reject the holistic interpretation of body, evidently because he thinks that that would rule out the physical connotation. See Brendan Byrne, "Sinning against One's Own Body: Paul's Understanding of the Sexual Relationship in 1 Corinthians 6:18," *Catholic Biblical Quarterly* 45 (1983): 610–12.

Byrne builds on Käsemann, who holds that body for Paul is that piece of the world which we are and for which we are responsible. It represents our solidarity with the corporeality of creation and our capacity for communication. See Ernst Käsemann, *New Testament Questions of Today,* trans. W. J. Montague (Philadelphia: Fortress, 1969), 135; *Perspectives on Paul,* trans. M. Kohl (Philadelphia: Fortress, 1971), 17–23. I would not put the stress where Käsemann puts it, but I do not think that the interpretations of body by Bultmann and Käsemann are necessarily as divergent as Käsemann thinks. The concept of relatedness embraces both Bultmann's self-relatedness and Käsemann's relatedness to the whole of creation.

Richard Hays has argued that in Galatians 3 Christians are justified not by their own faith but because they participate in Jesus Christ, who enacted the obedience of faith on their behalf (*The Faith of Jesus Christ,* 196). Hays then takes the faith by which Paul lives his life in the flesh in Gal. 2:20b to be not faith *in* the Son of God but the faith *of* the Son of God or the faith that comes from the Son of God (168). I would take the latter interpretation. It is consistent with Phil. 1:29, where it is given (by grace, *echaristhē*) to believe in Christ, and with Rom. 10:17, where faith is given by hearing the word of Christ. In both Gal. 2:20 and Phil. 1:29 faith is given to the believer, but in Gal. 2:20 the Son of God is implicitly the giver while in Phil. 1:29 he is the object. Hays is right that in Galatians 3 faith is not self-generated and even has an "objective" basis. But faith once given also operates subjectively in the believer.

70. See Gundry, *Soma,* 64.

71. Thus I am opposing the position of Robert Jewett, who argues that generally in Paul the human spirit is the divine Spirit apportioned to human beings so that it is theirs but without losing its divine character. There is no clear distinction

between the divine and human spirit (*Anthropological Terms,* 179, 183–85, 197–99). Jewett acknowledges that in 1 Cor. 2:11 Paul makes a rare distinction between human and divine spirit, but he denies that Paul here makes the human spirit the seat of self-consciousness (*Anthropological Terms,* 187–89, 194).

72. As claimed in Conzelmann, *1 Corinthians,* 66; Barrett (*First Corinthians,* 74) understands the human spirit in 2:11 as the organ by which one knows oneself.

73. Gundry (*Soma,* 70, 73) grants that throughout Greek literature *eis* with *hamartanō* (sin) regularly means "against." However, Gundry prefers "in" or "with" here.

74. See Eduard Schweizer, "Sōma," *Theological Dictionary of the New Testament,* ed. G. Friedrich, ed. and trans. G. Bromiley (Grand Rapids: Wm. B. Eerdmans, 1975), 7:1070. Gundry (*Soma,* 75) questions the probability of this interpretation because the church as the body of Christ had not yet been introduced in this letter.

75. Stowers, "Debate," 61, 69; C. F. D. Moule, *An Idiom Book of New Testament Greek* (Cambridge: Cambridge University Press, 1953), 196–97.

76. Barrett, *First Corinthians,* 150.

77. Ibid., 150–51; Byrne, "Sinning," 613.

78. See Countryman, *Dirt,* 210.

79. D. H. Lawrence, *Women in Love* (New York: Modern Library, 1950), 63–64.

## 4. SELF-DECEPTION IN MATTHEW

1. The idea of the wolf in sheep's clothing was traditional (see Aesop, for example) as was the wickedness of the wolf. See W. D. Davies and Dale C. Allison, Jr., *A Critical and Exegetical Commentary on the Gospel According to Saint Matthew* (Edinburgh: T. and T. Clark, 1988), 704.

2. See Käsemann, "The Beginnings of Christian Theology," in *New Testament Questions,* 83–84.

3. For the view that Matthew was opposing both Pharisees and antinomians, see Gerhard Barth, "Matthew's Understanding of the Law," in *Tradition and Interpretation in Matthew,* trans. P. Scott (Philadelphia: Westminster, 1963), 74–76, 85. The view that Matthew had only one opponent which was both legalistic and antinomian is held by Robert H. Gundry, *Matthew* (Grand Rapids: Wm. B. Eerdmans, 1982), 6, 132–33. Gundry does not distinguish, however, the historical situation from the narrative world nor does he use literary categories to explain the opponents as they appear in the text.

Davies and Allison (*Matthew,* 701–2) maintain that there is a unity between 7:15-20 and 7:21-23; therefore, the false prophets of the former are the confessing Christians of the latter, although we cannot be more precise about their identity. Georg Strecker denies that 7:21-23 is a clue to the identity of the false prophets. He does hold that the latter are Christians but that the text does not have a particular group in view. It speaks of a danger that always threatens the church. See Strecker, *The Sermon on the Mount,* trans. O. Dean, Jr. (Nashville: Abingdon, 1988), 161–62.

4. Daniel Patte, *The Gospel According to Matthew* (Philadelphia: Fortress, 1987), 99. See also Davies and Allison, *Matthew,* 705, 708.

5. See Wolfgang Iser, *The Act of Reading: A Theory of Aesthetic Response* (Baltimore: Johns Hopkins University Press, 1980), 21–25, 57, 38, 47–48, 74, 92, 141.

6. *Matthew,* 343.

7. I here give my own interpretation, but I have several discussions in the back of my mind, which I have both learned from and disagreed with. See G. Barth, "Law," 64–72; John P. Meier, *The Vision of Matthew* (New York: Paulist, 1979), 222–39; R. Pregeant, *Christology beyond Dogma,* 63–83; Georg Strecker, *Der Weg der Gerechtigkeit* (Göttingen: Vandenhoeck and Ruprecht, 1971), 143–47; Robert A. Guelich, *The Sermon on the Mount* (Waco, Tex.: Word Books, 1983), 134–74; Hans Dieter Betz, *Essays on the Sermon on the Mount* (Philadelphia: Fortress, 1985), 37–53.

8. See Thomas W. Ogletree, *The Use of the Bible in Christian Ethics* (Philadelphia: Fortress, 1983), 111.

9. As claimed by Guelich, *Sermon,* 84–87, 170, 301, 372. Guelich also recognizes the conduct side.

10. Davies and Allison, *Matthew,* 453; Strecker, *Sermon,* 37; Benno Przybylski, *Righteousness in Matthew and His World of Thought,* SNTSMS, 41 (Cambridge: Cambridge University Press, 1980), 87–88, 99, 105. We shall see that Matthew has an understanding of God's graciousness, but righteousness is not one of his terms for it.

11. *Righteousness,* 81–84.

12. Günther Bornkamm, "End-Expectation and Church in Matthew," in *Tradition and Interpretation in Matthew,* 25, 30–31; Davies and Allison, *Matthew,* 575–76; Strecker, *Sermon,* 40, 60–61, 175–76.

13. Leland J. White, "Grid and Group in Matthew's Community: The Righteousness/Honor Code in the Sermon on the Mount," *Semeia* 35 (1986): 63–64.

14. Ibid., 77–78, 82.

15. Ibid., 79–80, 82.

16. The same point I make about Matthew is made about Jesus by Marcus J. Borg, *Jesus: A New Vision* (San Francisco: Harper and Row, 1987), 105.

17. White, "Grid and Group," 80, 82, 83, 85.

18. Jane Schaberg argues that the story has a historical nucleus and that Mary could have been either raped or seduced. See *The Illegitimacy of Jesus* (San Francisco: Harper and Row, 1987), 151–56. Schaberg thinks that Matthew probably regarded the situation as rape (59–61).

19. See ibid., 72–76.

20. See Fred L. Horton, Jr., "Parenthetical Pregnancy: The Conception and Birth of Jesus in Matthew 1:18-25," *Society of Biblical Literature 1987 Seminar Papers* (Atlanta: Scholars Press, 1987), 179–86. Schaberg (*Illegitimacy,* 70–71) holds that Matthew understood Isa. 7:14 in the same way that the LXX did. There is no thought of a miraculous conception. The point is that one now a virgin will later conceive by natural means. But it seems to me that Matthew gives the reader

(but not Joseph) to understand that Mary was a virgin at the time of the conception and does so by the way he treats Isa. 7:14. In Isaiah the expiration of time between the birth and something else is the meaning of the sign. A child will be born, and before he reaches maturity, Syria and Israel will be defeated. The child is a sign of a relatively imminent future event. But Matthew omits the sign part, and the birth itself is the focus of attention. The birth will fulfill the prophecy, and it is not a sign of something else. The birth from the virgin (*parthenos*) seems to be the basis for Jesus' being Emmanuel. The time element plays no part, so perhaps the virgin idea was chosen as the basis for Jesus' being God with us. That is, virginity per se does not count for anything in the LXX of Isaiah, but it may in Matthew since he omits from Isa. 7:14-17 the time element that gives virginity its point in Isaiah.

21. See Frederick S. Carney, "Deciding in the Situation What Is Required," in *Norm and Context in Christian Ethics,* Outka and Ramsey, eds., 10; Outka; "Character, Conduct, and the Love Commandment," ibid., 46; Little and Twiss, *Comparative Religious Ethics,* 34–35; John Rawls, *A Theory of Justice* (Cambridge: Belknap Press, 1971), 131–33; Ogletree, *Bible,* 24–25, 111; Richard A. Horsley, *Jesus and the Spiral of Violence* (San Francisco: Harper and Row, 1987), 265.

22. Przybylski, *Righteousness,* 112–15.

23. Bornkamm ("End-Expectation," 24–25) thinks that Matthew maintained the unabridged validity of both written and oral law.

24. For a further discussion of the trace idea, see Dan O. Via, *The Ethics of Mark's Gospel,* 96–97, 135–36.

25. *Righteousness,* 107–15.

26. For a much fuller discussion of this passage see Dan O. Via, "Ethical Responsibility and Human Wholeness in Matthew 25:31-46," *Harvard Theological Review* 80 (1987).

27. See Davies and Allison, *Matthew,* 704.

28. David E. Garland, *The Intention of Matthew 23,* Supplements to Novum Testamentum, 52 (Leiden: E. J. Brill, 1979), 96.

29. Davies and Allison, *Matthew,* 580.

30. See U. Wilckens, "Hypocrites," *Theological Dictionary of the New Testament,* trans. G. Bromiley, abridged in one volume (Grand Rapids and Exeter: Wm. B. Eerdmans and Paternoster, 1985), 1235–36.

31. Garland, *Matthew 23,* 96.

32. See Francis W. Beare, *The Gospel According to Matthew* (San Francisco: Harper and Row, 1981), 165; Gundry, *Matthew,* 102.

33. See Eduard Schweizer, *The Good News According to Matthew,* trans. D. Green (Atlanta: John Knox, 1975), 143.

34. Garland, *Matthew 23,* 99–100. Many have taken this to be the meaning of hypocrisy in Matthew: Meier, *Matthew,* 160–61, 165; Strecker, *Sermon,* 99–100; Edward N. O'Neil on *De Cupiditate Divitiarum,* in Betz, ed., *Plutarch's Ethical Writing and Early Christian Literature,* 340; Davies and Allison, *Matthew,* 580–81, though with caution.

35. Garland, *Matthew 23,* 100–103.

36. Ibid., 111–12.

37. Guelich, *Sermon,* 278–79.

38. Bruce Wilshire, "Self-Deception," in *Perspectives,* 390–91.

39. See Davies and Allison, *Matthew,* 718–19; Meier, *Matthew,* 161.

40. John G. Gager, *Kingdom and Community* (Englewood Cliffs, N.J.: Prentice-Hall, 1975), 38–39, 42–43, 47. Bruce Malina is critical of Gager, arguing instead that what enabled Christianity to survive was not the attempt to resolve dissonance but rather that dissonance itself was normative in early Christianity. The value of normative inconsistency to groups is that it helps people to manage conflicting demands by letting them know that consistency is not necessary. Such understanding works against extreme behavior. See Bruce J. Malina, "Normative Dissonance and Christian Origins," *Semeia* 35 (1986): 35, 38–39, 44. While cognitive dissonance may be of limited value in explaining the survival of Christianity, as Gager acknowledges (*Kingdom,* 49), it is still a psychologically plausible theory that can explain certain phenomena.

41. Pregeant, *Christology beyond Dogma,* 48, 57–60, 81–82, 89–90, 122–23, 127, 130, 145, 147, 156–58.

42. Dan O. Via, "Structure, Christology, and Ethics in Matthew," in *Orientation by Disorientation,* 212–13.

## 5. THE RECOVERY OF WHOLENESS IN MATTHEW

1. See the chiastic diagram in H. J. Bernard Combrink, "The Structure of the Gospel of Matthew as Narrative," The Tyndale New Testament Lecture (1982), 71.

2. See Jack Dean Kingsbury, *The Parables of Jesus in Matthew 13* (Richmond: John Knox, 1969), 130–32.

3. This is true not only because of the structure of this particular passage but also because recitative *hoti* is uncharacteristic of Matthew. See Blass, Debrunner, and Funk, *A Greek Grammar of the New Testament,* 247. I earlier argued the causal interpretation in Dan O. Via, "Matthew on the Understandability of the Parables," *Journal of Biblical Literature* 84 (1965). This position is also taken by O. Lamar Cope, *Matthew: A Scribe Trained for the Kingdom of Heaven,* CBQ Monograph series, 5 (Washington, D.C.: The Catholic Biblical Association of America, 1976), 16. Also in basic agreement is David Hill, *The Gospel of Matthew* (Grand Rapids: Eerdmans, 1987), 226–27.

4. In Jewish apocalyptic the mysteries are the secrets about what is to happen at the end, especially as they affect human history. See Cope, *Matthew,* 17; Hill, *Matthew,* 226. In Matthew they undoubtedly take on the particularity given by the parables of the kingdom.

5. On parable as mysterious speech, riddle, or puzzle and the Old Testament and Jewish background of this, see Madeleine Boucher, *The Mysterious Parable,* CBQ Monograph series, 6 (Washington, D.C.: The Catholic Biblical Association of America, 1977), 24; James M. Robinson, *The Problem of History in Mark and Other Markan Studies* (Philadelphia: Fortress, 1982), 46–47.

6. Francis W. Beare takes the softening position and holds that in Matthew the disciples fail to understand because of their own culpable, self-willed blindness. See *The Gospel According to Matthew*, 293–94. A similar position is taken by John R. Donahue, *The Gospel in Parable* (Philadelphia: Fortress, 1988), 64–65. According to Kingsbury (*Parables*, 49), the incomprehensible riddles are the judgment of God against the Jews because they have already proved themselves hardened against the word of revelation, but Jesus does not speak to the crowd in parables in order to make them blind.

7. See Kingsbury, *Parables*, 89–90; Cope, *Matthew*, 22. Daniel Patte argues that the meaning of 13:34-35 is that the parables do in fact reveal to the crowd certain basic truths as distinguished from the mysteries that are revealed to the disciples (*The Gospel According to Matthew*, 195–96, 198–99). But Patte's interpretation depends on there being a distinction in Matthew between basic teachings and mysteries. Among the basic truths he includes such things as the hidden existence of the origin of evil and the hidden character of the kingdom. Among the mysteries he includes Jesus' being both the eschatological Son of Man and the meek one and the way Jesus' ministry is related to the eschatological judgment. I am not able to discern a real difference in principle between these two levels.

8. See Käsemann, *New Testament Questions*, 102–4.

9. Kingsbury (*Parables*, 30) observes that after 13:36 the parables to disciples are not designated as such.

10. At the same time the parables of 13:24, 31, 33 are also addressed to the crowd, as 13:34 shows.

11. Lamar Cope has pointed out that the elements in the interpretation that carry its meaning do not actually come from the parable. But all of them (with the exception of *logos* in 13:19) do occur in the dialogue about why Jesus speaks in parables (13:10-17). The key terms are "kingdom," "hear," and "understand." Matthew has linked together the parable of the sower, his parable theory, and his interpretation of the parable by means of careful allusions to Isa. 6:9-10 (*Matthew*, 20).

12. The Greek is *spareis*, the second aorist passive participle of *speirō*, "to sow."

13. *Esparmenon*, perfect passive participle.

14. *Spareis*, second aorist passive participle.

15. This is supported by the particular forms of the verb *speirō*. In episodes two through four it is *spareis*, where it is used of the hearer. Since it is *spareis* in 13:19d, it also should be connected to the hearer. But where it refers to the word (13:19c), it is *esparmenon*.

16. *Matthew*, 389.

17. Matthew 73 times; Mark 46 times; Luke 37; John 78. See Michael J. Wilkins, *The Concept of Disciple in Matthew's Gospel*, Supplement to Novum Testamentum, 59 (Leiden: E. J. Brill, 1988), 128.

18. The theme of forgiveness will be taken up in chapter 6.

19. For a fuller discussion and defense of these ideas see Dan O. Via, "Structure, Christology, and Ethics in Matthew," 202–10. Richard Edwards's reader-response

study of the disciples seems to make two basic points: (1) the evaluation of the disciples is ambiguous; (2) understanding is an important issue for the nature of discipleship. See Richard A. Edwards, "Uncertain Faith: Matthew's Portrait of the Disciples," in *Discipleship in the New Testament*, ed. Fernando F. Segovia (Philadelphia: Fortress, 1985), 52–59.

20. Georg Strecker, "The Concept of History in Matthew," in *The Interpretation of Matthew*, ed. Graham Stanton (Philadelphia and London: Fortress and SPCK, 1983), 70–73.

21. Wilkins argues (*Disciple*, 137, 143, 165) that the disciples' understanding magnifies the effectiveness of Jesus' teaching.

22. Bornkamm, "End-Expectation," 27–29; Barth, "Matthew's Understanding of the Law," 112–14; Heinz Joachim Held, "Matthew as Interpreter of the Miracle Stories," in *Tradition and Interpretation in Matthew*, 239–40; Gerd Theissen, *The Miracle Stories of the Early Christian Tradition*, trans. F. McDonagh (Philadelphia: Fortress, 1983), 137–38; Patte, *Matthew*, 114–15.

23. Barth, "Matthew's Understanding of the Law," 112.

24. Bornkamm, "End-Expectation," 27–28.

25. Held, "Miracle Stories," 275–77.

26. Ibid., 253–75.

27. Ibid., 253.

28. I think that Held tacitly acknowledges this (ibid., 196).

29. Barth, "Matthew's Understanding of the Law," 110, 113.

30. Ibid., 110. Barth is probably right that the plural "mysteries" in 13:11 as contrasted with the singular "mystery" in Mark 4:11 suggests the intellectual element in understanding—grasping doctrines (ibid., 107).

31. Ibid., 110–14. This position is followed in Peter J. Ellis, *Matthew: His Mind and His Message* (Collegeville, Minn.: The Liturgical Press, 1974), 147.

32. Ulrich Luz, "The Disciples in the Gospel According to Matthew," in *The Interpretation of Matthew*, ed. G. Stanton, 103–4, 107.

33. See Theissen, *Miracle Stories*, 139–40.

34. "Matthew's Understanding of the Law," 113.

35. See René Wellek and Austin Warren, *Theory of Literature* (New York: Harcourt, Brace, & Co., 1956), 14.

36. Samuel Taylor Coleridge, *The Complete Works*, vol. 3, *Biographia Literaria* (New York: Harper and Brothers, 1854), 363–64, 372–74. William K. Wimsatt and Cleanth Brooks, *Literary Criticism* (New York: Alfred A. Knopf, 1957), 392–93.

37. *Validity in Interpretation* (New Haven: Yale University Press, 1967).

38. *Interpretation* (Princeton: Princeton University Press, 1980).

39. *In Defense of the Imagination* (Cambridge: Harvard University Press, 1982).

40. See the classic new critical texts by William K. Wimsatt and Monroe C. Beardsley, "The Intentional Fallacy" and "The Affective Fallacy" in *The Verbal Icon* (Lexington: University of Kentucky Press, 1954). And see the more recent Murray Krieger, *Theory of Criticism* (Baltimore: Johns Hopkins University Press, 1976), 25–31.

41. See Jane P. Tompkins, "An Introduction to Reader-Response Criticism," in *Reader-Response Criticism*, ed. J. Tompkins (Baltimore: Johns Hopkins University Press, 1980), xi–xiii; Stanley Fish, "Introduction, or How I Stopped Worrying and Learned to Love Interpretation," in *Is There a Text in This Class?* (Cambridge: Harvard University Press, 1980), 2, 7.

42. Wolfgang Iser, *The Act of Reading* (Baltimore: Johns Hopkins University Press, 1978), 9–10, 14–15, 17, 19–21, 22–25, 27, 30, 38, 92, 135, 141, 150, 152; "The Reading Process: A Phenomenological Approach," in Tompkins, ed., *Reader-Response Criticism*, 50; Hans Robert Jauss, *Aesthetic Experience and Literary Hermeneutics*, trans. M. Shaw (Minneapolis: University of Minnesota Press, 1982), xxix–xxxii.

43. Stanley Fish, "Interpreting the Variorum," in Tompkins, ed., *Reader-Response Criticism*, 172, 176–79; *Is There a Text?* 12–14.

44. Wilkins (*Disciple*, 160) shows that the verb *mathēteuō* is a characteristically Matthean word. In ordinary Greek usage it had the intransitive meaning "to be or become a pupil." But in the New Testament it can mean transitively to make a disciple. Matthew, in Wilkins's judgment, has a transitive passive that should be understood in the sense "be instructed."

45. According to Cope, the old and new may have a double meaning (*Matthew*, 25). The new could be the eschatological secrets and the old, the things hidden since creation. Or the new could be Jesus' parables and the old, the storehouse of Old Testament texts. For Gundry (*Matthew*, 281) the new is the new understanding given by Jesus' parables, and the old is the understanding held prior to the parables. Patte (*Matthew*, 199) agrees, more or less, with Cope. While all of these seem plausible, I will pursue a slightly different angle.

46. Patte (*Matthew*, 222–23) holds Matthew to be interpreting the Canaanite woman (15:21–28) as also manifesting a human, secular wisdom—her resolve to seek the good for her daughter—which is not opposed to the will of God. But since Matthew interprets her persistent resolve as faith, which Patte recognizes, is Matthew here praising human, secular wisdom or the wit of faith?

47. This Markan material is discussed at length in Dan O. Via, *The Ethics of Mark's Gospel*, 182–88.

48. G. Barth ("Matthew's Understanding of the Law," 110) maintains that for Matthew understanding has no basis in the natural reason of humankind but is a gift of God, the act of God on a person. This is largely true but needs qualification.

49. *Ekballō*, Jesus casts out demons by his word (8:16; 12:27-28).

50. Strecker (*The Sermon on the Mount*, 42) basically denies that the twofold structure has any real significance for the meaning. I hope to show that this is wrong.

51. Roman Jacobson, "Linguistics and Poetics," in *Structuralists from Marx to Lévi-Strauss*, ed. R. T. De George and F. M. De George (Garden City, N.Y.: Doubleday, Anchor Books, 1972), 95, 109.

52. See F. Hauck, "Makarios," *Theological Dictionary of the New Testament, Abridged in One Volume*, 548–49; Samuel Terrien, *Till the Heart Sings*, 115; Strecker, *The Sermon on the Mount*, 30–31. On the meaning of "blessed" and on

the history of beatitudes see Davies and Allison, *Matthew*, 431–32. For the history of developing types of the beatitude, see Hans Dieter Betz, *Essays on the Sermon*, 25–34.

53. For example, see Robert A. Guelich, *Sermon*, 69, 74–75.

54. See Strecker, *The Sermon on the Mount*, 32; Guelich, *Sermon*, 75, 98. Davies and Allison seem to tend to this view. The term refers to the spiritually poor. It describes an internal disposition similar to that described in Pss. 24:4; 34:18; 11:2; Prov. 29:38 (*Matthew*, 444). It should be pointed out that Pss. 11:2; 24:4; Prov. 29:23 refer to people who are morally upright. Ps. 34:15-17 refers to people who are morally upright and also apparently crushed by circumstances (34:18). Betz's interpretation is puzzling. He seems to argue that the first Beatitude goes beyond the strictly religious type (blessed is he who keeps the law) and beyond the conventional secular type (blessed are the rich) and manifests the nonconventional wisdom type (*Essays on the Sermon*, 25–34). But Betz has missed the paradox involved and has attributed to Matt. 5:3 a fairly conventional Jewish piety of the poor: Blessed are those who accept the misery of existence with humility and find salvation in the kingdom.

55. Joachim Jeremias seems to hold that for Jesus the poor were the lost sinners. But he, too, argues that for Matthew they are the humble who are conscious of their spiritual poverty. See Joachim Jeremias, *New Testament Theology*, trans. J. Bowden (New York: Charles Scribner's Sons, 1971), 112–13.

56. Davies and Allison (*Matthew*, 430) hold that the ninth Beatitude (5:11-12), which also pronounces the persecuted blessed, should not be excluded from 5:3-10 and attached to 5:13-16. In my judgment it is not an either/or matter, for 5:11-12 has connections with both 5:3-10 and 5:13-16. It is rather a question of to which passage it is more strongly connected. It shares with 5:3-10 the beatitude form based on "blessed" and "because," and it has a content connection with the eighth Beatitude—persecution. But in my judgment its relationship to 5:13-16 is closer than its relationship to 5:3-10. It is excluded from 5:3-10 because it lies outside of the frame constituted by the reference to the kingdom in 5:3, 10. It is excluded, moreover, by its shift from the third to the second person. And it is excluded because it has added an imperative clause—rejoice and be glad—to the a part, and it has added a *houtōs* clause to the b part. In addition, 5:11-12 is organically connected to 5:13-16 as the first part of a three-member form: blessing, naming, commissioning. This construction has a parallel in Matt. 16:17-19 where we also have blessing (16:17), naming (16:18), commissioning (16:19). See M. Jack Suggs, *Wisdom, Christology, and Law in Matthew's Gospel* (Cambridge: Harvard University Press, 1970), 120–25.

57. Both Strecker (*The Sermon on the Mount*, 31) and Davies and Allison (*Matthew*, 445–46) assimilate the present tense in 5:3, 10 to the future tenses in 5:4-9, Strecker less subtly than Davies and Allison. But the present and future should both be allowed their full force. The presence of paradox in the first clauses prompts us to expect paradox in the second clauses and not to reduce the tension between present and future to synonymy.

58. As claimed, for example, by Hans Windisch, *The Meaning of the Sermon on the Mount*, trans. S. Gilmour (Philadelphia: Westminster, 1951), 26–29; Suggs, *Matthew's Gospel*, 122; Strecker, *The Sermon on the Mount*, 33.

59. Variations on this position may be seen in Guelich, *Sermon*, 110–11; Patte, *Matthew*, 67; Davies and Allison, *Matthew*, 432, 438–40, 449.

60. Strecker (*The Sermon on the Mount*, 179) maintains that Matthew and his community made no distinction between indicative and imperative such as we find in Paul. The eschatological kingdom is not the prior ground for the ethical imperative, but the gift rather exists in the demand and is identical with it (*Der Weg der Gerechtigkeit*, 166, 169–71, 174–75). Obviously I have argued a different interpretation.

61. See Bernard Brandon Scott, "The King's Accounting: Matthew 18:23-34," *Journal of Biblical Literature* 104 (September 1985): 439–40.

62. See Little and Twiss, *Comparative Religious Ethics*, 104, 179, 190, 194, 196.

## 6. CONCLUSION AND IMPLICATIONS

1. As claimed in Roger Mohrlang, *Matthew and Paul, A Comparison of Ethical Perspectives* (Cambridge: Cambridge University Press, 1984), 80, 114.

2. As claimed ibid., 114.

3. In an instructive paper delivered to the Society of New Testament Studies in 1980 ("Interpreting Paul: Demythologizing in Reverse") Hendrikus Boers argued that Paul is the canon within the canon because he alone saw that salvation is a matter of both faith and works. Only Paul expressed the experience of reality in terms of these two contradictory principles. Matthew, on the other hand, moved toward the extreme of a reversion to Judaism, and John approached the opposite extreme of gnosticism. I have argued that Paul is not exactly at the center of the New Testament, balancing faith and works, as Boers seems to imply, but rather that Paul is to the left of center, containing both principles while stressing faith, whereas Matthew is to the right of center, containing both principles but emphasizing works.

4. See John R. Donahue, *The Gospel in Parable*, 81.

5. It has been correctly observed that the thrust of this parable is very similar to Paul's justification by grace alone. So Eberhard Jüngel, *Paulus and Jesus* (Tübingen: J. C. B. Mohr, 1967), 165.

# Index

# AUTHORS

## SUBJECTS